九寨沟形象标识：九寨之眼

寓意为："放眼看九寨山水""像保护自己的眼睛一样保护九寨沟的山水、生物多样性"

Jiuzhaigou's image logo: The Eye of Jiuzhaigou

Meaning: "Look at Jiuzhaigou's landscape"

"Protect Jiuzhaigou's landscape and biodiversity as you protect your own eyes"

九寨沟图志

JIUZHAIGOU PICTORIAL ANNALS

四川省地方志工作办公室
阿坝州地方志办公室　编著
九寨沟风景名胜区管理局

Compiled by
The Office of Sichuan Province Local Records
The Office of Aba Prefecture Local Records
The Management Bureau of Jiuzhaigou Scenic and Historic Area

方志出版社
Publishing House of Local Records

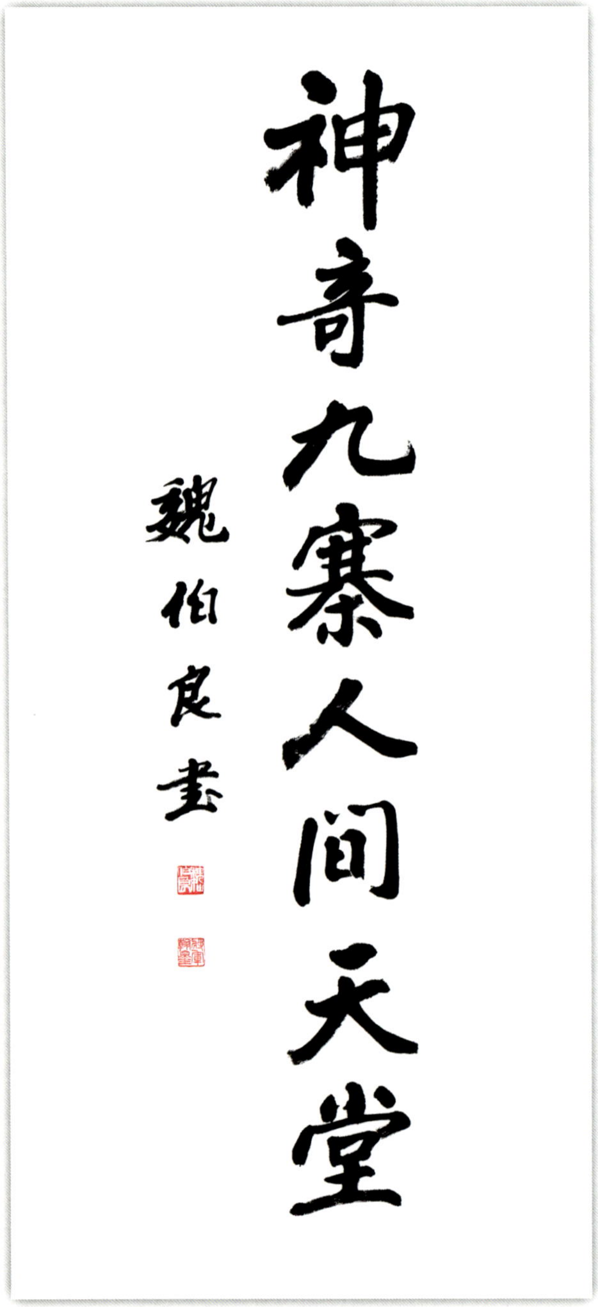

书法《神奇九寨人间天堂》，138cm×69cm（2023 年，魏伯良 作品）
Magical Jiuzhai–An Earthly Paradise, calligraphy, 138cm×69cm (by Wei Boliang, 2023)

篆刻《九寨天堂》，3.4cm×2.4cm（上），3.2cm×3cm（中），3.3cm×3.3cm（下）（2023 年，王道义 作品）
Heavenly Nine Villages, seal cutting, 3.4cm×2.4cm (top), 3.2cm×3cm (middle), 3.3cm×3.3cm (bottom) (by Wang Daoyi, 2023)

九寨金秋
壬寅年新春笑秋作

彩墨《九寨金秋》
370cm×260cm
（2022 年，邱笑秋 作品）

Golden Autumn in Jiuzhai, color ink painting, 370cm×260cm (by Qiu Xiaoqiu, 2022)

《九寨沟图志》编纂机构

Compiling Team for *JIUZHAIGOU PICTORIAL ANNALS*

凡　例

一、本图志编纂工作以马克思列宁主义、毛泽东思想、邓小平理论、“三个代表”重要思想、科学发展观、习近平新时代中国特色社会主义思想为指导，坚持辩证唯物主义和历史唯物主义的立场、观点和方法，全面客观地记述九寨沟的自然地理、人文历史、景观资源以及对九寨沟的研究、保护、开发、管理和灾后重建的历史与现状。

二、本图志采用篇、章结构，分为九篇，每篇设有卷首语和若干章，每章下有正文和知识点。

三、本图志以图片和照片为主要记述方式，上限起于1970年，下限截至2023年。另根据本图志编纂的实际时间和九寨沟发展史上重大事件的实际记述需要，部分内容适当上溯，大事记记述时间上溯至1924年。图片和照片文字说明包括图所反映的主要内容、拍摄者、时间、来源等信息。记述的行政区域以阿坝藏族羌族自治州为主，兼及四川省内其他市（州）。

四、本图志中的地名、机构等均用当时的名称记载，若名称有过变化，通过注释加以说明。机构或文件名等首次出现时用全称，并括注简称，此后一般用简称。省级人民政府、省级林业管理机构与国家部、委、局联合发文及组织有关活动时，机构名称用全称；在外事活动中机构名称用全称。科学技术术语以国家有关机关审定的为准，未经审定的遵从习惯。有关法律名称，首次出现时用全称，之后用简称。图志中所用地图，遵循《地图管理条例》相关规定。

五、本图志资料主要来源于现存档案和公开出版的志书、年鉴，以及相关单位报送及编写人员征集的材料。所用资料经反复核对和考证，其中涉及的相关数据，以历史文献、政府公布的资料、职能部门公布的数字为准，均符合有关保密规定；对志稿中的人物、事件，依当时习惯提法及实际情况记载。

六、本图志使用规范的现代语体文记述，遵循行文严谨、朴实、简洁、流畅的要求。

七、本图志使用公元纪年，各篇正文采用第三人称表述。除涉及人名、地名、纪年和简称等项采用括注外，其余采用页下或页边脚注。

八、数字用法、标点符号用法分别采用国家标准《出版物上数字用法》（GB/T 15835—2011）、《标点符号用法》（GB/T 15834—2011），计量单位采用国家技术监督局1993年12月发布的《量和单位》系列国家标准。

To Our Readers

1. Guided by Marxism-Leninism, Mao Zedong Thought, Deng Xiaoping Theory, the Important Thought of "Three Represents", the Scientific Outlook on Development and Xi Jinping Thought on Socialism with Chinese Characteristics for a New Era, the compilation of the current pictorial annals adheres to the position, viewpoint and method of historical materialism while comprehensively and objectively recording the natural geography, human history, landscape resources of Jiuzhaigou and history and status quo of Jiuzhaigou concerning its research, protection, development, management and post-quake reconstruction.

2. The annals are made up of nine episodes, each having a preface and several chapters composed of the main text and knowledge points.

3. Mainly covered by pictures and photos taken from 1970 to 2023, the annals, required by the actual time and description of major events in the development of the valley, have part of the contents appropriately extended beyond these limits. The description of each picture and photo includes information such as its main content, photographer, year, and source. In this book, the administrative region covered herein primarily focuses on Aba Zang and Qiang Autonomous Prefecture while also encompassing other cities (prefectures) within Sichuan Province, and the recording of Key Events dates to 1924.

4. The names of places and institutions herein are all recorded as they were at that time. If done differently, some notes shall be given. When an institution or document name is mentioned for the first time, the full name is provided along with its abbreviation, and the abbreviation is generally used thereafter. When the provincial people's government, provincial forestry management institution and national ministry, committee, and bureau jointly issue any documents and organize related events concerned, the full name of each institution is used; in foreign affairs, the institution concerned is used in full name. Scientific and technical terminologies are subject to the approval of the relevant national agencies, and the unapproved ones are to the customary terminologies. For legal titles, the full name is used when it first appears, and its abbreviation is used thereafter. The maps used in the annals are in compliance with the relevant provisions of *The Map Management Regulations.*

5. The information concerned is mainly from the existing archives and publicly published chronicles and yearbooks, as well as materials submitted by the relevant units and collected by the compilers. The materials used have been repeatedly checked and verified, and the relevant data involved are based on historical documents, government-published materials, and figures published by functional departments and all in compliance with relevant confidentiality regulations; all persons and events concerned are provided in accordance with the custom at the time and factual records.

6. Standardized modern writing style is used in the annals in an effort to satisfy the requirements of precise, concise and fluent writing.

7. The chronology of Common Era (CE) is used and the text of each chapter is expressed in the third person. Except for personal names, place names, dates, and abbreviations, which are in parentheses, all other information is referenced using footnotes at the bottom or in the margins of the page.

8. The national standards of *General Rules for Writing Numerals in Public Texts* (GB/T 15835-2011) and *General Rules for Punctuation* (GB/T 15834-2011) are respectively adopted in numbers and punctuation marks, so are those of *Quantities and Units* issued by the State Bureau of Quality and Technology Supervision in December, 1993 in the unit of measurement.

目录 CONTENTS

火花海（2023 年，桑吉 供图）
Sparkling Lake (photo by Sangji, 2023)

九看九寨之二

Episode Two

Grotesque Peaks and Wonderful Valleys

奇峰异谷

九看九寨之三

Episode Three

A Kingdom of Flora

植物王国

九看九寨之四 Episode Four
A Treasure House of Fauna
动物宝库

九看九寨之五 Episode Five
Customs of the Zang Ethnic Villages
风情藏寨

九看九寨之六 Episode Six
A Pioneer in Scientific Research
科考当先

九看九寨之七 Episode Seven
Heritage Well Protected
遗产呵护

九看九寨之八 Episode Eight

Tourism in the Easy Way

安逸畅游

九看九寨之九 Episode Nine

Nirvana and Rebirth

涅槃重生

1 | 2

1 热西寨新民居（2005 年，来源于《四川省志·九寨沟志》）

2 树正寨磨房（2019 年，来源于《四川省志·九寨沟志》）

1 New dwellings in Rexi Village (photo from *Sichuan Provincial Records–Jiuzhaigou Records*, 2005)

2 Mill at Shuzheng Village (photo from *Sichuan Provincial Records–Jiuzhaigou Records*, 2019)

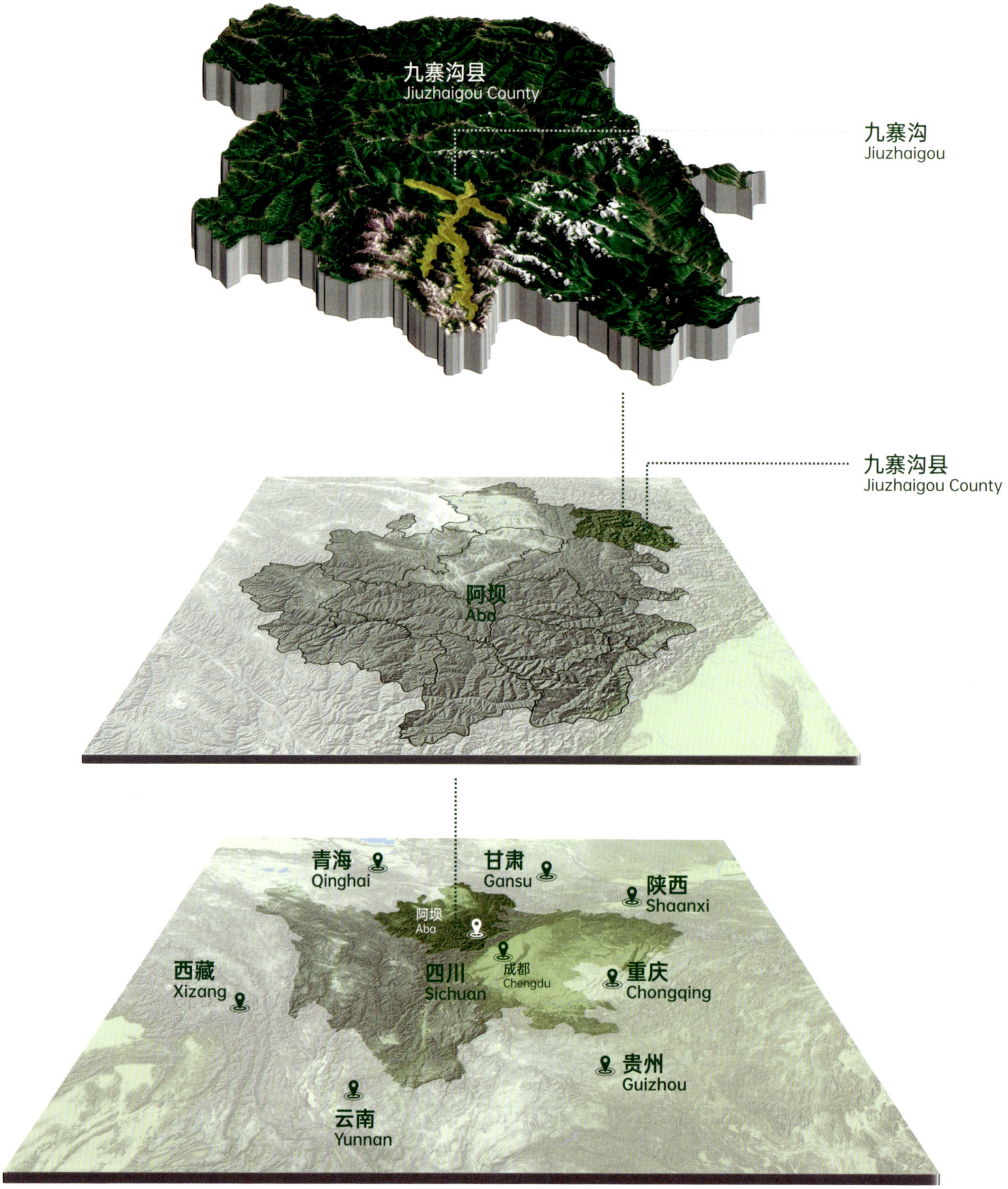

九寨沟位置、地形示意图

Sketch Maps of the Position and Landform of Jiuzhaigou

序　神奇九寨宜九看

九寨沟是全球罕有、中国唯一的以高山湖泊群、瀑布群和钙华滩流为主体的世界级、国家级自然保护区、风景名胜区。她是天赐华夏的珍宝，与三星堆、大熊猫、黄龙、峨眉山、乐山大佛、青城山、都江堰等一起处于巴蜀旅游的核心地位。

当今的九寨沟以色彩斑斓之翠海流滩，巍峨壮丽之圣洁群峰，造山运动之地质遗迹，丰富多样之珍稀物种，茂密完整之森林生态，神秘多姿之藏寨风情而闻名遐迩。而在四十年前，她还蒙着神秘的面纱，一直藏在深闺人未识。是改革开放的浩荡东风催她苏醒，是我们伟大的祖国和人民，开展了多次科学考察，发现了她的多重稀世价值，使其免遭斧钺之灾，同时以“尊重自然，生态优先”为准则，走向了独特的保护开发之路。在全民持续努力之下，九寨沟方能集多项桂冠于一身，不仅是国家级自然保护区、国家地质公园，国家 AAAAA 级旅游景区，更在 1992 年和 1997 年成为世界自然遗产和世界生物圈保护区的成员。2017 年遭受一场强烈地震后，在中央的关怀下，九寨沟没有被压趴下。她像凤凰涅槃一样，在恢复重建中补妆归来，更加美丽夺目了！

我有幸多次游九寨，赞赏她的四季美景各具神韵：初春的妩媚，仲夏的绚丽，深秋的浓艳，隆冬的圣洁。而这次读到四川省地方志工作办公室和阿坝州地方志办公室、九寨沟风景名胜区管理局编著的这部《九寨沟图志》书稿，才领悟到了神奇九寨宜九看的门径。这本书广搜精选，以图文并茂、文史交融的图志形式，按九寨沟的特色和广大读者的关注点，分列碧水、青山、植物、动物、风俗、科研、保护、旅游、灾后重建这九个版块，揭示对神奇、神秘、神妙的九寨宜于九看之道。对有心人来说，每看一番都是难得的奇异旅程，都会带来浮想联翩，回味不尽的体悟和惊喜。

分而言之：一看九寨，看的是她雾海叠瀑，溪涧回环；二看九寨，看的是她山境奇绝，雪峰巍峨；三看九寨，看的是她彩林蓊郁，植物多样；四看九寨，看的是她熊猫栖息，动物珍稀；五看九寨，看的是她民俗淳厚，风格独特；六看九寨，看的是她科研不懈，持续创新；七看九寨，看的是她成功申遗，和谐发展；八看九寨，看的是她文明畅游，永续利用；九看九寨，看的是她柔韧坚毅，涅槃重生。

九寨沟得天地厚爱，聚宇宙绝观，移步都是美景，处处融入人文。受限于篇幅，这本图志展示的可能仅是她优美景色和风土人情部分代表，恐怕还有更多或雄浑、或妩媚、或纯净、或多彩的内容未能收录。但我相信，在祖国和人民的珍爱与保护下，九寨沟必将永续发展并越来越美，地球村不同肤色的人们都会有足够多的机会与她邂逅，亲自体验聚大美而不言的九寨沟。

章玉钧

2023 年 8 月 31 日

Foreword: Magical Jiuzhaigou in Nine Episodes

Jiuzhaigou is a rarity of rarities in the world and the only national nature reserve and scenic spot in China dominated by alpine lakes, waterfalls, and travertine beach streams; and as a treasure bestowed upon China, it stays at the core of Ba-Shu tourism together with the Sanxingdui Site, the giant panda, Huanglong, Mount Emei, Leshan Giant Buddha, Qingcheng Mountain, Dujiangyan and so on.

Today's Jiuzhaigou is famous for its colorful emerald beaches, majestic and holy peaks, geological relics of orogeny, rich and diverse rare species, dense and complete forest ecology, and mysterious and colorful Zang customs; and yet, it had been in deep slumber under a veil of mystery until four decades ago, when there blew the mighty east wind of China's reform and opening up; it is our great motherland and people that, through numerous scientific investigations, have discovered and kept its multiple rare values from any man-made harm, while leading it to a unique road of protection and development based on "respecting nature and prioritizing ecology". It is through the continued efforts of the whole society that Jiuzhaigou has scored such laurels as nature reserve, geological park, and national AAAAA-level tourist attraction at the national level, as well as a member of world natural heritages and world biosphere in 1992 and 1997, respectively. Despite the strong earthquake in 2017, Jiuzhaigou was not crushed, thanks to the great care of the central government. Like a phoenix nirvana, it has got restored, and even more beautiful and eye-catching than ever before!

I have been fortunate enough to frequent Jiuzhaigou, and admire its beauty in each season: charm in early spring, splendor in midsummer, richness in late autumn, and sacredness in midwinter. This time, upon scanning the manuscript of Jiuzhaigou Pictorial Annals compiled by the Offices of Sichuan Province and Aba Prefecture Local Records, and the Management Bureau of Jiuzhaigou Scenic and Historic Area, I have come to learn nine episodes of admiring the magical Jiuzhaigou. According to the characteristics of Jiuzhaigou and focuses of readers, this book, widely collected and exquisitely selected, is a blend of literature and history illustrated with rich pictures and texts, which falls into such nines episodes as clear waters, green mountains, flora and fauna, customs, scientific research, protection, tourism, and post-quake reconstruction, displaying to the full how Jiuzhaigou is magical and marvelous. For those who are interested, each reading makes an unusual and exotic journey, which brings imaginative, endless insights and surprises.

To put it in a nutshell: first, one can see its sea of clouds, waterfalls, and streams; second, one can see its amazing mountains and snow-capped peaks; third, one can see its colorful forests; fourth, one can see its habitat of pandas and other rare animals; fifth, one can see its simple folk customs and unique style; sixth, one can see its unremitting technology and continuous innovation; seventh, one can see its success in applying for world natural heritage; eighth, one can see its civilization and sustainable use; ninth, one can see its perseverance and rebirth.

In Jiuzhaigou, so blessed as to gather the spectacular view of the universe, every step means breathtaking beauty, and humanities are felt everywhere. Due to limited space, Jiuzhaigou Pictorial Annals may but show part of its scenes and local customs, and there are far more sights waiting to be included. But I believe that with the constant love and protection of the motherland and people, it will develop better and become more and more enchanting, so that all in the global village will have enough opportunities to meet and experience it to their hearts' content.

章玉钧

Zhang Yujun
August 31, 2023

前言　世界只有一个九寨沟

九寨沟隐藏于中国川西北高原的群山之间，是大自然慷慨赠予人类的无价珍宝，素有“童话世界，人间仙境”的美誉。亿万年来，一系列构造运动塑造了九寨沟奇绝地貌的骨架，又有第四纪冰川或侵蚀，或堆积，或搬运，奠定了九寨沟自然风景的地貌基础，还有岩溶作用、气候影响、生物作用等细笔勾勒，绘就九寨沟的惊世容颜。

从空中俯瞰九寨沟，树正沟、日则沟、则查洼沟三条主沟呈“Y”形躺卧于大地之上，波光粼粼的火花海、水波不兴的镜海、水势浩大的诺日朗瀑布、小而艳丽的五彩池等海子、瀑布镶嵌其间，宛如一条拥有无数晶莹钻石的项链。

纵横于巍峨高山之间的沟谷，汇集了九寨沟的主要景观地貌，奇水荟萃、彩林掩映、珍禽穿梭、异兽出没，具有独特风情的藏族村寨与之交相辉映，人与自然共同谱写出一曲和谐的九寨乐章。

在九寨沟，与自然奇景来一场浪漫邂逅。在这里，人们能看到古冰斗、冰蚀湖、冰川谷、角峰、刃脊等众多冰川侵蚀遗迹，透过冰蚀U形谷厚厚的冰碛物堆积层，感悟百万年来的光阴流变；清澈见底的海子好比情人温柔的眸子，只一眼，心底里就涌起难以言喻的喜爱；原始森林里，冷杉、云杉、铁杉、槭树、桦木等种类繁多的植物竞相生长，长松萝附生在树枝上，厚厚的苔藓植物像一块巨大的绿地毯布满林地……

春风渐暖，万物自冬之封印中苏醒。大地染绿，山花吐芳，瀑布解冻，水花迸射，湖面冰融，涟漪层现。鸟雀也为这活力四射的时节感到欢欣，一个个动人的音符自婉转的歌喉间流泻而出，奏响了大自然的交响乐。九寨沟的春天，被新绿包裹，被空灵渲染，被生机充盈。

盛夏草木长，山雨撼山谷。充沛的阳光和雨露，为植物提供了肆意生长的自然条件，而茂盛的植被，又为生活在其间的动物提供了充足的食物来源和休憩场所。九寨沟的夏天，是热情的季节，是酣畅的季节，是生长的季节。

湖水晶莹澄净，溪涧叮咚潺流，天渐渐高远起来，树木的色彩渐渐绚丽起来，一串串成熟的野果挂上枝头，像爱美的小姑娘戴上了精美头饰。九寨沟的秋天，充满色彩，充满甜蜜，充满收获。

气温持续走低，神奇的变化悄然出现。瀑布停止歌唱，冰凌悬垂，冰湖如玉，雪峰似画。皎洁的明月在不冻的溪流和清波中投射她的影子，清峻空寂中便添了洒脱疏朗。九寨沟的冬天，拥有韵味，拥有闲情，拥有智慧。

一年四季，四时之景不同。“一千个读者就有一千个哈姆雷特”，一千个游客就有一千个九寨沟。九寨沟的美，即便是千言万语也仅能道出十之一二。

九寨沟民俗文化丰富多彩。藏族先民们迁徙至此，在生产生活中与其他民族不断交融发展，形成了其独特的传统民俗。精美的服饰，香醇的青稞酒、酥油茶，高耸的喇嘛塔，循环不息的转经轮，为九寨沟人文增添许多温暖与厚度。

自 20 世纪 80 年代以来，原本“养在深闺”的九寨沟逐渐揭开面纱、走向人前，成为世界级的旅游新地标。来自全球各地的游客将惊艳的目光投射至这片“人间仙境”，即便是最挑剔的评论家，也不会对九寨沟吝惜夸赞之语。

九寨沟于 1978 年建立自然保护区，1982 年被列为第一批国家重点风景名胜区，1992 年被列入《世界遗产名录》，1994 年被确认为国家级自然保护区，1997 年成为“世界生物圈保护区网络”成员，2007 年成为全国首批 AAAAA 级旅游景区。

“绿水青山就是金山银山。”九寨沟是环境保护与经济发展相辅相成、和谐共生的典范。无论是推行退耕还林、天然林保护工程，还是创新利用太阳能、风能等清洁能源，抑或是实行“沟内游，沟外住”政策，都是九寨沟人民为追求更加美好的生活，同时也不破坏当地生态环境所做的努力。

2017 年 8 月 8 日，一场 7.0 级地震突袭九寨沟。一日之间，地动山摇、水流震荡、湖泊决堤、瀑布震裂……遭受重创后，“童话世界”将不复存在吗？时间给出了最好的答案：在各方力量的共同努力下，“补妆”归来的九寨沟以全新的面貌重现人前，继续构建人与自然和谐共生的大美生态。

九寨沟是坚韧的。冰川剥蚀、地震侵崩、流水冲击……足以摧毁一切的力量反而成为九寨沟美景的创造之源。但同时，九寨沟也是脆弱的。无论是地震、岩石崩塌、滑坡、泥石流等自然灾害，还是污水排放、空气污染等人为影响，都可能造成九寨沟生态失衡。世界上只有一个九寨沟，人类只有小心呵护，才能使这颗璀璨明珠永远夺目。

四川省地方志工作办公室

阿坝州地方志办公室

九寨沟风景名胜区管理局

2023 年 8 月 31 日

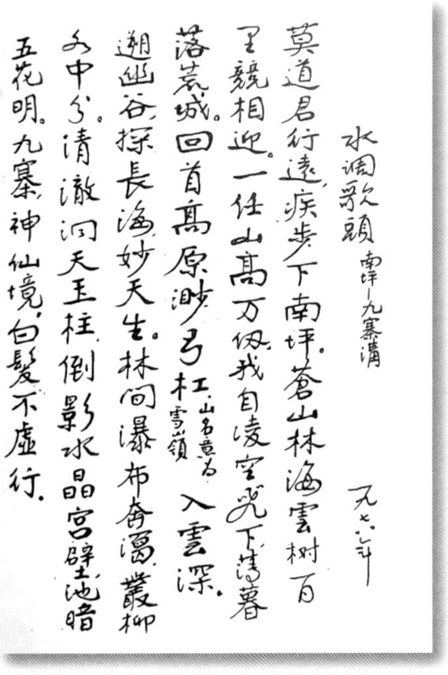

《水调歌头 南坪—九寨沟》（1978 年，何郝炬 作品）

Nanping–Jiuzhaigou, to the tune of Prelude to Water Melody

(by He Haoju, 1978)

Preface: Jiuzhaigou, the One and Only on Earth

Known as a Fairytale World and Fairyland on Earth, Jiuzhaigou, hidden among the mountains of the plateau in China's Northwest Sichuan, is a priceless treasure generously bestowed by nature on human beings. For hundreds of millions of years, one tectonic movement after another has shaped the valley's extraordinary landform, the erosion, accumulation, or transport of Quaternary glaciers laid the foundation for its natural landscape of Jiuzhaigou and the karstification, climate influence, biological effect outlined its stunning appearance.

An aerial view of Jiuzhaigou presents such three gullies of Shuzheng, Rize and Zezhawa lying aground in a "Y" shape, along with the shimmering Sparkling Lake, the undisturbed Mirrior Lake, the raging Waterfalls at Nourilang Lake and the cute Wucai Pool, which look like a necklace with countless crystal diamonds.

The ravines and valleys crisscrossing the majestic mountains bring together the main landscape and landforms of Jiuzhaigou filled with unique waters, colorful forests, rare birds and strange beasts. The Zang villages with ethnic customs complement each other, where man and nature form a harmonious movement.

Do greet the valley for a romantic encounter with natural wonders. Here, one can feast his eyes on ancient ice cirques, glacial lakes, glacial valleys, horn peaks, knife-edge crest and the like glacial erosion relics. Through the thick accumulation of moraines in the glacial U-shaped valley, one can feel the change owing to the flow of time for millions of years; the crystal-clear lakes are like the gentle eyes of a beholder, who is brimming with unspeakable love at one glance; in the virgin forest, a wide variety of flora such as fir, spruce, hemlock, maple and birch with each other for growth and longipinia grows on the branches, while thick moss covers the woodland like a giant green carpet...

As the spring breeze gets warm, everything wakes up from winter. The earth is dyed green, the mountain flowers bloom, the waterfall thaws, the water splashes, the lake melts and ripples appear. Birds also rejoice in this energetic season and moving notes flow out from their melodious voices, playing the symphony of nature. Jiuzhaigou in the spring is wrapped in fresh green, rendered ethereal and filled with vitality.

In midsummer, all vegetation grows and mountain rains shake the valley. Abundant sunshine and rain provide natural conditions for the free growth of flora, while lush vegetation provides sufficient food sources and resting places for fauna. The summer here is of enthusiasm, joy and growth.

The lake is crystal clear, the streams are flowing, the sky is getting higher and higher, the trees get more colorful and strings of ripe wild fruits hang on the branches, like a beautiful maiden in an exquisite headdress. And in autumn, the valley is full of colors, sweetness and harvest.

As its temperature continues to drop, magical changes appear quietly. Waterfalls stay silent, icicles hang still, lakes are like jades and snowy peaks paintings. The bright and clear moon casts the valley's shadow in the ice-free stream and clear waves, adding a sense of freedom and ease to the solitude and emptiness. The winter here has charm, leisure and wisdom.

"There are a thousand Hamlets in a thousand people's eyes", as the famous saying goes, so is the case of varied landscapes throughout the year in Jiuzhaigou, the beauty of which may fail the mightiest pen.

Jiuzhaigou boasts a rich and colorful folk culture. The Zang ancestors migrated here and continued to blend and develop with other ethnic groups in production and life, forming their unique traditional folk customs. Their exquisite costumes, mellow highland barley wine, buttered tea, towering Lama pagodas, and endless prayer-wheels have provided the humanities of Jiuzhaigou with plenty of warmth and depth.

Since the 1980s, Jiuzhaigou, little known to the outside, has gradually lifted its veil and stepped forward, as a new world-class tourist landmark. Tourists from all over the world have turned their astonished eyes to this "Wonderland on Earth". Even the most critical critics will not hesitate to give it a thumbs-up.

Jiuzhaigou, established as a nature reserve in 1978, was listed among the first national key scenic spots in 1982, included in the "World Heritage List" in 1992, confirmed as a national nature reserve in 1994, served on "World Network of Biosphere Reserves" in 1997 and entered the First Batch of National AAAAA-level Tourist Attractions in 2007.

"Clean waters and green mountains are invaluable assets." Jiuzhaigou is a model of the complementary and harmonious coexistence of environmental protection and economic development. Whether in line with the projects of farmland returning to forests, natural forest protection, innovative use of solar energy and wind energy, or the policy of "touring in but lodging outside the valley", these have all been the efforts by the local people in the hope of a better life while leaving the environment intact.

Unfortunately, a magnitude 7.0 earthquake struck the valley on August 8, 2017. On that very day, the earth trembled, the mountains swayed, both the lakes and the waterfalls broke... Will the Fairytale World cease to exist upon such a hard blow? Time gives the best answer: With the concerted efforts of all sectors, Jiuzhaigou, upon some "repairing", has reappeared with a brand-new look, with its plan for building a better ecology in which man and nature coexist harmoniously.

So tenacious is Jiuzhaigou before the erosion of glacier, collapse and erosion by earthquake and the impact of flowing water, which are powerful enough to destroy everything, but they have turned into the source of creation of its beauty. But at the same time, Jiuzhaigou is also vulnerable. Yet it is so fragile before natural disasters such as earthquakes, rock collapses, landslides, mudslides, or man-made impacts like sewage discharge and air pollution, all of which may result in its ecological imbalance. As it is the only one of its kind in the world, human beings cannot be too careful enough to let this bright pearl dazzle forever.

The Office of Sichuan Province Local Records

The Office of Aba Prefecture Local Records

The Management Bureau of Jiuzhaigou Scenic and Historic Area

August 31, 2023

大事记

1924

《松潘县志》记载："翠海，县东北一百余里，中羊峒番部内。海狭长数里，水光浮翠，倒映林岚。"描述了九寨沟的地理位置、景观规模、美学价值。

1942

传统的上、中、下羊峒（羊峒，南坪县古称）分别更名为上塘乡、永安乡、下塘乡，何药九寨（今九寨沟）在永安乡境内。

1949

12月16日，何药九寨随南坪县和平解放而解放。

1953

南坪县人民政府成立，何药九寨属塔藏乡，由南坪县管辖。

1956—1973

建立公社期间，何药九寨所在的扎如大队、荷叶大队、树正大队属隆康公社。

1956

四川省林业局王志强、傅春华进入九寨沟调查森林储备量，他们撰写的报告首次将塔藏乡扎如村、荷叶村和树正村所在林区称为九寨沟林区，这是"九寨沟"称谓首次出现在政府文件中。

1959

10月，南（坪）松（潘）公路建成通车。

1966

7月6日，白龙江林业管理局南坪林业局筹备处成立。

1967

南坪林业局在九寨沟中心位置组建哲泽（124）林场（名称出自《阿坝州南坪林业局志（1966—2015）》）。

1970

8月，四川省薯蓣（山药）资源调查科研人员进入九寨沟，开展薯蓣资源科研考察。

1972

南坪林业局在日则沟中心位置建立日则（126）林场。

1975

四川省革命委员会林业组向南坪林业局发出《关于日则、格泽沿沟200米以下禁止砍伐的通知》。

1978

12月15日，国务院批准建立南坪九寨沟自然保护区。

1979

1月31日，《四川日报》第3版发表公开介绍九寨风光的第一篇文章《童话世界九寨沟》。中共四川省委领导在《四川日报》转发的《情况反映》上批示："请阿坝州和省林业局采取措施保护。"中共阿坝州委决定：凡距九寨沟风景区1000米之内的地区一律禁止采伐森林，现仍在景区内采伐的应立即停止。

3月28日，四川省革命委员会印发《关于加强自然保护区建设的通知》，要求迅速将南坪九寨沟自然保护区建立起来。

1980

年初，九寨沟自然保护区管理所在九寨沟挂牌成立。

1982

10月7日，四川省林业厅正式通知南坪林业局，所属哲泽林场、日则林场于年底前从九寨沟自然保护区撤出。

11月8日，黄龙寺—九寨沟被列入国家第一批重点风景名胜区。

1983

7月，林业部同意九寨沟有限度发展旅游。同年秋，九寨沟正式开始国际旅游接待工作。九寨沟正式印制门票。

9月8日，四川省人民政府发布《关于加强南坪九寨沟自然保护和风景名胜区管理工作的决定》。

1984

1月，九寨沟风景名胜管理局（简称“九寨沟管理局”）成立，九寨沟正式对外开放。

1985

九寨沟管理局设旅游公司，对旅游工作进行统一管理。

1986

九寨沟管理局开工建设诺日朗给排水工程，架设羊峒至诺日朗、日则的电话线路，修建珍珠滩、五彩池等景点游路，拓宽羊峒至诺日朗公路，实施第一期泥石流治理工程。

1987

1月20日，城乡建设环境保护部批准《九寨沟风景名胜区总体规划》，规划年限为1985—2000年。

6月20—21日，四川省人民政府在南坪县召开九寨沟黄龙现场办公会，副省长顾金池主持，研究落实国务院旅游协调小组第七次会议精神和保护开发九寨沟、黄龙事宜。

1988

8月，南坪县设立九寨沟镇。

1990

建立长海、日则、树正、诺日朗、荷叶、扎如、沟口7个保护组。

1991

12月18日，九寨沟获颁“中国旅游胜地四十佳”证书。

1992

10月，塔藏、隆康两乡合并到九寨沟镇。

12月14日，经联合国教科文组织世界遗产委员会第十六届会议批准，将九寨沟风景名胜区作为自然遗产列入《世界遗产名录》。

1993

9月13—17日，九寨沟管理局参加第一届东亚地区国家公园与保护区会议。

1994

7月28日，林业部发文确认九寨沟保护区为森林和野生动物类型国家级自然保护区。

1995

9月14日，联合国教科文组织“人与生物圈计划”(MAB) 中国委员会将九寨沟纳入“中国生物圈保护区”序列，并列入“世界生物圈保护区”推荐名单。

10 月 10—15 日，四川省人民政府副省长徐世群在九寨沟召开现场办公会，阿坝州及省直有关部门负责人参加。会议以落实国务院批准的“沟内游，沟外住”总体规划为主题，坚持“保护第一”，开发、保护、利用有机结合，议定有关事项，还对九寨沟环线公路改造、九寨沟通信条件等提出意见。

11 月，四川省林业厅批准建立九寨国家森林公园，公园位于九寨沟风景区的外围地带。

1997

10 月 27—29 日，联合国教科文组织“人与生物圈计划”国际协调理事会执行局会议接纳九寨沟为“世界生物圈保护区”组织正式成员。

1998

6 月 19 日，经国务院批准，南坪县正式更名为“九寨沟县”。

7 月，九寨沟镇更名为“漳扎镇”。

1999

3 月 26 日，九寨沟绿色旅游观光有限责任公司在九寨沟沟口举行剪彩仪式，九寨沟开通绿色旅游环保观光车，除景区居民生活车和景区巡查车辆外，其余车辆全部停放在景区外。

2000

10 月 20 日，阿坝州机构编制委员会决定，九寨沟国家级自然保护区管理局、九寨沟风景名胜区管理局为州政府直属正县级事业单位，实行“两块牌子、一套人马”的管理体制。

11 月 20 日，九寨沟景区沟口综合工程项目建设完成，游客中心、游客中转中心、管理中心、中心广场等工程基本竣工，成为九寨沟的标志性建筑。

2001

5 月 1 日，九寨沟景区内宾馆饭店停止经营，景区实行“沟内游，沟外住”。

7 月 1 日，九寨沟景区实行限量游览措施，单日进沟游客控制在 1.2 万人次以内。

2002

9 月 3—8 日，首届中国（四川）国际熊猫节在九寨沟举行。

是年，九寨沟管理局完成并开通景区内近 60 千米的架空式木质栈道。

2003

10 月 20 日，九寨—黄龙机场正式通航。

2004

1 月 9 日，中国（四川）第四届南国冰雪节暨首届阿坝大九寨冰瀑旅游节开幕式在九寨沟举行。

10月16日，九寨沟国家地质公园开园揭碑。

2005

6月19日，“数字九寨沟”示范工程一期工程通过建设部验收。

7月28日，九寨沟管理局增挂世界遗产管理局牌子。

11—12月，阿坝州文物管理所与九寨沟县文化体育局组成的考古调查组，在九寨沟内发现荷叶寨遗址。

2006

6月14日，九寨沟管理局与克罗地亚普利特维采湖群国家公园签署合作议定书。

8月30日，“九寨沟生态环境与可持续发展国际联合实验室”挂牌成立。

是日，九寨沟管理局举行世界遗产管理局揭牌仪式。

2007

4月12日，“九寨沟生态环境与可持续发展战略规划国际研讨会”在九寨沟顺利召开。

5月8日，国家旅游局授予九寨沟全国首批国家AAAAA级旅游景区称号。

“十一”黄金周前夕，九寨沟景区自行研发并试用全国景区第一台自动售票机。

10月，九寨沟全自动水文监测站建成。

2008

5月12日14:28，汶川发生8.0级特大地震，九寨沟震感明显。九寨沟管理局立即启动应急预案，开展抗震救灾工作。

8月6日，九寨沟灾后旅游恢复启动仪式在九寨沟生态广场举行。

2009

7月14日，九寨沟扎如景区生态旅游项目正式对外开放。

7月18日，九寨沟国家级自然保护区首批通过“全国林业科普基地”审验。

2010

1月9日，“九寨沟旅游发展恳谈会暨战略合作联盟签字仪式”、中国九寨沟“智慧景区”暨国家“863”重大项目实施研讨会在九寨沟举行。

10月29日，九寨沟景区智能化管理与服务平台正式通过科技部专家验收，成为全国第一家实行网格化管理的景区。

12月24日，首届“中国旅游景区标准化建设论坛”在九寨沟召开。

2011

5月5日，中共阿坝州委机构编制委员会批准成立九寨沟国家地质公园管理局。

5月19日，首个“中国旅游日”暨“银发旅游月”启动仪式在九寨沟生态广场举行。

7月8日，九寨沟国家AAAAA级旅游景区管理局成立。至此形成九寨沟国家级自然保护区管理局、九寨沟风景名胜区管理局、九寨沟世界遗产管理局、九寨沟国家地质公园管理局、九寨沟国家AAAAA级旅游景区管理局“五块牌子、一套人马”的管理体制。

2012

3月26日，九寨沟管理局被国家旅游局确定为首批“全国旅游标准化示范单位”。

9月16日，九寨沟被中华环保联合会和中国旅游景区协会等单位评为首批全国低碳旅游示范区。

9月26日，科技部同意批准九寨沟生态保

护国际联合研究中心为国家国际科技合作基地。

2013

7月1日，阿坝州首批区域性地方涉旅标准——九寨沟景区编制的《旅游景区木制游步道建设规范》《旅游景区环境清洁质量要求与作业规程》正式实施。

7月3日，"九寨沟水资源与生态安全保护关键技术合作研究"项目启动仪式在九寨沟举行。

2014

5月24日，中国—克罗地亚生态保护国际联合研究中心在克罗地亚的普利特维采湖群国家公园举行揭牌仪式。

10月24日，首批"全国中小学环境教育社会实践基地"授牌仪式在九寨沟举行。

2015

4月1日，九寨沟管理局启动《四川省志·九寨沟志》编纂工作。

10月20日，九寨沟管理局应邀参加纪念中国世界遗产30周年、联合国教科文组织70周年暨建立国家公园体制专题研讨会，作题为《规范提升，常态管理，做世界遗产管理典范》的交流报告。

2016

7月6日，"国际科技合作专项中期会议暨水生态保护研讨会"在九寨沟召开。

10月24日，中国科学院·水利部成都山地灾害与环境研究所召集的第二届地球科学论坛在九寨沟举办，会议宣布成立九寨沟科学技术协会。

2017

7月1日，四川省安全科学技术研究院和九寨沟风景名胜区管理局共同起草编制的两部地方标准《旅游景区突发事件（事故）应急救援指南》《旅游景区安全防护设施基本规范》正式实施。

8月8日，21：19，九寨沟县发生7.0级地震。震中位于九寨沟景区丹祖沟北侧支沟北端。

8月8日，九寨沟管理局启动Ⅰ级应急响应，成立"8·8"九寨沟地震抗震救灾领导小组，全面推进抗震救灾工作；发布通告，九寨沟景区从8月9日起停止游客接待。

9月7日，九寨沟管理局成立"8·8"九寨沟地震灾后恢复重建领导小组。

12月1日，九寨沟"8·8"地震后地质灾害勘查、设计承包单位入驻九寨沟景区对各标段灾害点进行现场确认，标志着九寨沟景区灾后保护与地震灾后恢复重建项目勘察设计工作全面启动。

12月17日，九寨沟风景名胜区管理局参与起草的行业标准《景区游客高峰时段应对规范》（LB/T 068—2017）由国家旅游局发布，2018年5月1日实施。

2018

3月8日，九寨沟"8·8"地震后，九寨沟景区按照"限区域、限流量、限时段、限方式"的原则，分区域开放沟口经诺日朗瀑布至长海、扎如沟的扎如寺及日则沟的镜海。

11月13日，九寨沟景区下季节海公路边坡上部崩塌治理工程主体顺利完工，标志着地质灾害治理一期项目中最重要的地质灾害治理工作取得阶段性成果。

12月29日，九寨沟景区沟口立体式游客服务设施建设项目正式开工。至此，以九寨沟管理局为实施主体的29个灾后恢复重建项目全部开工，标志着九寨沟景区灾后恢复重建全面进入新阶段。

2019

9 月，四川省地方志编纂委员会编纂、九寨沟风景区管理局承编的《四川省志·九寨沟志》由方志出版社出版发行。

9 月 27 日，灾后恢复重建两年的九寨沟景区部分区域正式对外开放 (试运行)，实行单日最大限量 5000 人次，接待对象为旅行社团队游客，全网实名制预购景区门票、车票。

11 月 28 日，九寨沟管理局开放散客旅游，开放区域单日游客接待最大限量 2 万人次。

2020

1 月 28 日，九寨沟管理局开展新型冠状病毒感染的肺炎疫情防控工作，九寨沟景区暂停对外开放。

3 月 31 日，九寨沟景区分区域对外开放（试运行），每天入园限量 1 万人次，接待境内团队和散客，暂不接待入境游客。

10 月 16 日，联合国教科文组织国际自然与文化遗产空间技术中心（HIST）九寨沟工作站成立仪式在九寨沟举行，开启九寨沟自然遗产保护工作新篇章。

2021

7 月 16 日，九寨沟火花海作为世界遗产自然生态环境的保护与修复成功案例，亮相第 44 届世界遗产大会。

9 月 26 日，世界自然遗产地韧性能力建设与可持续发展国际研讨会在九寨沟举行。

是日，“中国—克罗地亚生物多样性和生态系统服务‘一带一路’联合实验室（筹）九寨沟科研基地”揭牌仪式在九寨沟举行。

9 月 28 日，第七届中国（四川）国际旅游投资大会开幕式暨九寨沟景区全域恢复开放仪式在九寨沟景区沟口立体式游客服务中心举行。

2022

4 月 24 日，九寨沟管理局沟口立体式游客服务设施建设项目荣获 LEED 金级认证（世界绿色建筑认证最高标准）。

5 月 6 日，四川省地方志工作办公室、阿坝州地方志办公室、九寨沟管理局在成都召开《九寨沟图志》编纂座谈会，正式启动《九寨沟图志》编纂工作。

11 月 22 日，九寨沟管理局决策咨询委员会（简称决咨委）正式成立。

11 月 25 日，九寨沟管理局组织开展九寨沟国家级风景名胜区设立 40 周年、列入《世界遗产名录》30 周年庆祝活动。

Memorabilia

1924

The Records of Songpan County stated, "Cuihai (meaning Blue Lake) is located some one hundred *li* northeast of the County, within the Middle Yangdong Tribe. The Lake is narrow but lasts several *li* and bright and blue is the water with the forest and haze reflected." This shows the geographic location, landscape scale and aesthetic value of Jiuzhaigou.

1942

The traditional Upper, Middle and Lower Yangdong (ancient name of Nanping County) got renamed Townships of Shangtang, Yong'an and Xiatang respectively, and Heyaojiuzhai (present-day Jiuzhaigou) was in Yong'an Township.

1949

On December 16, Heyaojiuzhai was liberated peacefully right after Nanping County.

1953

The People's Government of Nanping County was established, Heyaojiuzhai, which was part of Tazang Township, was put under the jurisdiction of Nanping County.

1956-1973

During the period of communes, the brigades of Zharu, Heye and Shuzheng where Heyaojiuzhai was located, belonged to Longkang Commune.

1956

Wang Zhiqiang and Fu Chunhua from the Forestry Bureau of Sichuan Province entered Jiuzhaigou to investigate forest reserves. For the first time, their report named the forest area where Zharu, Heye and Shuzheng Villages in Tazang Township as the Jiuzhaigou Forest Area. This was the first time that the title "Jiuzhaigou" appeared in a government document.

1959

In October, the Nanping-Songpan Highway was completed and opened to traffic.

1966

On July 6, the Preparatory Office of Nanping Forestry Bureau of Bailongjiang Forestry Administration was established.

1967

Nanping Forestry Bureau established Zheze (124) Forest Farm in the center of Jiuzhaigou (name from Annals of Nanping Forestry Bureau, Aba Prefecture (1966~2015) Forest Farm in the center of Jiuzhaigou.

1970

In August, scientific research personnel of Sichuan yam resource investigation entered Jiuzhaigou for scientific research.

1972

Nanping Forestry Bureau established Rize (126) Forest Farm in the center of Rize Gully.

1975

Sichuan Revolutionary Committee's Forestry Group issued the *Notice on the Prohibition of Logging Below 200 Meters Along Rize and Geze Gullies* to Nanping Forestry Bureau.

1978

On December 15, the State Council approved the establishment of Nanping Jiuzhaigou Nature Reserve.

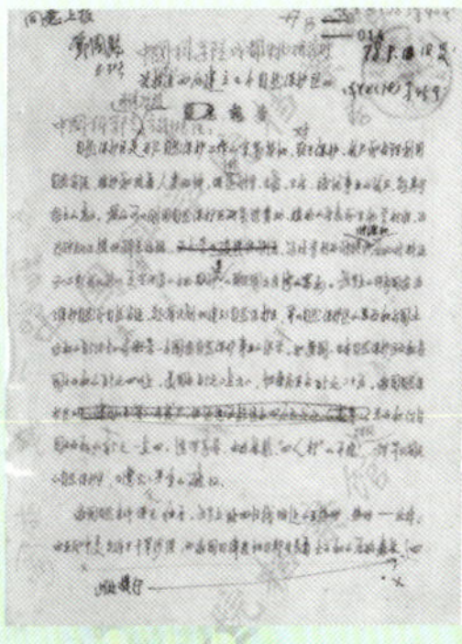

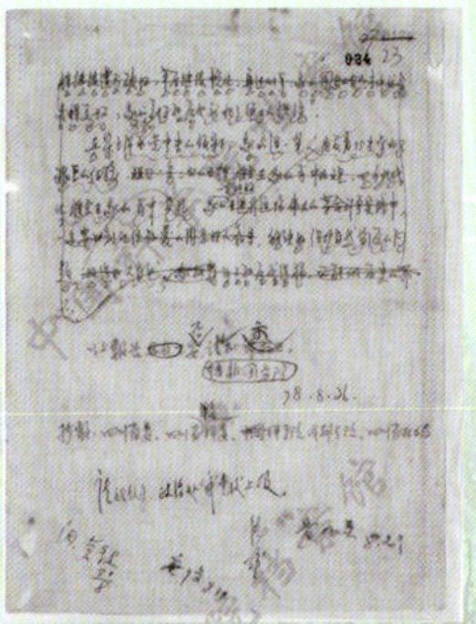

1979

On January 31, *Sichuan Daily* published its first article to introduce the great scenery of Jiuzhaigou named *A Fairytale World of Jiuzhaigou* on the third page, and forwarded it to the leadership of the Communist Party of China (CPC) Sichuan Provincial Committee by way of the *Condition Report*, which instructed that "Measures must be taken by Aba Prefecture and the Provincial Forestry Bureau." "Deforestation 1,000 meters within the scenic area of Jiuzhaigou is prohibited and tree-felling must be stopped with no delay," was the order from CPC Aba Prefecture Committee.

On March 28, the Revolutionary Committee of Sichuan Province issued *The Notice on Strengthening the Construction of Nature Reserves*, calling for the rapid establishment of Nanping Jiuzhaigou Nature Reserve.

1980

At its beginning, the Management Office of Jiuzhaigou Nature Reserve was established.

1982

On October 7, Sichuan Povincial Department of Forestry officially notified Nanping Forestry Bureau that its Forest Farms of Zheze and Rize be withdrawn from Jiuzhaigou Nature Reserve by the end of the year.

On November 8, Huanglong Temple-Jiuzhaigou entered the first batch of national key scenic spots.

1983

In July, the Ministry of Forestry approved the limited development of tourism in Jiuzhaigou. In the autumn of the same year, it officially began to receive international tourists and print tickets.

On September 8, the People's Government of Sichuan Province issued *the Decision on Strengthening Jiuzhaigou Nature Protection and Scenic Area Management in Nanping*.

1984

In January, the Management Bureau of Jiuzhaigou Scenic and Historic Area was established (Jiuzhaigou Management Bureau, for short), which indicates that it was officially opened to the outside world.

1985

Jiuzhaigou Management Bureau set up its tourism company to unify tourism management.

1986

Jiuzhaigou Management Bureau started Nuorilang Water Supply and Drainage Project, erected telephone lines from Yangdong to Nuorilang and Rize, built scenic spots such as Pearl Shoal and Wucai Pool, widened the highway from Yangdong to Nuorilang and implemented the first-phase project on debris flow control.

1987

On January 20, the Ministry of Urban and Rural Construction and Environmental Protection of the PRC approved *Master Plan for Jiuzhaigou Scenic and Historic Area*, with a planning period of 1985~2000.

From June 20 to 21, the People's Government of Sichuan Province held an on-site office meeting in Nanping County, chaired by vice governor Gu Jinchi, studying and implementing the spirit of the 7th meeting of Tourism Coordination Group under the State Council on the protection and development of Jiuzhaigou and Huanglong.

1988

In August, Nanping County established Jiuzhaigou Town.

1990

7 protection groups of Long Lake, Rize, Shuzheng, Nuorilang, Heye, Zharu and Entrance were established.

1991

On December 18, Jiuzhaigou received its certificate for "One of the Forty Best Chinese Tourist Attractions".

1992

In October, Tazang and Longkang Townships were merged into Jiuzhaigou Town.

On December 14, buttered was approved at the 16th session of the United Nations Educational, Scientific, and Cultural Organization (UNESCO) World Heritage Committee (WHC) to be on the *World Heritage List*.

1993

From September 13 to 17, Jiuzhaigou Management Bureau participated in the 1st on Conference East Asia National Parks and Protected Areas.

1994

On July 28, the Ministry of Forestry issued a document confirming that Jiuzhaigou Reserve is a national nature reserve for forests and wild animals.

1995

On September 14, "Man and the Biosphere Program" (MAB) of the Chinese Committee of UNESCO included Jiuzhaigou into "China Biosphere Reserves" and the recommended list of "World Biosphere Reserves".

From October 10 to 15, vice governor of Sichuan province Xu Shiqun, held an on-site office meeting in Jiuzhaigou, attended by the heads of Aba Prefecture and the relevant provincial departments. Its theme was to implement the overall plan of "touring in but lodging outside the valley" approved by the State Council, insisting on "Protection First", and organic combination development, protection and utilization; relevant matters were discussed, and views were expressed on the improvement of the Jiuzhaigou tourist ring road renovation and telecom conditions.

In November, Sichuan Povincial Department of Forestry approved the establishment of Jiuzhaigou National Forest Park what is located in the fringe zone of Jiuzhaigou Scenic Area.

1997

From October 27 to 29, Jiuzhaigou was accepted as a full member of the "World Biosphere Reserve" Organization at the meeting of the Executive Board of the International Coordinating Council of UNESCO Biosphere Program.

1998

On June 19, approved by the State Council, Nanping County was officially renamed "Jiuzhaigou County".

In July, Jiuzhaigou Town was renamed "Zhangzha Town".

1999

On March 26, Jiuzhaigou Green Sightseeing Co., Ltd. held a ribbon-cutting ceremony at its entrance. Jiuzhaigou opened green tourism and environment-friendly sightseeing vehicles. No other vehicles are to be parked inside the scenic spot but those for patrol and by the residents.

2000

On October 20, the Administration of Establishment Committee of Aba Prefecture decided that Jiuzhaigou National Nature Reserve and Scenic Area Management Bureaus should be county-level institutions directly under the Prefecture Government, operating on a system managed by the same contingent of personnel but under two names.

On November 20, with the completion of its comprehensive project on the entrance, its tourist, transfer, management centers, central square and so on came into being as landmark buildings.

2001

On May 1, all hotels and restaurants within the Scenic Area ceased operations owing to the implementation of "touring in but lodging outside the valley".

On July 1, the Scenic Area began to implement a measure to restrict tourists within 12,000 on a single day.

2002

From September 3 to 8, the First China (Sichuan) International Panda Festival was held in Jiuzhaigou.

This year, Jiuzhaigou Management Bureau completed and opened a nearly 60km elevated wooden plank road in the scenic area.

2003

On October 20, Jiuzhai-Huanglong Airport was officially opened to air traffic.

2004

On January 9, the opening ceremony of the 4th Southern China Ice and Snow Festival and the 1st Aba Great Jiuzhaigou Icefall Tourism Festival were held in Jiuzhaigou.

On October 16, Jiuzhaigou National Geological Park was opened.

2005

On June 19, the first phase of "Digital Jiuzhaigou" project was accepted by the Ministry of Construction.

On July 28, the Jiuzhaigou added the World Heritage Administration board.

From November to December, an archaeological survey team composed of Aba Prefecture Cultural Relics Management Office and Jiuzhaigou County Culture and Sports Bureau discovered the Heye Village site in Jiuzhaigou.

2006

On June 14, Jiuzhaigou Management Bureau and Croatian Plitvice Lakes National Park signed a cooperation agreement.

On August 30, "International Joint Lab for Jiuzhaigou Ecological Environment and Sustainable Development" was established.

On the same day, the unveiling ceremony of the Jiuzhaigou Management Bureau was held.

2007

On April 12, "International Symposium on Jiuzhaigou Ecological Environment and Sustainable Development Strategic Planning" was held in Jiuzhaigou.

On May 8, National Tourism Administration awarded Jiuzhaigou the First Batch of National AAAAA-level Tourist Attractions.

On the eve of "October 1" Golden Week, Jiuzhaigou led China in testing the first automatic ticket vendor of its independent development in scenic areas.

In October, Jiuzhaigou automatic hydrological monitoring station was completed.

2008

At 14:28 on May 12, a magnitude 8.0 earthquake occurred in Wenchuan and Jiuzhaigou felt the quake distinctly. Its Management Bureau immediately launched the emergency plan on earthquake relief.

On August 6, the launching ceremony of Jiuzhaigou post-quake tourism recovery was held in its Ecological Plaza.

2009

On July 14, its eco-tourism project of Zharu Scenic Area was officially opened to the public.

On July 18, Jiuzhaigou National Nature Reserve was among the first to pass the inspection of "National Forestry Science Popularization Base".

2010

On January 9, "Symposium on Jiuzhaigou Tourism Development and Signing Ceremony on Strategic Cooperation Alliance", China Jiuzhaigou "Smart Scenic Spot" and Seminar on National "863" Major Project Implementation were held in Jiuzhaigou.

On October 29, the intelligent management and service platform of Jiuzhaigou Scenic Spot officially passed the inspection and acceptance by experts from the Ministry of Science and Technology, making it the first of its kind across the country to implement its grid management.

On December 24, the first "Forum on Tourism Scenic Spots Standardization Construction in China" was held in Jiuzhaigou.

2011

On May 5, the Administraion of Establishment Committee of the CPC Aba Prefecture Committee approved the establishment of Jiuzhaigou National Geopark Management Bureau.

On May 19, the launching ceremony of the first "China Tourism Day" and "Silver Hair Tourism Month" was held at Jiuzhaigou's Ecological Plaza.

On July 8, Jiuzhaigou National AAAAA-level Tourist Scenic Area Management Bureau was established, hence the coexistence of the system of the Management Bureau of Jiuzhaigou Scenic and Historic Area, World Heritage Administration, National Geopark and National AAAAA-level Tourist Scenic Area Management Bureaus by the same contingent of personnel.

2012

On March 26, Jiuzhaigou Management Bureau was included in the first "National Tourism Standardization Demonstration Units" by China National Tourism Administration.

On September 16, Jiuzhaigou was rated as one of the first national low-carbon tourism demonstration areas by All-China Environment Federation and China Tourist Attractions Association.

On September 26, the Ministry of Science and Technology approved International Joint Research Center for Jiuzhaigou Ecological Protection as a national base for international sci-tech cooperation.

2013

On July 1, the first batch of regional tourism-related standards in Aba Prefecture were officially implemented in the *Specifications for Construction of Wooden Trails in Tourist Scenic Spots* and *Requirements and Operational Regulations for Environmental Cleanliness in Tourist Scenic Spots* compiled by Jiuzhaigou Scenic Area.

On July 3, the launching ceremony of "Key Technology Cooperation Research on Jiuzhaigou Water Resources and Ecological Security Protection" was held in Jiuzhaigou.

2014

On May 24, the International Joint Research Center for China-Croatia Ecological Conservation held an inauguration ceremony in the latter's Plitvice Lakes National Park.

On October 24, the awarding ceremony for the first "National Elementary and Middle School Environmental Education Social Practice Base" was held in Jiuzhaigou.

2015

On April 1, Jiuzhaigou Management Bureau started compiling *Sichuan Provincial Records–Jiu-*

zhaigou Records*.

On October 20, Jiuzhaigou Management Bureau, invited to the symposium on the commemoration of the 30th anniversary of China's World Heritage, the 70th anniversary of UNESCO and the establishment of national park system, made a report entitled *Standard Improvement, Normal Management and Be a Model of World Heritage Management.*

2016

On July 6, "Interim Conference on International Science and Technology Cooperation and Seminar on Water Ecological Protection" was held in Jiuzhaigou.

On October 24, the second Earth Science Forum, convened by Chengdu Institute of Mountain Hazards and Environment, Ministry of Water Resources, and Chinese Academy of Sciences, was held in Jiuzhaigou. The meeting announced the establishment of Jiuzhaigou Science and Technology Association.

2017

On July 1, the two local standards of *Guidelines for Emergency Rescue in Tourist Scenic Spots (Accidents)* and *Basic Specifications for Safety and Protection Facilities in Tourist Scenic Spots* jointly drafted and compiled by Sichuan Institute of Safety Science and Technology and the Management Bureau of Jiuzhaigou Scenic and Historic Area were implemented.

On August 8, at 21:19, an earthquake of magnitude 7.0 occurred in Jiuzhaigou County, with epicenter at the northern end of the branch gully on the north side of Danzu Gully in Jiuzhaigou Scenic Area.

On August 8, Jiuzhaigou Management Bureau initiated a Level I emergency response, established a leading group to relieve this earthquake and comprehensively promoted comprehensively promoted related work of the "8·8" Earthquake; issued a notice that the scenic area was to stop receiving tourists from August 9 onward.

On September 7, the Bureau above established a leading group for post-quake recovery and reconstruction of the "8·8" Earthquake.

On December 1, after the "8·8" Earthquake, geological disaster survey and design contractors settled down in the scenic area to confirm the disaster's point in each bid section, kicking off a full start of its survey and design work for post-quake protection and recovery.

On December 17, the Management Bureau of Jiuzhaigou Scenic and Historic Area participated in the drafting of the industry standard *Regulations on Standards of Responding to Tourist Scenic Area During Peak Hours* (LB/T 068-2017), which was issued by the National Tourism Administration and implemented on May 1, 2018.

2018

On March 8, after the "8·8" Earthquake, the scenic area opened its entrance to the Long Lake via Nuorilang Waterfall, Zharu Temple in the Zharu Gully and the Mirror Lake in the Rize Gully based on "restricted area, flow, time and means principle."

On November 13, the main works of the collapse control above the highway slope along the Lower Seasonal Lake in Jiuzhaigou Scenic Area was completed, marking the phased results of greatest importance in the first-phase geological disaster control.

On December 29, construction of the tridimensional tourist service facility at the entrance to Jiuzhaigou Scenic Area officially started. So far, the 29 post-quake restoration and reconstruction projects in the charge of the Management Bureau had all begun, which marked that the post-quake restoration and reconstruction of the scenic area had entered a new stage.

2019

In September, the very first *Sichuan Provincial Records–Jiuzhaigou Records*, edited by Sichuan Provincial Local Records Compilation Committee and undertaken by the Management Bureau of Jiuzhaigou Scenic and Historic Area, was published by Publishing House of Local Records.

On September 27, part of the scenic area, restored and reconstructed two years after the earthquake, was officially opened to the public (for trial operation), its daily maximum number reaching 5,000 group tourists from travel agencies. Entrance tickets and bus tickets for the scenic spot can be pre-purchased online through the real-name system.

On November 28, the Management Bureau opened to individual tourists, receiving a daily maximum number of 20,000 ones.

2020

On January 28, the scenic area was temporarily closed in response to the prevention and control of Covid-19 carried out by Jiuzhaigou Management Bureau.

On March 31, Jiuzhaigou Scenic Area was partially opened to the public (for trial operation), with a daily number of 10,000 (domestic groups and individuals only) tourists.

On October 16, the inauguration ceremony of Jiuzhaigou Work Station of UNESCO International Center for Natural and Cultural Heritage Space Technology (HIST) was held here, which marked a new chapter in the protection of its natural heritage.

2021

On July 16, the Sparkling Lake in Jiuzhaigou was unveiled at the 44th World Heritage Conference as a successful case of protection and restoration of natural eco-environment.

On September 26, International Symposium on Resilience Capacity Building and Sustainable Development at World Natural Heritage Sites was held in Jiuzhaigou.

On the same day, the unveiling ceremony of "China-Croatia Biodiversity and Ecosystem Services and Jiuzhaigou Research Base for 'Belt and Road' Joint Lab (Preparatory)" was held in Jiuzhaigou.

On September 28, the opening ceremonies of the 7th China (Sichuan) International Tourism Investment Conference and Restoration of Jiuzhaigou Scenic Area were held at its tridimensional Tourist Service Center of the entrance to Jiuzhaigou.

2022

On April 24, its construction project of tridimensional Tourist Service Facility at the entrance won LEED Gold Certification–the world's highest standard for green building.

On May 6, Sichuan and Aba Prefecture Local Record Offices, together with Jiuzhaigou Management Bureau, held a symposium on the compiling of *Jiuzhaigou Pictorial Annals* in Chengdu, hence the official launch of this book.

On November 22, the Jiuzhaigou management Bureau's Decision Consulting Committee (Consulting Committee, for short) was formally established.

On November 25, the Jiuzhaigou Management Bureau organized the celebration of the 40th anniversary of the establishment of the Jiuzhaigou National Scenic and Historic Area and the 30th anniversary of its inclusion on *World Heritage List*.

四季长海（春：2022 年，周正强 摄；夏：2009 年，桑吉 摄；秋：2008 年，九寨沟管理局 供图；冬：2007 年，于宁 摄）

冬
Winter

五花海彩林（2020 年，梁峰 摄）　Colorful forest at Wuhua Lake (photo by Liang Feng, 2020)

诺日朗群海（2019 年，高华康 摄）
Nuorilang Lake Cluster (photo by Gao Huakang, 2019)

珍珠滩（2019 年，高华康 摄）

Pearl Shoal (photo by Gao Huakang, 2019)

冬日五花海（2019年，梁峰 摄）

Wuhua Lake in winter (photo by Liang Feng, 2019)

九看
Jiuzhaigou in Nine Episodes
九寨

之一
Episode One

水景之最

A Crown of Waterscapes

长海左岸（2017 年，桑吉 摄）

The left bank of the Long Lake (photo by Sangji, 2017)

九寨沟位于阿坝藏族羌族自治州九寨沟县漳扎镇境内。4 亿年前，这里还是一片汪洋。此后在燕山运动的反复作用下，海平面持续下降，陆地裸露而出，随后发生的喜马拉雅运动加快地壳的抬升速度，频繁的地震与多变的气候进一步塑造着这里的地形。

伴随第四纪全球性的气温骤降，大规模的山岳冰川在九寨沟孕育、生长。冰期往复、冷暖变动，河流沿着构造薄弱带侵蚀发育，冰碛物在流水、岩溶和生物作用下形成稳固的堤坝，阶梯状的湖泊和海子群逐渐成形，湖水超出堤坝的承载上限后，外溢成高大的瀑布或低矮的跌水。在漫长的时光里，流水、钙华和生物等更为柔和的力量对九寨沟进行着一次次精细的雕刻，最终呈现出一个如梦似幻的“童话世界”“人间仙境”。

如今的九寨沟，既是中国第一个以保护自然风景为主要目的的自然保护区和“世界生物圈保护区”成员，又是国家级风景名胜区和国家 AAAAA 级旅游景区，被列入《世界遗产名录》，还是以地质遗迹和森林生态系统为内容的国家地质公园。这片地处川西北群山中的大美之地，正期待着更多关注的目光。

火花海（2022 年，桑吉 摄）
Sparkling Lake (photo by Sangji, 2022)

Jiuzhaigou, located in Zhangzha Town, Jiuzhaigou County, Aba Zang and Qiang Autonomous Prefecture, was still part of a vast ocean 400 million years ago. Since then, under the repeated action of the Yanshan Movement, the sea level continued to drop and the land was exposed, while the subsequent Himalayan Movement accelerated the uplift of the crust and the frequent earthquakes and the everchanging climate further shaped the terrain here.

With the sudden drop in global temperature in the Quaternary, large-scale mountain glaciers were conceived and grown right here. With the reciprocation of ice periods, cold and warm changes, rivers eroded and developed along the unsubstantial tectonic belts, moraines formed stable dams under the action of flowing water, karstification and living things; stepped lakes and clusters of Haizi gradually formed; when water therein got higher than the dams, it overflowed in the form of a huge waterfall or head fall. Over a long period of time, softer forces such as flowing water, travertine and living things engraved the valley time and time again and finally brought into being a dreamlike Fairytale World and Fairyland on Earth .

Jiuzhaigou today, not only a national nature reserve and a member of the “World Biosphere Reserve”, but also a national scenic spot and National AAAAA-level Tourist Attractions, is on the *World Heritage List* and a national geopark with geological relics and forest ecosystem. This beautiful land located in the mountains of northwest Sichuan is looking forward to more attention.

长海左岸褶曲（2013 年，蹇代君 摄）
Folds on the left bank of the Long Lake (photo by Jian Daijun, 2013)

喜马拉雅运动

简称“喜山运动”，以造山运动、断裂运动和岩浆活动为主要特征。1945 年，中国地质学家黄汲清提出用“喜马拉雅运动”表示中国境内新生代的造山运动。九寨沟经历多期构造运动，其中喜山运动对九寨沟的地质演化影响最为强烈。印度洋板块与亚欧板块的碰撞使整个古地中海出现强烈褶皱，青藏高原强烈隆起，受其影响，九寨沟地区海拔急剧抬升，断裂活动加剧，冰川作用显著，气候变化异常剧烈。

Himalayan Movement

It is characterized by orogeny, fault movements and magmatic activities. In 1945, Chinese geologist Huang Jiqing proposed the use of “Himalayan Movement” to describe the Cenozoic orogeny in China. Jiuzhaigou has experienced multiple tectonic movements, among which the Himalayan movement had the strongest impact on its geological evolution. The collision between the Indian Ocean plate and the Eurasian plate caused strong folds in the entire Paleo-Teyhys Ocean and strong uplift of the Qinghai-Xizang Plateau. Thus affected, Jiuzhaigou received a sharp rise in altitude, intensified faulting activities, significant glaciation and extremely severe climate changes.

第四纪冰川遗存的 U 形谷（2011 年，周正强 摄）
U-shaped valley of Quaternary glacial remnants (photo by Zhou Zhengqiang, 2011)

第四纪冰期

也称“第四纪大冰期”，是地质史上距今最近的一次地球表面覆盖有大规模冰川的地质时期。这一时期大约始于距今 200 万～ 300 万年前，结束于 1 万～ 2 万年前。第四纪冰期的冰川活动奠定了九寨沟自然风景的地貌基础，也是这里形成许多湖泊与瀑布的重要成因。

Quaternary Ice Age

As the most recent geological period in geological history when the earth’s surface was covered with large-scale glaciers, the Quaternary Ice Age began about 2~3 million years ago and ended 10,000~20,000 years before now. It is these glacial activities that have laid the foundation of the Jiuzhaigou’s natural scenery, hence the key cause of formation of various lakes and waterfalls here.

九寨沟旅游区

位于阿坝州东北部，九寨沟县西南部，涵盖九寨沟风景名胜区、九寨国家森林公园和漳扎镇域，总面积约 1200 平方千米。其中，九寨国家森林公园于 1995 年经林业部批准建立，位于九寨沟旅游区西部边缘，属九寨沟风景区外围地带，总面积 370 平方千米。

Jiuzhaigou Tourist Area

Located in the northeast of Aba Prefecture and the southwest of Jiuzhaigou County, it covers the Jiuzhaigou Scenic and Historic Area, Jiuzhai National Forest Park and Zhangzha Town, totaling about 1,200 square kilometers. Among them, the Jiuzhaigou National Forest Park that was established with the approval of the Ministry of Forestry in 1995, is located on the western edge of the Tourist Area and belongs to the peripheral area of the scenic spot, with a total area of 370 square kilometers.

九寨沟国家级风景名胜区区位关系图（2017 年，九寨沟管理局 供图）

Location map of Jiuzhaigou National Scenic and Historie Area (photo by courtesy of Jiuzhaigou Management Bureau, 2017)

1978 年 12 月 15 日，国家林业局所颁四川九寨沟国家级自然保护区（牌）（九寨沟管理局 供图）

Sichuan Jiuzhaigou National Nature Reserve awarded by State Forestry Administration on December 15, 1978 (photo by courtesy of Jiuzhaigou Management Bureau)

2004 年 1 月，中华人民共和国国土资源部所颁四川九寨沟国家地质公园（牌）（九寨沟管理局 供图）

Sichuan Jiuzhaigou National Geopark of China awarded by the Ministry of Land and Resources of the People's Republic of China (PRC) in January, 2004 (photo by courtesy of Jiuzhaigou Management Bureau)

四川九寨沟国家级自然保护区

位于岷山山脉南段弓杠岭东北侧，南北长 40.5 千米，东西宽 35.4 千米，总面积 642.97 平方千米。范围东界为甘孜公盖山顶、马家乡行政界线、王朗保护区界，南与松潘县境内的黄龙寺保护区相邻，西界为松潘县县界沿扎玛且莫普德山主山脊而下到比芒，再顺塔藏乡行政区划界线至九寨沟沟口，北以扎如沟北面的大山脊为界。

Sichuan Jiuzhaigou National Nature Reserve

Located on the northeast side of Ridge Gonggang in the southern section of the Minshan Mountains, it is 40.5 kilometers long from north to south and 35.4 kilometers wide from east to west, with a total area of 642.97 square kilometers. It ends in the east from the top of Ganzi Gonggai Mountain, the administrative boundary of Majia Township and the boundary of Wanglang Reserve, abuts in the south on Huanglong Temple Reserve in Songpan County and in the west on the main ridge of Zamaqiemopude Mountain along the boundary of Songpan County and down to Bimang and then along the administrative boundary of Tazang Township to the entrance of Jiuzhaigou and terminates in the north at the big ridge north of the Zharu Gully.

四川九寨沟国家地质公园

位于九寨沟县西部，南北长 38 千米，东西宽 23 千米，总面积约 729.6 平方千米。范围南至尕尔纳峰，以九寨沟县和松潘县县界为界，西界为藏马龙里沟沟尾山脊—扎玛且莫普德—中查沟山脊—永和塘一线，北界为永和塘至隆康段北侧分水岭，东至红海（红池）、黑海（青池），接白河自然保护区和王朗自然保护区界。

Sichuan Jiuzhaigou National Geopark

Located in the west of Jiuzhaigou County, it is 38 kilometers long from north to south and 23 kilometers wide from east to west, about 729.6 square kilometers in total. It extends from Gaerna Peak in the south, where the counties of Jiuzhaigou and Songpan meet, ends in the west along the ridge above Zangmalongli Gully-Zamaqiemopude Mountain-ridge of Zhongcha Gully-Yonghetang. Its north boundary is the section where Yonghetang and Longkang divide the watershed on the north side, while in the east, reaching the Red Lake (Red Pond) and Black Lake (Blue Pond) and abuts on the nature reserves of Baihe and Wanglang.

九寨飘雪（2011 年，周正强 摄）

气象水文
Meteorology and Hydrology

Snow across Jiuzhaigou (photo by Zhou Zhengqiang, 2011)

九寨沟位于川西北高原、岷山山脉南段。东南方龙门山阻挡来自太平洋的暖湿气流，使这里降雨偏少；北面秦岭山脉屏护，大大削弱冬季蒙古高原冷高压寒潮影响。在高原季风和热带海洋季风影响下，九寨沟气候总体表现为冷凉干燥的温带季风气候特征，气候垂直分带明显，海拔 2500 米以上为山地寒温带季风气候，2500 米以下为温带季风气候，平坝为亚热带季风气候，焚风效应明显。

九寨沟冬无严寒，夏无酷暑，最热月（7 月）平均温度 16.8 ℃，最冷月（1 月）平均温度 -3.7 ℃。年降水量为 700 ～ 800 毫米，年降水日超 150 天，主要集中在 5—10 月，占全年降水量的 75% 以上。夏半年多暴雨，多偏南风；冬半年多雪，多偏北风。日照充足，紫外线强，很少见雾。

九寨沟位于岷江、嘉陵江、涪江三江分水岭地区，最远支流发源于区域南缘的岷山尕尔纳峰，距沟口直线距离约 30 千米，主流全长约 45 千米，全流域面积约 643 平方千米，河网密度大，水系切割深。

地表径流和地下径流共同构成九寨沟水系，其中，地表径流表现为呈阶梯状交替分布的一系列湖泊（海子）、瀑布、河流和涌泉。次级水文单元之间的地下补给和排泄关系，使九寨沟形成复杂的隐蔽水系结构，也为区内地貌和景观塑造提供重要的水动力。

焚风效应（2023 年，云何视觉 制图）
Foehn Effect (by Yunhe Vision, 2023)

Jiuzhaigou, located on the northwestern plateau of Sichuan and the southern section of the Minshan Mountains, gets a slight rainfall, owing to the facts that Longmen Mountain in the southeast blocks the warm and humid airflow from the Pacific Ocean. At the same time, under the protection of the Qinling Mountains in the north, the impact of the cold wave caused by cold high pressure over the Mongolian Plateau on Jiuzhaigou in winter is greatly weakened. Under the influence of plateau monsoon and tropical marine monsoon, the climate here is generally characterized by a cool and dry temperate monsoon climate, with obvious altitudinal zoning. Places over 2,500 meters above sea level witness a mountainous cold temperate monsoon climate, below that is temperate monsoon climate and flatlands is subtropical monsoon climate, where the Foehn Effect is obvious.

Its winter and summer are neither too cold nor hot, with an average temperature of 16.8°C (hottest in July) and −3.7°C (coldest in January). The annual precipitation is 700~800mm here and its rainy days exceed 150, mainly in May to October, which accounts for over 75% of the whole year. The summer half of the year witnesses heavy rains and southerly winds, while the winter half sees more snow and northerly winds. There is plenty of sunshine, strong ultraviolet rays and rare fog.

Jiuzhaigou is located in the watershed area of the Minjiang River, the Jialing River and the Fujiang River. Its farthest tributary originates from the Gaerna Peak in the Minshan Mountains on the southern edge, which is about 30 kilometers from the valley's entrance. Jiuzaigou's main stream lasts around 45 kilometers and covers about 643 square kilometers, with a dense network, the water system here cuts deep.

The water system here is constituted of both surface and underground runoff, in which the former appears as a cluster of lakes (or called Haizi), waterfalls, rivers and springs distributed alternately as a ladder does. The subsurface recharge and discharge relationship between the secondary hydrological units helps the Jiuzhaigou form a complex hidden water system structure, providing an important hydrodynamic force for the shaping of landforms and landscapes in the area.

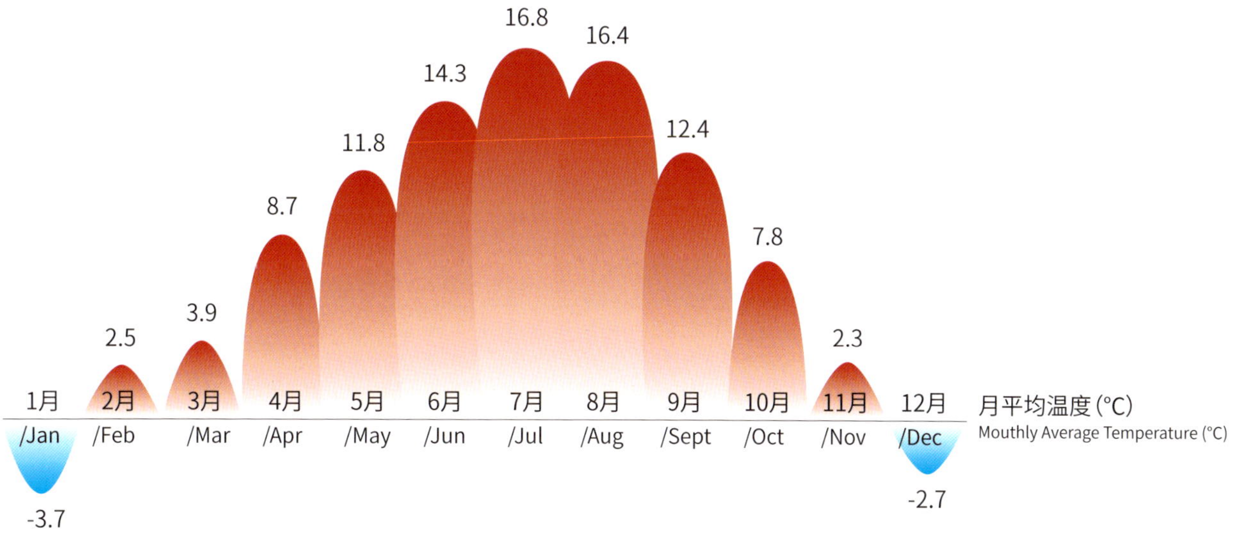

九寨沟多年月平均温度统计图（2023 年，云何视觉 制图）
Statistical Chart of Years' Monthly Mean Temperature in Jiuzhaigou (by Yunhe Vision, 2023)

焚风效应

地理领域术语，一般指“焚风”，是空气作绝热下沉运动时，因温度升高、湿度降低形成的一种干热风。焚风是山高谷深山区特有的天气现象，每下降 1000 米，温度平均升高 6.5 °C，九寨沟区域东侧有海拔 3800 米的野猪关梁子等山梁作屏障，气流越过高山后沿山坡向下吹，使河谷平坝地带的气温快速升高 20 °C以上，促进冰雪消融、植物生长，也容易引起森林野火、干旱等灾害。

Foehn Effect

As a geographic term, foehn generally refers to a dry hot wind formed when air moves adiabatically and sinks due to the rise in temperature and drop in humidity. It is a weather phenomenon typical of mountainous areas with deep valleys. As the altitude drops by 1,000 meters, the temperature rises by 6.5°C. On the east of the Jiuzhaigou area stand mountain ridges at an altitude of 3,800 meters such as Yezhuguan (Boar Pass) as barriers. The temperature in the surrounding flat and dam area, once air flows down the slope after crossing the mountains, will rise rapidly by 20°C and above and promote the melting of ice and snow and the growth of flora, hence the immediate cause of forest fires, droughts and the like.

五彩水色成因

九寨沟流水清澈、水质优良。阳光投射清澈水体后，近红外的长波段暖光被大量吸收，近紫外的短波段冷光穿透水体，再经反射、折射、散射等方式进入人的眼睛，呈现出以蓝绿色为主调的多彩水色。此外，湖底的灰白色钙华、黄绿色藻类对透射光的选择性吸收和反射，以及水生植物群落所含叶绿素深浅的不同，也增加了湖水色彩的层次和变化。

Cause of Colorful Water

Jiuzhaigou boasts clear and quality water. When the Sun shines on the clear water, it absorbs plenty of near-infrared long-wavelength warm light and the near-ultraviolet short-wavelength cold light penetrates the water and then enters the human eye through reflection, refraction and scattering, showing colorful water (dominantly blue-green). In addition, selective absorption and reflection of transmitted light by gray-white travertine and yellow-green algae at the lake bottom, as well as the difference in the depth of chlorophyll contained in the aquatic vegetation can increase the level and change of water color.

蓝冰奇观

蓝冰，学名冰川冰，因冬季粒雪经成冰作用形成的冰体中富含微小气泡，蓝光波长较短易被散射，而使冰块呈现蓝色。低温、洁净的空气和水是形成蓝冰的基础条件，温度越低，冰层越厚，蓝冰越明显。蓝冰是九寨沟六绝之一，只在每年 1 月底和 2 月初出现，且在特定条件下才可见，最佳观赏期仅短短十余天。

Blue Ice Wonder

Blue ice (glacier ice by scientific name), is thus called because the ice body formed of grain snow in winter through ice formation is rich in tiny air bubbles and the blue light with a short wavelength is easily scattered, making the ice appear blue. Low temperature, clean air and water are the basic conditions for the formation of blue ice. And the lower the temperature, the thicker the ice and the more obvious the blue ice. As one of the six wonders in the Jiuzhaigou, blue ice appears only at the juncture of January and February every year and this phenomenon can be seen only under certain conditions, the best viewing period no more than ten days.

1 珍珠滩蓝冰（2009 年，桑吉 摄）
2 纯水的总散射系数随入射波波长的变化情况一览表（2023 年，云何视觉 制图）
资料来源：四川省地方志编纂委员会编《四川省志 • 九寨沟志》，方志出版社，2019 年

1 Blue ice across the Pearl Shoal (photo by Sangji, 2009)
2 A List of How Total Scattering Coefficient of Pure Water Changes with Incident Wavelength (by Yunhe Vision, 2023)
Source: *Sichuan Provincial Records–Jiuzhaigou Records* by Sichuan Provincial Local Records Compilation Committee, Publishing House of Local Records, 2019

1

2

紫光 Violet light	蓝光 Blue light	青光 Cyan light	绿光 Green light	橙光 Orange light	红光 Red light
波长 Wavelength 400~425纳米(nm)	波长 Wavelength 450纳米(nm)	波长 Wavelength 475纳米(nm)	波长 Wavelength 500~575纳米(nm)	波长 Wavelength 600纳米(nm)	波长 Wavelength 650~760纳米(nm)
散射系数 Scattering coefficient 58.1~44.7	散射系数 Scattering coefficient 34.9	散射系数 Scattering coefficient 27.6	散射系数 Scattering coefficient 22.2~12.5	散射系数 Scattering coefficient 10.9	散射系数 Scattering coefficient 8.3~4.3

树正群海秋韵（2020 年，夏雪东尔 摄）

湖泊（海子）

Lakes (Haizi)

Autumnal charm of Shuzheng Lake Cluster (photo by Xiaxue Dong'er, 2020)

九寨沟的景观资源以水域风光为主体，其中又以湖泊（民间称“海子”）为核心。九寨沟内有 114 个海子，包括 16 个季节性和沼泽性湖泊，累计容积约 6330 万立方米，主要集中于“Y”形的主干沟谷中，尤其以日则沟和树正沟数量最多。两条沟谷中密集分布的湖泊群被人们称之为“群海”。

树正沟的湖泊除卧龙海、双龙海两个湖泊更具顺沟向的特征外，其他湖泊都以横向分布为主。日则沟内群湖与叠瀑顺沟的走向相间呈梯级分布，层湖叠瀑、美不胜收。则查洼沟分布有九寨沟最大、最长、最深的湖泊——长海。长海沿沟谷走向呈“S”形分布，是九寨沟湖泊群重要的天然调节水库。

九寨沟纵横交错的沟谷内，湖泊星罗棋布，湖面光滑如镜，湖水清澈见底，林岚倒影入水，清晰可见。关于九寨沟的海子，当地还流传有动人的传说：男神达戈爱上女神沃洛色嫫，将一面宝镜作为定情信物赠送给她。不料魔鬼插足，女神不慎打碎宝镜，其碎片散落人间，变成 114 个海子，于是便有了仙境——九寨沟。

镜海（2022 年，桑吉 摄）
Mirror Lake (photo by Sangji, 2022)

The landscape resources here are dominated by waterscapes and lakes (generally called "Haizi" among the folks) as the core. There are 114 lakes in Jiuzhaigou, including 16 seasonal and marsh lakes, with a total volume of about 63.3 million cubic meters. These lakes mainly concentrate along the Y-shaped major Gully, especially in the Rize Gully and the Shuzheng Gully. The densely distributed group of lakes in these two valleys is called the "lake cluster".

The lakes in the Shuzheng Gully are all distributed horizontally, except Wolong (sleeping dragon) Lake and the Shuanglong (double dragon) Lake. The lake cluster and waterfalls in the Rize Gully are distributed all along the gully in the shape of a ladder, with a breath-taking scene of one lake and waterfalls after another. Zezhawa Gully is distributed with the Long Lake, the largest, longest and deepest one in Jiuzhaigou; the Long Lake is in an "S" shape along the gully and serves as a key natural regulating reservoir for all the lake clusters in Jiuzhaigou.

In the crisscrossing gullies of Jiuzhaigou lie dotted lakes, each lake is smooth as a mirror, its water is crystal clear and reflection of trees is so clearly visible. As for the lakes nestled in Jiuzhaigou, there goes a moving legend: the male god Da'ge fell in love with the goddess Woluosemo and presented her with a precious mirror as a token of love. Unexpectedly, when the devil intervened, the goddess accidentally broke the precious mirror and its fragments scattered around the world, becoming 114 lakes, so there is a fairyland–Jiuzhaigou.

芦苇海

海拔 2192 米，长 1520 米，宽 124 ～ 186 米，深 3 米，是树正沟下游半沼泽化的水流通道湿地，呈条带状分布。河道两侧丛生有许多芦苇，引来鸟儿在此觅食、繁衍、栖息。芦苇随季节变化由绿转黄，雪白的芦苇花盛放，一簇簇，一丛丛，将九寨沟的秋天装点得越发迷人。

Reed Lake

2,192 meters above sea level, 1,520 meters long, 124~186 meters wide and 3 meters deep, it is a semi-swamp water channel wetland on the lower reaches of the Shuzheng Gully, distributed linearly. There are many reeds clustered on both sides of the river, attracting birds to forage, reproduce and inhabit here. All the reeds change with each season from green to yellow and their snow-white flowers bloom in clusters, making the autumnal Jiuzhaigou more charming.

（芦苇海（2009 年，桑吉 摄））

Reed Lake (photo by Sangji, 2009)

双龙海（2011 年，周正强 摄）
Shuanglong Lake (photo by Zhou Zhengqiang, 2011)

双龙海

海拔 2200 米，长 290 米，宽 247 米，深 9 米，位于吉玉朗瀑布下。两条呈带状的生物钙华礁堤在海子底部若隐若现，湖堤上部为钙华，下部为冰碛物，似双蛟龙隐伏海底。

Shuanglong (Double Dragon) Lake

Located below the Jiyulang Waterfall, it is 2,200 meters above sea level, 290 meters long, 247 meters wide and 9 meters deep. Two belt-shaped biological travertine reefs loom at its bottom, while the upper part of its dike is travertine and lower part is moraine, resembling two dragons in hiding.

火花海（2005 年，于宁 摄）
Sparkling Lake (photo by Yu Ning, 2005)

火花海

海拔 2211 米，长 294 米，宽 232 米，深 16 米，位于双龙海与卧龙海之间。因晴日晨昏阳光斜射时，湖面上浮现粼粼波光，宛如朵朵火花燃烧、跳跃闪烁而得名。晨昏之外，火花海一湖碧波，静如处子。

Sparkling Lake

2,211 meters above sea level, 294 meters long, 232 meters wide and 16 meters deep, it is located between Shuanglong and Wolong Lakes. It is thus named because, when the Sun shines obliquely at dawn and dusk on a clear day, sparkles appear on the lake, like sparks burning, jumping and flickering. All the rest of time, the lake, with its blue waves, stays still as a maiden.

卧龙海

海拔 2220 米，长 253 米，宽 2255 米，深 24 米，因湖底有一条形似卧龙的乳黄色钙华堤埂而得名。无风时，巨龙身影清晰可见，似沉睡于湖底。微风乍起，湖面荡起层层涟漪，龙身微动。风强时，水波激荡，波光迷离，龙影消失，仿佛临空飞升。

树正群海

海拔 2187 ～ 2280 米，是位于树正寨前的阶梯状湖群，由大小 19 个海子组成，高差 100 余米，逶迤相连长达 1000 米。群海总体呈椭圆形或近椭圆形分布，大小、形状、深度等各有不同。最大的海子长 201 米，宽 40 米；最小的海子长 24 米，宽 10 米。海子水深多在 7 ～ 14 米，最深处 16.2 米，最浅处 1.5 米。

Wolong (Sleeping Dragon) Lake

2,220 meters above sea level, 253 meters long, 2,255 meters wide and 24 meters deep, it is thus called just because of its milky yellow travertine embankment at the bottom, which takes after a sleeping dragon. When there is no wind, the figure of the giant dragon is clearly visible, as if lying asleep there. In case of a breeze, the lake is rippled layer upon layer and the dragon moves slightly. Once the water is stirred by a strong wind, the dragon may seem lost owing to waves, as if flying into the sky.

Shuzheng Lake Cluster

At an altitude of 2,187~2,280 meters, there is a terraced lake cluster located in front of Shuzheng Village. This cluster contains 19 lakes (or called "Haizi") of different sizes, with a height difference of over 100 meters and a winding length of 1,000 meters. It is generally distributed in an elliptical shape or nearly so, with varied sizes, shapes and depths. The largest lake is 201 meters long and 40 meters wide and the smallest one is just 24 meters long and 10 meters wide. The depth of a here lake is mostly between 7 and 14 meters, with the deepest being 16.2 meters and the shallowest 1.5 meters only.

1 | 2

1 卧龙海（2017 年，桑吉 摄）
2 树正群海（2023 年，于宁 摄）

1 Wolong Lake (photo by Sangji, 2017)
2 Shuzheng Lake Cluster (photo by Yu Ning, 2023)

犀牛海

海拔 2301 米，长 2000 米，宽 225 米，深 17 米，是九寨沟内第二大湖泊。因传说有位西藏的喇嘛骑犀牛到此，留恋神水，驱坐骑入水而得名。犀牛海湖水湛蓝，山光水色交织，令人迷醉。岸畔山泉列布，其中中段东侧岸边海拔 2350 米处，有达戈神山上流下来的“神水”。泉水自林间石隙渗出，清冽甘甜，传说能够美容延寿、祛病消灾。

Rhinoceros Lake

2,301 meters above sea level, 2,000 meters long, 225 meters wide and 17 meters deep, it is the second largest lake in Jiuzhaigou. It owes its name to the legend that a Xizang lama, who came here on the back of a rhinoceros in pursuit of this magic water, went into it. This very lake is so fascinating owing to its blue water mixed with the reflection of mountains nearby. It boasts springs along its shore, yet in the middle section on the east bank stands a holy mountain called Dage of 2,350 meters above sea level, from which flows “magic water”. Cool and sweet water that oozes from the stone gaps in the forest, according to legend, can bring the drinker not only good looks and prolonged life, but also cure diseases and eliminate disasters.

1 | 2

1　犀牛海（2011 年，周正强　摄）
2　老虎海（2021 年，梁峰　摄）
1　Rhinoceros Lake (photo by Zhou Zhengqiang, 2011)
2　Tiger Lake (photo by Liang Feng, 2021)

老虎海

海拔 2298 米，长 310 米，宽 194 米，深 23 米，是位于树正瀑布之上、犀牛海下游的一处冰川堰塞湖。深秋时节，湖边山上彩林倒映于清澈的湖水之中，光影斑驳，犹如斑斓的虎纹。不远处，树正瀑布水声浑厚，宛若虎啸。

Tiger Lake

2,298 meters above sea level, 310 meters long, 194 meters wide and 23 meters deep, it is a glacial dammed lake situated above the Shuzheng Waterfall and below the Rhinoceros Lake. In late autumn, the colorful forests on the surrounding mountains are reflected in its clear water and the mottled light and shadow are just like the colorful stripes of a tiger, while the Shuzheng Waterfall close by makes a thick roar just like that of a tiger.

诺日朗群海（2009 年，桑吉 摄）
Nuorilang Lake Cluster (photo by Sangji, 2009)

诺日朗群海

海拔 2353 ～ 2365 米，是位于日则沟与树正沟、则查洼沟交会处的冰川堰塞湖群，由大小 20 个钙华湖泊组成，有钙华溶蚀现象。总体呈椭圆形、近椭圆形分布，湖泊大小、形状、深度等各有不同。最大的海子长 185 米，宽 45 米；最小的海子长 20 米，宽 15 米。海子水深多在 7 ～ 20 米，最深处 23 米。

Nuorilang Lake Cluster

Where the gullies of Rize, Shuzheng and Zezhawa meet at an altitude of 2,353~2,365 meters lies a glacial barrier lake cluster, which totals 20 in different sizes and depths, all with developmental travertine dissolution. The overall distribution of each is elliptical or nearly elliptical. The largest one is 185 meters long and 45 meters wide while the smallest is 20 meters long and 15 meters wide. Their water depth is between 7~20 meters and the deepest is 23 meters.

镜海

海拔 2367 米，长 1155 米，宽 241 米，深 31 米，与诺日朗群海紧密相连，是九寨沟内第三大湖泊，因无风时水平如镜而得名。平面上呈宽"V"形分布，根据水深特点分为入口段、中段和出口段三个部分。中部有一处明显转折点，是海子分段的主要标志。

Mirror Lake

The lake, as its name indicates, is placid as a mirror in case of no wind. 2,367 meters above sea level, 1,155 meters long, 241 meters wide and 31 meters deep, it abuts on Nuorilang Lake Cluster as the third largest of its kind in Jiuzhaigou. Distributed like a wide "V", it is divided into such three parts as entrance, middle and exit according to its water depth. The obvious turning point in the middle makes its main sign of the lake segment.

1 2020 年的镜海（梁峰 摄）
2 1982 年的镜海（牟航远 摄，牟薇 供图）
1 Mirror Lake in 2020 (photo by Liang Feng)
2 Mirror Lake in 1982 (photo by Mou Hangyuan, by courtesy of Mou Wei)

金铃海

海拔 2452 米，长 97 米，平均宽度 169 米，平均深度 14.99 米，由大小金铃海组成。两个紧密相连的湖泊一大一小，形似金铃，传说是万山之祖扎依扎嘎的金铃所化。

Jinling (Golden Bell) Lake

2,452 meters above sea level, 97 meters long, 169 meters wide and 14.99 meters deep in average, it is composed of large and small Jinling Lake. The two closely connected lakes, one big and one small, are shaped like a golden bell. Legend has it that they were transformed by the golden bell of Zhayi Zhaga, the ancestor of all mountains.

金铃海（2005 年，王庆九 摄）
Jinling Lake (photo by Wang Qingjiu, 2005)

1　五花海（2021 年，梁峰 摄）

2　五花海栈桥（1985 年，来源于《四川省志・九寨沟志》）

1　Wuhua Lake in 2021 (photo by Liang Feng, 2021)

2　Wuhua Lake Trestle (photo from *Sichuan Provincial Records–Jiuzhaigou Records*, 1985)

五花海

海拔 2462 米，长 450 米，宽 313 米，深 9 米。平面呈圆瓶形，出口处因巨大的崩滑体堵塞而变窄。从空中俯瞰，形如孔雀五彩斑斓的巨大尾屏。湖水常年呈现出鹅黄、翠绿、天蓝、藏青等多种色调，是九寨沟内色彩最丰富的海子。

Wuhua (Five-flower) Lake

2,462 meters above sea level, 450 meters long, 313 meters wide and 9 meters deep, it is shaped like a round bottle, the exit narrowed due to the blockage of a huge landslide mass. An aerial look shows it resembles the huge colorful tail screen of a peacock, which presents a variety of colors like light yellow, emerald green, sky blue and navy blue all year round, it is the most colorful of its kind in Jiuzhaigou.

1 2008 年的熊猫海（桑吉 摄）
2 1982 年的熊猫海（牟航远 摄，牟薇供图）

1 Panda Lake in 2008 (photo by Sangji)
2 Panda Lake in 1982 (photo by Mou Hangyuan, by courtesy of Mou Wei)

熊猫海

海拔 2574 米，总长 670 米，宽 109 ～ 237 米，均深 15.6 米，是九寨沟水位年变幅最大的湖泊之一，变幅 5 ～ 7 米，仅次于长海。丰水期，湖水越堤形成高瀑布；枯水期，大片金黄色钙华滩出露。因曾有大熊猫常在此饮水而得名。

Panda Lake

2,547 meters above sea level, 670 meters long in total, 109~237 meters wide and 15.6 meters deep in average, it possesses the largest annual change (5~7 meters) in water level here, second only to the Long Lake. During the wet season, its water brims over the embankment to form high waterfalls and during the dry season, a large expanse of golden travertine shoal is exposed. It is named so because the giant panda once frequently drink at here.

长海

海拔 3101 米，总长约 4350 米，宽 300 米，深 90 米，位于九寨沟南端东侧。长海汇集南面雪峰的雪水和四周的流泉，无出水口，湖水除蒸发外，通过潜流进入五彩池、五花海等下游景点。夏秋遇暴雨不溢堤，冬春旱季不干涸，被称为“装不满、漏不干的宝葫芦”。

Long Lake

3,101 meters above sea level, 4,350 meters long in total, 300 meters wide and 90 meters deep, it is located on the east side of the southern end of Jiuzhaigou. This lake, which gathers the snow water from the snowy peak in the south and the surrounding springs, has no water outlet. Apart from evaporation, its undercurrent enters scenic spots downstream such as Wucai Pool and Wuhua Lake. In summer and autumn, the dike will not overflow even in the case of rainstorm, and it will not dry up in winter, spring and dry season, it is therefore called “a precious gourd that gets neither full nor empty”.

1 | 2

1 2009 年的长海（桑吉 摄）
2 2022 年的长海（梁峰 摄）
1 Long Lake in 2009 (photo by Sangji)
2 Long Lake in 2022 (photo by Liang Feng)

仙女池（2023 年，梁峰 摄）
Fairy Pool (photo by Liang Feng, 2023)

仙女池

海拔 3150 米，长 100 米，宽 80 米，深 2 米，位于长海东侧厄波山半山处的原始森林中，距长海口 1500 米。湖水漫过堤埂，形成 10 米宽的跌水，湖岸修长，池水明净，湖心处有一株古树横卧，上面生长着一排小树，传说为仙女沐浴的场所。

五彩池

海拔 3010 米，长约 100 米，宽 60 米，深 6.6 米，位于长海末端堰塞堤的冰碛物夹缝中，是九寨沟内最小的海子，被誉为“九寨之眼”。在阳光、藻类等因素的综合作用下，湖水以翠蓝色为主色，镶嵌有淡绿、乳白、鹅黄、瓦灰等多彩色块，宛如一颗瑰丽宝石。

Fairy Pool

3,150 meters above sea level, 100 meters long, 80 meters wide and 2 meters deep, it is located in the virgin forest and halfway up Ebo Mountain east of the Long Lake (1,500 meters off its entrance). As its water overflows the embankment, a 10-meter-wide drop will appear. Legend has it that fairies used to bathe themselves in this clear lake, which has a long shore, an ancient tree lying in the center and a row of small ones growing out of it.

Wucai (Colorful) Pool

3,010 meters above sea level, about 100 meters long, 60 meters wide and 6.6 meters deep, it is located in the crevices of moraines at the end of the Long Lake. As the smallest lake of its kind, it is known as the “Eye of Jiuzhaigou”. Under the combined effect of sunlight, algae and other factors, its water is mainly emerald blue, mixed with light green, milky white, light yellow, slate grey and so on and resembles a brilliant gem.

1 2

3

1 五彩池，这是九寨沟第一张彩色照片（1975 年，吕荣森 摄）
2 2009 年的五彩池（桑吉 摄）
3 2020 年的五彩池（梁峰 摄）
1 Wucai Pool, the first color photograph of Jiuzhaigou (photo by Lv Rongsen, 1975)
2 Wucai Pool in 2009 (photo by Sangji)
3 Wucai Pool in 2020 (photo by Liang Feng)

上季节海（2019 年，梁峰 摄）
Upper Seasonal Lake (photo by Liang Feng, 2019)

上季节海

海拔 2910 米，长 680 米，宽 200 米，深 3 米，位于五彩池下方。因湖水量随季节变化时盈时干而得名。一年中，6 月端午节时从地下出水、涨水，1—5 月为枯水期。

Upper Seasonal Lake

2,910 meters above sea level, 680 meters long, 200 meters wide and 3 meters deep, the lake is located under Wucai Pool. It is so named because the water volume here changes with the seasons. The water rises from underground during the Dragon Boat Festival in June every year and the dry season lasts from January to May.

下季节海

当地人称为干海。海拔 2560 米，长约 750 米，宽 240 米，位于则查洼沟山坳，距则查洼寨约 4000 米，是因崩塌、泥石流堆积物阻塞河谷形成的季节性湖泊。一年中大部分时段有水，水位变化幅度较大。秋季雨量充沛时，湖水盈池，水色湛蓝；初夏时节，水位渐低，水色翠绿。每年端午节时涨水，1—5 月为枯水期。

Lower Seasonal Lake

Also called Dry Lake by the locals, it is 2,560 meters above sea level, about 750 meters long and 240 meters wide. As a seasonal one formed due to landslides and debris flow blocking the gully, this lake is located in the depression of Zezhawa Gully, about 4,000 meters away from the village of the same name. It holds water most of the year, but with a greatly varied water level. With its abundant rainfall in autumn, the lake stays full in blue; in early summer, its water level lowers gradually and gets emerald green. The water rises during the Dragon Boat Festival every year and the dry season lasts from January to May.

1 下季节海（2013 年，杜杰 摄）
2 黑海（2006 年，于宁 摄）
1 Lower Seasonal Lake (photo by Du Jie, 2013)
2 Black Lake (photo by Yu Ning, 2006)

黑海

藏名“措拉”。海拔 3850 米，深 8 米，面积 3330 平方米，位于褡裢海对面山坳中的原始森林中，距热西寨 25000 米。因湖底土质呈黑色，湖水深黑而得名。黑海变幻莫测，忽而一池湛青，忽而一片乳白，有时黑白杂陈，上空常有乌云笼罩，是藏民天旱求雨的地方。

Black Lake

“Cuola” in Xizang refers to the lake. 3,850 meters above sea level, 8 meters deep and covering an area of 3,330 square meters, this lake is located opposite Dalian Lake in the virgin forest, 25,000 meters away from Rexi Village. It is so named because the lake looks deep black due to its black soil at the bottom. Black Lake is unpredictable, sometimes it is clear blue, sometimes milky white, sometimes black and white and often covered with dark clouds, it is where the Zang villgers pray for rain.

箭竹海瀑布（2010 年，桑吉 摄）

Nuorilang Waterfall

2,343 meters above sea level, 24.5 meters high and 320 meters wide, this waterfall, the widest one of alpine travertine in China, is located at the end of the Shuzheng Gully, where gullies of Rize and Zezhawa meet. "Nuorilang" means "splendor" in the Zang language. The broad and mighty water pours down from the bushes above, just like covering the stone wall with countless white hada. In winter, so unique is the occasional spectacle of blue ice when waterflow appears together with icicles.

珍珠滩瀑布（2009 年，周正强 摄）
Pearl Shoal waterfall (photo by Zhou Zhengqiang, 2009)

珍珠滩瀑布

海拔 2433 米，均高 21 米，宽 270 米，位于日则沟镜海和金铃海之间。瀑面略向后凹，呈新月状。珍珠滩一坡流水跌落谷底，形成高大飞瀑，水声震耳欲聋、气势磅礴、动人心魄。

Pearl Shoal Waterfall

2,433 meters above sea level, with an average height of 21 meters and a width of 270 meters, it is located between the Mirror and the Jinling Lakes in the Rize Gully. It looks slightly concave and crescent-shaped. A tremendous waterfall forms when its water flies right down the bottom and its deafening noise stays imposing and moving.

珍珠滩

海拔 2450 米，滩面长 189 米，宽 112.3 米，平均坡度 20 度，相对高差 15 米，位于日则沟中段。因湍流在由鳞片波纹状钙华体组成的滩面上翻滚而下，激起数以万计的水珠，在阳光下宛如无数洁白的珍珠而得名。传说女神沃洛色嫫与恶魔大战时，所戴项链被扯断，珍珠洒落此处。

Pearl Shoal

At an altitude of 2,450 meters, it is 189 meters long and 112.3 meters wide, with an average slope of 20 degrees and a relative height difference of 15 meters. Located in the middle of the Rize Gully, the shoal gets its name because the turbulent current rolls down here composed of scales and corrugated travertine, arousing tens of thousands of water droplets, which look like countless white pearls in the sunlight. Legend has it that when Goddess Woluosemo fought Demon, her necklace was torn off and its pearls scattered here.

珍珠滩（2022 年，建措 摄）
Pearl Shoal (photo by Jiancuo, 2022)

1 | 2

1　熊猫海瀑布（2010 年，周正强　摄）
2　扎如瀑布（2023 年，肖维阳　摄）

1　Panda Lake Waterfall (photo by Zhou Zhengqiang, 2010)
2　Zharu Waterfall (photo by Xiao Weiyang, 2023)

熊猫海瀑布

海拔 2574 米，高 65 米，宽 75 米，位于日则沟熊猫海出水口，是九寨沟内落差最大的瀑布，又名高瀑布。丰水期，湖水从熊猫海翻越堤坎，分三道自悬崖飞泻而下，又分三段跌落，如万马奔腾，声彻峡谷。枯水期，瀑布断流，底部溶洞显露，形成天然冰雕，仿佛一座水晶宫殿。

扎如瀑布

总高 35 米，瀑布自扎如沟内扎依扎嘎山腰密林间悬崖飞出，因岩石差异性风化形成 4 级。一级宽 7 米，高 19 米；二级宽 3 米，高 5 米；三级宽 3 米，高 9 米；四级宽 3 米，高 2 米。

Panda Lake Waterfall

2,574 meters above sea level, 65 meters high and 75 meters wide, it is located at the outlet of the Panda Lake in the Rize Gully. With its largest vertical drop in Jiuzhaigou, it is also known as the High Waterfall. During the wet season, water climbs over the embankment, falls down the cliff in three ways and then in three sections, reminding one of ten thousand horses galloping, the sound of which pierces the whole gully. During the dry season, the waterfall stops flowing and the karst caves at the bottom are exposed, forming natural ice sculptures in a crystal palace.

Zharu Waterfall

With a total height of 35 meters, the waterfall darts out from the cliff in the dense forest on the Zhayi Zhaga mountainside in the Zharu Gully, forming a 4-layer waterfall due to the differential weathering of rocks. The first is 7 meters wide and 19 meters high; the second is 3 meters wide and 5 meters high; the third is 3 meters wide and 9 meters high; and the fourth 3 meters wide and 2 meters high.

盆景滩

海拔 2190 米，滩长 218 米，宽 98 米，平均水深 0.8 米，最深处 10 米，是进入九寨沟看到的第一个滩流景观。乳白色的钙华浅滩上，杨、柳、松、柏、杜鹃等植物丛生，钙华沉积于植物根部，形成天然盆堤，远望如一组组盆景。

Bonsai Shoal

2,190 meters above sea level, 218 meters long, 98 meters wide and 0.8 meters deep on average (the deepest being 10 meters), it is the first shoal stream one sees when entering Jiuzhaigou. On the milky white travertine shoal, plants such as poplar, willow, pine, cypress and azalea grow in clusters. The travertine, deposited on the roots of the plants, forms a natural basin embankment, which looks like groups of bonsai from a distance.

盆景滩（2007 年，于宁 摄）
Bonsai Shoal (photo by Yu Ning, 2007)

九看九寨

Jiuzhaigou in Nine Episodes

之二

Episode Two

奇峰异谷

Grotesque Peaks and Wonderful Valleys

单面山(2011年，周正强 摄)

地质地貌

Geology and Landforms

Cuesta (photo by Zhou Zhengqiang, 2011)

北纬 32° 是中国地理上一条重要的分界线。中国地势西高东低，沿着这条纬线由西往东走，地势呈三级阶梯逐渐下降。九寨沟便位于北纬 32°，处于第一级阶梯向第二级阶梯过渡、青藏高原向四川盆地过渡的区域。

九寨沟属四川盆地外围山地区、嘉陵江上游白水江流域山地区。作为白河流域中最大的支沟，九寨沟主区域内沟谷纵横，沟谷主轴大致呈南北走向，从北部沟口经树正沟、诺日朗、则查洼沟至南部长海一线，纵深约 40 千米。

从高空中俯瞰，树正沟、日则沟和则查洼沟 3 条主沟呈不规则的"Y"形躺卧于九寨沟起伏的峰峦之间。树正沟从九寨沟沟口到诺日朗，长约 14 千米，到诺日朗后向南分成两条支沟。其中，东南支沟为则查洼沟，长约 31 千米，西南支沟为日则沟，长约 30 千米。

从形态上看，九寨沟地貌类型丰富，有高山、坡地、峡谷、湖泊、瀑布、溪流、山间平坝等。整个区域重峦叠嶂，波光水影，奇峰妙壁，怪石嶙峋，雪山连绵，林岚飞瀑，恍若童话。

Along the 32° parallel north latitude, an important geographical dividing line, China's terrain is high in the west and low in the east and therefore, it gradually descends in three space, Jiuzhaigou, by chance, is located at this north latitude, that is, the transitional area from the first step to the second one, namely, from Qinghai-Xizang Plateau to Sichuan Basin.

Jiuzhaigou belongs to the mountainous area outside the Sichuan Basin and the Baishui River Basin on the upper reaches of the Jialing River. As its largest tributary of the Baihe River, the main area of Jiuzhaigou is crisscrossed with gullies roughly going north-south, from the northern entrance through the Shuzheng Gully, the Nuorilang Gully, the Zezhawa Gully to the southern Long Lake, in a depth of about 40 kilometers.

An aerial look shows that the three main gullies of Shuzheng, Rize and Zezhawa, lie in an irregular "Y" shape among the undulating peaks of Jiuzhaigou. The Shuzheng Gully is about 14 kilometers away from the entrance of Jiuzhaigou to the Nuorilang Gully. At Nuorilang, it is divided into two branches to the south: the southeast branch is the Zezhawa Gully of about 31 kilometers in length and the southwest branch is the Rize Gully of about 30 kilometers in length.

In terms of morphology, Jiuzhaigou is rich in landform types such as high mountains, slopes, gorges, lakes, waterfalls, streams and flat dams within mountains. The entire area is full of mountains, wavy water, strange peaks, jagged rocks, snowy mountains, forests and waterfalls, as if seen in fairy tales.

九寨沟山谷（2010 年，桑吉 摄）
The gorges of Jiuzhaigou (photo by Sangji, 2010)

表 1 九寨沟褶皱构造一览表

Table 1 List of Jiuzhaigou Folded Structures

名称 Name	延伸方向 Extension direction	轴向倾向 Axial tendency	延伸长度（千米） Extended length (km)	岩溶作用特征 Karstification features
卧龙海向斜 Syncline of Wolong Lake	北西向 North-west	南西 South-west	16.0	促进卧龙海南东侧岩溶沟谷及群海的形成 It promoted the formation of karst gullies and lake clusters on the south-east side of the Wolong Lake
熊猫海瀑布向斜 Syncline of Panda Lake Waterfall	北北西向 North-north-west	南西 South-west	9.0	有利于箭竹海、熊猫海等湖泊的岩溶下蚀 It benefited the karst erosion of lakes such as Arrow Bamboo, Panda and others
丹祖沟向斜 Syncline of Danzu Gully	北西向 North-west	南西 South-west	5.5	使丹祖沟中游北东侧地下水向丹祖沟补充，地下水位抬高，丹祖沟地表水不致迅速转入地下 It supplemented the middle reaches of the Danzu Gully with groundwater from the northeast side, the raised groundwater level of which prevented it from going underground so soon
丹祖沟背斜 Anticline of Danzu Gully	东西向 East-west	南 South	3.0	有助于地下水向丹祖沟向斜补充 It helped groundwater supplement the Danzu Gully in a synclinal way
五花海向斜 Syncline of Wuhua Lake	北西向 North-west	南西 South-west	7.0	促进五花海内溶凹及岩溶泉的形成 It promoted the formation of karst depressions and karst springs in the Wuhua Lake

九寨沟所在的北纬 32° 剖面图

Sectional Map of Jiuzhaigou at 32° North Latitude

资料来源：四川省地方志编纂委员会编《四川省志·九寨沟志》，方志出版社，2019 年

Source: *Sichuan Provincial Records–Jiuzhaigou Records* by Sichuan Provincial Local Records Compilation Committee, Publishing House of Local Records, 2019

九寨沟湖堤成堤阶段地质模式表

Geological Model Table for Stages of Lake Embankment in Jiuzhaigou

起始阶段

地壳抬升，形成高山峡谷，沟谷两岸形成卸荷带，沟谷受早期的冰川刨蚀，形成波状起伏的纵断面。

Initial stage

The crust was uplifted to form alpine gullies, unloading zones formed on both sides, and the gullies eroded by early glaciers, forming undulating longitudinal sections.

成坝阶段

沟谷一侧或两侧的卸荷带在重力改变或地震诱发下产生崩塌，形成锥形湖堤，并有一定的蓄水功能。

Damming stage

The unloading zones on one or both sides of the gullies collapsed under the change of gravity or induced by an earthquake, forming a conical lake embankment with a certain water storage function.

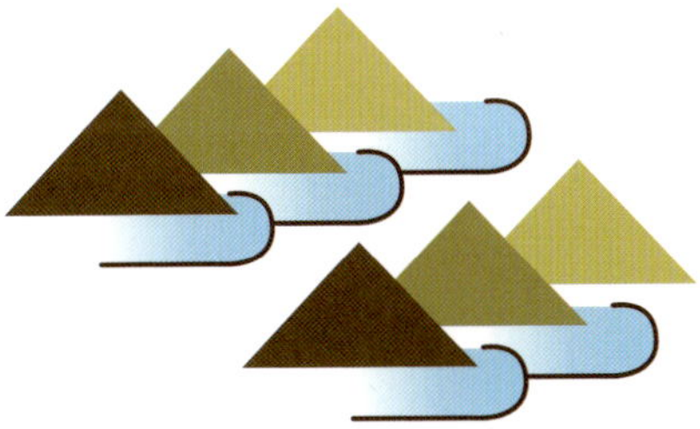

填充阶段

在地表水和地下水的作用下，湖堤内的空隙被泥沙、碎块石和碳酸钙充填，湖水水位逐渐上升。

Filling stage

Under the action of surface water and groundwater, the gaps in the lake embankment were filled with sediments, broken stones and calcium carbonate, and the water level of the lake gradually rose.

固结阶段

湖堤被碳酸钙充填、胶结，碳酸钙在湖堤外侧结壳堆积，湖水从湖堤上浸流。

Consolidation stage

The lake embankment was filled and cemented with calcium carbonate, and the calcium carbonate crusted and accumulated on the outside of the lake embankment, and the lake water flowed from the lake embankment.

资料来源：四川省地方志编纂委员会编《四川省志·九寨沟志》，方志出版社，2019 年

Source: *Sichuan Provincial Records–Jiuzhaigou Records* by Sichuan Provincial Local Records Compilation Committee, Publishing House of Local Records, 2019

冰蚀 U 形谷

因冰川侵蚀而形成的冰川谷。冰川在沿着由地面径流侵蚀形成的沟谷移动时，夹带的大量碎冰和石块会缓慢侵蚀两侧山壁，使原来的沟谷加深、加宽，形成广阔的 U 形谷。U 形谷谷底或两壁常见磨光面和冰川擦痕。

Glacial U-shaped Valley

Glacial valleys formed by glacial erosion. When the glacier moves along the valley formed by the erosion of surface runoff, a large amount of crushed ice and stones will gradually erode the mountain walls on both sides, deepening and widening the original valley into a broad U-shaped one. Polished surfaces and glacier scratches are common on the bottom or walls of U-shaped valley.

长海冰蚀 U 形谷
（2022 年，桑吉 摄）
Glacial U-shaped valley at the Long Lake (photo by Sangji, 2022)

火花海钙华堆积体（2009 年，桑吉 摄）
Travertine deposits in the Sparkling Lake (photo by Sangji, 2009)

钙华堤埂

九寨沟的出露地层主要为碳酸盐岩地层，岩性以灰岩为主。地下水在流动过程中，将碳酸盐岩中的钙质不断溶蚀。地下水溢出地表后，由于大量二氧化碳逸出，水中富含的碳酸钙在沿途不断沉淀析出，形成钙华。由于谷地两侧的崩塌和滑坡体物质堵塞谷底，导致河床起伏变化，改变了水动力条件，从而使局部地区钙华快速沉积、固结，最终形成钙华堤埂。

Travertine Dam

The outcropping strata in Jiuzhaigou are mainly carbonate strata and its lithology is mainly limestone. During the flow of groundwater, the calcium in carbonate rocks is continuously dissolved. After the groundwater overflows the surface and due to the escape of a large amount of carbon dioxide, the rich calcium carbonate in the water is continuously precipitated along the way, forming travertine. The collapse and landslide materials on both sides of the valley block its bottom, resulting in undulating changes in the riverbed, changing the hydrodynamic conditions, causing rapid deposition and consolidation of travertine in some areas and finally forming travertine dams.

云海中的冰斗 (2009 年，桑吉 摄)

巍峨高峰
Towering Peaks

Glacier-cirque landform in the sea of clouds (photo by Sangji, 2009)

九寨沟地处岷山山脉南段，随着板块运动和冰川活动对山峰产生强烈的挤压剥蚀，逐渐形成扎依扎嘎神山、达戈神山、沃洛色嫫神山等山峰。

由于气候、海拔等原因，这些高耸的山峦大部分时间都有积雪覆盖，周围云雾缭绕，营造出一幅如梦似幻的景象，身处其间，让人恍若置身于仙境。这些或奇特、或峻拔、或雄浑、或高险的多姿山体林立于沟谷两岸，苍莽的绿林遍布其间，皑皑的白雪覆盖纵横脊岭，苍绿与雪白的和谐色彩造就了九寨沟六绝之一的雪峰绝景。

古往今来，内外营力的综合作用促成九寨沟独一无二的奇绝山景。这些巍峨的高峰既是难得的景观资源，也是当地藏族同胞们朴实的情感寄托——许多山峰都有着与之相关的、被口口相传的神话传说。当地居民将宗教信仰寄托于充满灵性的峰峦，向它们祈求着幸福安康。

Jiuzhaigou is located in the southern section of the Minshan Mountains. As plate movements and glacial activities have strongly squeezed and eroded the peaks, various peaks such as Zhayi Zhaga, Dage and Woluosemo have gradually formed.

Due to climate, altitude and other factors, these towering mountains are covered with snow most of the time and surrounded by clouds and mist, creating a dreamlike scene as if in a fairyland. These strange, steep, majestic, or highly precipitous mountains stand on both sides of the valley, with lush green forests all over and white snow across vertical and horizontal ridges. The harmonious color of green and white has become one of the six wonders of Jiuzhaigou: superb snow-clad peaks.

Throughout the ages, the comprehensive effect of internal and external forces has brought Jiuzhaigou this unique scenery. These majestic peaks are not only rare landscape resources, but also the simple emotional sustenance of the local Zang compatriots, as many of the peaks have related myths and legends that have been passed down by word of mouth. The residents here place their religious beliefs on the spiritual peaks and pray to them for happiness and well-being.

达戈神山

位于九寨沟西北的树正寨背后，主峰海拔 4200 米，是九寨沟居民最崇拜的神山之一，传说达戈是阿尼玛卿神山部下一位武艺高强的将军。历史上 9 个寨子的土官出于达戈神山下的荷叶寨和树正寨。山形似金字塔，山势挺拔雄健，出露山岩为石灰岩。

Dage Holy Mountain

This mountain is located behind the Shuzheng Village in the northwest of Jiuzhaigou. Its main peak, 4,200 meters above sea level, is a most sacred one worshiped by the local villagers. People say that Dage was a highly-skilled general under the sacred mountain of Animaqing. In history, the native officials of the nine villages came from Heye Village and Shuzheng Village at the foot of the Dage Mountain, which looks like a pyramid, tall and strong with its exposed rock of limestone.

沃洛色嫫神山（2022 年，桑吉 摄）
Wolosemo Holy Mountain
(photo by Sangji, 2022)

干孜公盖山

位于诺日朗进则查洼沟 9000 米处至长海的左面，主峰海拔 4548 米。山中有 3 条沟谷和 3 座小山，冰斗、冰川 U 形谷等第四纪古冰川遗迹隐于山林之间。

Ganzi Gonggai Mountain

This mountain is located at 9,000 meters left of the Zezhawa Gully to the Long Lake from Nuorilang, its main peak is 4,548 meters above sea level. In this mountain, there are 3 gullies, 3 hills and Quatemary glacier relics such as glacier cirques and glacier U-shaped valley nestled among the forest.

厄波山

位于长海东侧，主峰海拔 4326 米。厄波山上部常见奇峰怪石和古冰川遗迹，山腰遍布苍莽的原始森林，山脚长约 7000 米。

Ebo Mountain

This mountain is located on the east side of the Long Lake, and its main peak is 4,326 meters above sea level. In its upper part, strange peaks and rocks and relics of ancient glaciers are common, its side is covered with vast virgin forests and its foot stretches about 7,000 meters long.

扎依扎嘎山 (2009 年，桑吉 摄)
Zhayi Zhaga Mountain (photo by Sangji, 2009)

尕尔纳峰

位于九寨沟南端，主峰海拔 4780 米，是九寨沟最高峰。山势起伏，怪石嶙峋，悬崖壁立，保存着丰富的古冰川遗迹。

扎依扎嘎神山

位于扎如沟内，主峰海拔 4400 米，山峰尖削峥嵘，与松潘小西天“萨德”、白螺圣山“雪宝顶”等神山齐名。农历每月十五等良辰吉日，九寨沟当地信众在此绕转神山，朝拜祈福。每年的嘛智节期间，是此地一年中转山活动的高潮。节日当天，男女老少成群结队，或骑马，或步行，一路念八字真言等心咒，撒龙达，高诵祈神词，自山脚向山顶沿扎依扎嘎神山逆时针转一周。

Ga'erna Peak

4,780 meters above sea level, the highest in Jiuzhaigou, this mountain is located at the southern end. In this undulating mountain with strange rocks and sheer cliffs lie rich relics of ancient glaciers.

Zhayi Zhaga Holy Mountain

This mountain is located in the Zharu Gully, its sharp and towering main peak, being 4,400 meters above sea level, enjoys the same great fame as Sade in Songpan's Xiaoxitian and Bailuo Holy Mountain Xuebaoding. On the auspicious day on the fifteenth day of every month in the lunar calendar, local believers in Jiuzhaigou will circle around it to pray for blessings. The annual Mazhi Festival is the climax of this tour. On this big occasion, groups of men, women, elder and children gather either on horseback or foot, reciting eight-character mantras, throwing Longda and chanting prayers and walk counterclockwise from the foot to the top of the mountain.

沃洛色嫫神山

位于九寨沟东南的则查洼沟与日则沟之间，主峰海拔4134米，与达戈神山遥遥相望，是传说中的女神山，九寨沟湖泊的主人，其四周被湖泊和河流围绕。山脚从诺日朗延伸至悬泉、长海一带，蜿蜒48000米。

Woluosemo Holy Mountain

This mountain is located between the Zezhawa and Rize Gullies in the southeast of Jiuzhaigou. Its main peak, standing 4,134 meters above the sea level, faces the Dage Mountains from afar. This goddess mountain, owner of all lakes in Jiuzhaigou according to some legend, winds 48,000 meters long at its foot from Nuorilang to the Hanging Spring and Long Lake.

图波雪峰

位于日则沟底部，原始森林西侧，主峰海拔 4452 米。山势挺拔，角峰如刃，山脚蜿蜒 11000 米。每至冬春季节，银装素裹的图波雪峰圣洁雄伟，风景如画。

Tubo Snowy Peak

This mountain is located at the bottom of the Rize Gully, on the west side of the virgin forest. Its main peak is 4,452 meters above sea level. This 11,000-meter long winding mountain is tall and strong, with its horn peak like a blade. Every winter and spring, its snow-covered peak looks holy, majestic and picturesque.

裸岩（2011 年，周正强 摄）

奇异山石
Grotesque Rocks

Bare Rocks (photo by Zhou Zhengqiang, 2011)

九寨沟区内岩石古老，地质作用复杂，主要分布有浅变质碎屑岩及碳酸盐岩，面积占整个区域面积的 96%。泥质成分含量较高是九寨沟碳酸盐岩的特点之一，也是九寨沟景观形成的物质基础。

板块运动为九寨沟塑造了起伏不断的山峦，冰川侵蚀为九寨沟雕刻了道道沟壑，再加上风化、流水、重力等多重因素的影响，以碳酸盐岩为主的山体岩石形成形态各异的外观。这些千姿百态的山石是大自然以鬼斧神工之力精心雕琢的艺术品，观之则令人生出无限遐思，比如形状似剑劈的剑岩，黑白分明、浑圆似大熊猫的熊猫戏水石，如万卷书页整齐排列的万卷书山峰，等等。

斗转星移，沧海桑田，这些原本或深埋地底，或隐于雪山之间的岩石，经历了天翻地覆的变化，不仅成为九寨沟奇异的山石之景，还为科研工作者提供了地质历史变迁的证据。

The rocks in Jiuzhaigou are old and the geological processes are complex, the valley area mainly contains shallow metamorphic clastic and carbonate rocks, accounting for about 96%. One of the characteristics here is its high content of muddy components in carbonating rocks, which makes the material basis for the formation of its landscape.

Plate movements have shaped Jiuzhaigou's undulating mountains and glacier erosion carved its ravines. In addition, affected by multiple factors such as weathering, flowing water and gravity, the mountain rocks dominated by carbonate rocks have taken on various appearances. These rocks in various poses and with different expressions are works of art carefully carved by nature with uncanny workmanship. A view of each will give rise to such infinite reveries as if it is a rock split by sword, a stone with round and distinct black and white like a giant panda, and volumes of books with neatly arranged pages, and so on.

Years have gone by and the world has undergone a complete transformation. These rocks, originally buried deep underground or hidden among the snow-capped mountains, having undergone earth-shaking changes, have not only became the strange scenery here in Jiuzhaigou, but also provided scientific researchers with evidence of geological and historical changes.

宝镜岩

位于扎如沟沟口北侧，受地壳表层的差异运动及地震活动的影响，岩体断裂抬升，形成宽约 1300 米、最大高差达 500 米的石灰岩断面，在常年的滑坡、风化等作用下，岩面呈现出各种天然纹路，形似十二生肖和藏族吉祥八宝图案。因岩面平坦、光滑得像一面镜子，故名，是游览九寨沟的起点。

Treasure Mirror Crag

It stands on the north side of the entrance to the Zharu Gully, affected by the differential movements of crustal surface and seismic activities, its rock mass has suffered fracture and uplift, forming a limestone section with a width of about 1,300 meters and a maximum height difference of 500 meters. Under the action of landslides and weathering for years, its rock surface takes on various natural patterns, resembling those of the twelve zodiac signs and auspicious eight treasures of the Zang nationality. It gets this name just because it looks like a flat and smooth mirror, and it is the starting point for the tour of Jiuzhaigou.

宝镜岩 (2008 年，阿冬 摄)

Treasure Mirror Crag (photo by A Dong, 2008)

沃洛色嫫女神像（2011 年，杜杰 摄）
Statue of Goddess Wolosemo (photo by Du Jie, 2011)

沃洛色嫫女神像

位于芦苇海东侧对面石灰岩崖壁上，海拔 2192 米，高约 15 米，宽约 10 米，又称“美人岩”。由于该处崖壁岩石自然风化，凹凸不平，其上的阴影线条组合恰似少女脸庞，故被当地传为沃洛色嫫女神像。

回音壁

位于芦苇海上游尽头的甲勿神山脚下，长约 200 米，高 150 米。游人在对面的山坡面对回音壁高声呼喊，很快就能听到清晰的回声。此地原来有一座高约 5 米的佛塔，如今仅存塔座遗址，被沟内居民视为“圣坛”，经常前来祈求神灵驱邪灭灾。每月农历十五或藏族民间节日，当地居民还会在此举行带有原始宗教色彩的拜山拜水仪式。

Statue of Goddess Woluosemo

Located on the limestone cliff opposite to the east side of the Reed Lake, it is 2,192 meters above sea level, about 15 meters high and 10 meters wide, also known as “Beauty Rock”. Due to the natural weathering and unevenness of the cliff rock, its crosshatches combined resemble the face of a girl, so it is said locally to be the statue of Goddess Woluosemo.

Echo Wall

Located at the foot of Jiawu Mountain at the upper end of the Reed Lake, it is about 200 meters long and 150 meters high. After a loud shout toward the echo wall on the opposite hillside, it can be heard clearly in no time. There used to be a 5-meter-high pagoda here, but now there lies only its ruins, which is regarded as a “holy altar” by the locals, who often come to pray for the gods to rid them of evil spirits and disasters. On the fifteenth day of the lunar calendar every month or the Zang ethnic folk festival, local residents worship mountains and water by means of a ceremony with primitive religious overtones.

鹰爪洞（2004 年，蹇代君 摄）
Talon Cave (photo by Jian Daijun, 2004)

剑岩（2006 年，于宁 摄）
Sword Rock (photo by Yu Ning, 2006)

鹰爪洞

位于日则沟天鹅海北缘东侧路边，海拔 2900 米，洞高 4 米，宽 4 米，深 6 米，因洞壁有 50 多处菊花状天青石风化线条似鹰爪抓痕而得名。据当地传说，这些抓痕是格萨尔王化鹰与恶魔所化的鹞在此恶战时所留。

剑岩

位于日则沟芳草海南端，是一处断层三角面岩体，高 500 多米，因岩面光滑如削，上尖下宽，形如宝剑而得名。据当地传说，剑岩是格萨尔王的宝剑，为保护神泉、降伏盗宝妖魔，倒插地面所化。

Talon Cave

Located on the east roadside and northern edge of the Swan Lake in the Rize Gully, at an altitude of 2,900 meters, this cave is 4 meters high, 4 meters wide and 6 meters deep. It is so named owing to 50-odd weathered lines of chrysanthemum-shaped celestite on the wall, which look like scratches made by eagle talon. According to the local legend, these marks were left in the fierce battle here between King Gesar who turned into an eagle and the devil who turned into a harrier.

Sword Rock

Located at the southern end of the Fragrant Grass Lake in the Rize Gully, it is a fault triangular rock mass with a height of over 500 meters. Because the rock surface is smooth as if cut so, the top being sharp and the bottom wide, it is named for its shape like a sword. According to the local legend, it was transformed from King Gesar's sword in order to protect the holy spring and subdue evil treasure robbers.

九看
Jiuzhaigou in
Nine Episodes
九寨

之三
Episode Three

植物王国

A Kingdom of Flora

彩林奇观（2022 年，肖维阳 摄）

珍稀植物

Rare Plants

Spectacle of Colorful Forest (photo by Xiao Weiyang, 2022)

九寨沟地处中国植物分布区位的南北向和东西向过渡地带，得天独厚的地理位置孕育了植物资源的丰富多样。这里植被覆盖率超过 85%，有 2659 种植物繁衍栖息于此，是当之无愧的植物王国。

由于山高谷深，地形起伏大，高差悬殊，九寨沟的植物群落表现出明显的垂直变化，落叶阔叶林、高山耐旱灌丛、针阔叶混交林、针叶林、高山灌丛草甸等植物群落由低到高依次分布。

除常见的植物种类，九寨沟还孕育了许多珍稀植物，有“树中寿星”之称的红豆杉、古老的孑遗植物独叶草、生长于沟谷中的中国特有植物四川红杉等。它们沐浴着九寨沟的阳光和雨露，历经风吹雨打仍自在生长，成为九寨沟庇护下的“幸运儿”，得以播撒生命的种子，将基因延续至今，为科研人员研究九寨沟植物系统的演化和植物区系的演变提供重要的科考价值。

九寨沟内有国家一级保护野生植物 1 种，国家二级保护野生植物 38 种 3 变种。这些珍稀植物对海拔高度、温度、湿度、酸碱度等要求不一，却不约而同地选择在九寨沟扎根，千百年来共同见证此地的沧桑变迁。

Jiuzhaigou is located in the north-south and east-west transitional zone of China's plant distribution and its unique geographical location develops rich and diverse plant resources. The vegetation coverage here exceeds 85%, with 2,659 species of plants living here, which is a well-deserved kingdom of flora and fauna.

Due to its high mountains and deep valleys, large undulations of the terrain and great difference in latitude, Jiuzhaigou's plant communities show clear-cut vertical changes, such as deciduous broad-leaved forests, alpine drought-tolerant shrubs, mixed coniferous and broad-leaved forests, coniferous forests and alpine shrub meadows and the like are distributed in order from low to high latitude.

Besides the common plant species, Jiuzhaigou breeds many other rare plants, such as yew *(Taxus wallichiana* var. *chinensis)* known for its "longevity among trees", ancient relict plant oneflower kingdonia *(Kingdonia uniflora)*, unique Chinese plant of masters larch (*Larix mastersiana)* growing in the valley and so on. Bathed in the sunshine and rain, they still grow freely, however weather-beaten as the lucky ones under the protection of Jiuzhaigou, sow the seeds of life and pass their genes down to today and provide important value for scientific researchers.

Jiuzhaigou boasts one specie of wild plants under national first-level protection and 38 species and 3 varieties under national second-level protection. These rare plants, with different requirements of altitude, temperature, humidity, soil PH, choose to take root here, bearing silent witness to its vicissitudes for thousands of years.

原始森林（2021 年，梁峰 摄）
Virgin forest (photo by Liang Feng, 2021)

红豆杉

属红豆杉科，国家一级保护植物。常绿乔木。树皮呈灰褐色、红褐色或暗褐色，裂成条片脱落。小枝至秋季变黄绿色或淡红褐色。叶两列式，常微弯，镰形，边缘微反曲。雌雄异株，大孢子叶球仅有胚珠一个。种子扁卵形，两侧各有一不明显的棱脊，围有红色肉质杯状假种皮。

Yew (*Taxus wallichiana* var. *chinensis*)

It is in the family Taxaeae and is a plant and evergreen sylvae under first-level national protection. With a bark taupe, reddish brown or dark brown, it splits into strips and falls off. Its branchlets turn yellow-green or reddish-brown in autumn. Its leaf is dichotomous, often slightly curved, sickle-shaped, with slightly recurved margins. Dioecious, it has only one ovule in the megasporophyll. Its seed is flat ovoid, with an inconspicuous ridge on each side, surrounded by a red fleshy cup-shaped aril.

独叶草

属毛茛科，国家二级保护植物。

Oneflower Kingdonia (*Kingdonia uniflora*)

It is in the family Ranunculaceae under national second-level protection.

连香树

属连香树科，国家二级保护植物。

Katsura Tree (*Cercidiphyllum japonicum*)

It is in the family Cercidiphyllaceae under national second-level protection.

1
2
3

1 红豆杉（2022 年，九寨沟管理局 供图）
2 独叶草（2020 年，肖维阳 摄）
3 连香树（2022 年，张跃 摄）
1 Yew (*Taxus wallichiana* var. *chinensis*) (photo by courtesy of Jiuzhaigou Management Bureau, 2022)
2 Oneflower kingdonia (*Kingdonia uniflora*) (photo by Xiao Weiyang, 2020)
3 Katsura tree (*Cercidiphyllum japonicum*) (photo by Zhang Yue, 2022)

桃儿七

属小檗科，国家二级保护植物。

Chinese May-apple *(Sinopodophyllum hexandrum)*

It is in the family Berberidaceae under national second-level protection.

四川红杉

属松科。

Masters Larch *(Larix mastersiana)*

It is in the family Pinaceae.

星叶草

属星叶草科。

Filed Circa-easter *(Circaeaster agrestis)*

It is in the family Circaeasteraceae.

1 桃儿七（2022 年，张跃 摄）
2 四川红杉（2023 年，张跃 摄）
3 星叶草（2022 年，张跃 摄）

1 Chinese may-apple *(Sinopodophyllum hexandrum)* (photo by Zhang Yue, 2022)
2 Masters larch (*Larix mastersiana*) (photo by Zhang Yue, 2023)
3 Filed circa-easter (*Circaeaster agrestis*) (photo by Zhang Yue, 2022)

展枝沙参（2022 年，张跃 摄）

药用植物
Medicinal Plants

Adenophora divaricata (photo by Zhang Yue, 2022)

九寨沟是四川重要的中药材主产地之一，大量的药用植物孕育于此，如毛叶草芍药、蓝白龙胆、七叶一枝花、一把伞南星等，在九寨沟沟谷、山腰、雪峰等地肆意生长。生长于山地灌木丛中的党参根可入药，性平味甘，补中益气；分布在山地林缘半阴湿地带的大黄以根状茎入药，性寒味苦，行瘀通经；生于阴湿林下的天麻以块茎入药，性平味甘，熄风定惊。

九寨沟野生药用维管植物资源丰富，以世界广布和北温带分布的科属为主，热带广布成分也占很大比例，充分显示热带亚热带山区植物区系特征，具有极为明显的水平替代和垂直替代的替代现象和新老并存但以新为主的特有现象。[1] 值得一提的是，这些药用植物中，有许多是野生川产道地药材，比如川贝母、川赤芍等。这些珍贵的野生药用植物功效各不相同，千百年来，当地的居民们利用这些植物来解除病痛。

1 叶霄，贾国夫，闫利军等 . 九寨沟县野生药用维管植物资源初步调查 [J]. 中国中医药信息杂志，2022，29（6）：1-7.

Jiuzhaigou is one of the main producers of traditional Chinese medicine in Sichuan, where a large number of medicinal plants are distributed, such as woodland peony (*Paeonia obovata)*, blue and white gentiana *(Gentiana leucomelaena)*, *Paris polyphylla* and cobra lily (*Arisaema erubescens)*, that grows wantonly in every gully, mountainside and snow peak. *Codonopsis pilosula* root growing among the mountain shrubs can be used as medicine, which is mild in nature and sweet in taste, nourishing the spleen and stomach; *Rheum officinale* distributed in the semi-shady and humid areas on the edge of the mountain and forest is used as medicine in rhizomes, cold in nature and bitter in taste, promoting blood stasis and menstruation; and Tall gastrodia (*Gastrodia elata*) in damp forests used as medicine with tubers, is mild in nature and sweet in taste, suppressing cold and calming shock.

Jiuzhaigou is rich in wild medicinal vascular plant resources, dominated by families and genera distributed in the world and north temperate zones and tropical widespread components also account for a large proportion, fully showing the floristic characteristics of tropical and subtropical mountainous areas, with extremely obvious horizontal vicariation. The phenomenon of vertical vicariation and that of coexistence of the old and new but dominated by the new.[1] It is worth mentioning that many of these medicinal plants are wild Sichuan medicinal materials, such as tendrilleaf fritillary *(Fritillaria cirrhosa)* and veitch peony *(Paeonia veitchii).* Such precious wild medicinal plants have different effects. For thousands of years, local residents have used them to relieve pain.

1 Ye Xiao, Jia Guofu, Yan Lijun, etc. *Preliminary Investigation Research of Wild Medicinal Vascular Plants in Jiuzhaigou County* [J]. *Chinese Journal of Traditional Chinese Medicine Information*, 2022, 29 (6) :1-7.

1　水母雪兔子（2019 年，九寨沟管理局 供图）
2　川贝母（2022 年，张跃 摄）
3　天麻（2022 年，张跃 摄）
4　川赤芍（2009 年，桑吉 摄）

1　Jellyfish snow hare (*Saussurea medusa)* (photo by courtesy of Jiuzhaigou Management Bureau, 2019)
2　Tendrilleaf fritillary (*Fritillaria cirrhosa)* (photo by Zhang Yue, 2022)
3　Tall gastrodia (*Gastrodia elata*) (photo by Zhang Yue, 2022)
4　Veitch peony (*Paeonia veitchii*) (photo by Sangji, 2009)

水母雪兔子

属菊科，国家二级保护植物，因外观类似莲花又名雪莲花，珍贵药材。

川贝母

属百合科，国家二级保护植物，多年生草本植物，药用植物中的“名门望族”。

天麻

属兰科，国家二级保护植物，腐生草本植物，名贵中药材。

川赤芍

属芍药科，多年生草本，中国特有植物，根可药用。

Jellyfish Snow Hare *(Saussurea medusa)*

A precious medicinal material in the family Compositae under national second-level protection, it is also known as snow lotus flower because it resembles a lotus flower.

Tendrilleaf Fritillary *(Fritillaria cirrhosa)*

A perennial herb in the family Liliaceae under national second-level protection, a “noble family” among medicinal plants.

Tall Gastrodia *(Gastrodia elata)*

It is in the family Orchidaceae under national second-level protection, a saprophytic herb and valuable traditional Chinese medicine.

Veitch Peony *(Paeonia veitchii)*

A perennial herb in the family Paeoniaceae, it is a endemic plant in China, with its root used for medicine.

毛叶草芍药

属芍药科，多年生草本，根可入药。

陕南龙胆

属龙胆科，一年生草本，中草药。

一把伞南星

属天南星科，多年生草本，有毒，块茎可入药。

五脉绿绒蒿

属罂粟科，多年生草本，全草入药。

展枝沙参

属桔梗科，多年生草本植物，根可入药。

紫菀

属菊科，多年生草本，中草药。

1 | 2 | 3 | 4 | 5 | 6

1 毛叶草芍药（2022 年，周正强 摄）
2 陕南龙胆（2020 年，张跃 摄）
3 一把伞南星（2022 年，张跃 摄）
4 五脉绿绒蒿（2022 年，张跃 摄）
5 展枝沙参（2022 年，张跃 摄）
6 紫菀（2022 年，孙鸿鸥 摄）

Woodland Peony *(Paeonia obovata)*

It is in the family Paeoniaceae, a perennial herb with its root used as medicine.

Piasezki's Gentian *(Gentiana piasezkii)*

It is in the family Gentianaceae, an annual herb as Chinese herbal medicine.

Cobra Lily *(Arisaema erubescens)*

It is in the family Araceae, a poisonous perennial herb, with its tuber used as medicine.

Harebell Poppy *(Meconopsis quintuplinervia)*

It is in the family Papaveraceae, a perennial herb that can be wholly used as medicine.

Spreading-branch Ladybell *(Adenophora divaricata)*

It is in the family Campanulaceae, a perennial herb with its roots used as medicine.

Aster *(Aster* spp.*)*

It is in the family Aster setchuenensise, a perennial herb as Chinese herbal medicine.

1 Woodland peony *(Paeonia obovata)* (photo by Zhou Zhengqiang, 2022)
2 Piasezki's Gentian (*Gentiana piasezkii*) (photo by Zhang Yue, 2020)
3 Cobra lily *(Arisaema erubescens)* (photo by Zhang Yue, 2022)
4 Harebell poppy *(Meconopsis quintuplinervia)* (photo by Zhang Yue, 2022)
5 Spreading-branch ladybell *(Adenophora divaricata)* (photo by Zhang Yue, 2022)
6 Aster. *(Aster* spp.*)* (photo by Sun Hong'ou, 2022)

原始森林苔藓（2010 年，阿冬 摄）

苔藓植物
Bryophytes

Moss in the virgin forest (photo by A Dong, 2010)

苔藓植物广泛分布于九寨沟内森林的树干、树枝、腐木、地表、灌丛地带、裸露的岩石、道路旁、房屋等环境，除此之外，在珍珠滩、五花海等水域中也有部分苔藓种类分布。

九寨沟苔藓植物的垂直分布多样性差异不明显，但在种类构成上有变化，随着海拔升高，温带性成分物种逐渐增加，热带性成分物种逐渐减少。不同植被类型中的苔藓植物类群组成差异较为明显，温性针叶林，尤其是油松林中的苔藓植物种类较少。相同海拔的近水源森林与灌丛内苔藓植物种类、种群数量均高于远水区域，流石滩区和裸露的岩石地带种类较少。

九寨沟苔藓植物生境大致分为树附生、土生（包括地表凋落物层生）、石生、倒 / 腐 / 朽木生和水生 5 种。其中，树附生种类 78 种，约占总种数的 36%；土生（包括地表凋落物层生）种类 54 种，约占总种数的 25%；石生种类 45 种，约占总种数的 21%；倒 / 腐 / 朽木生种类 55 种，约占总种数的 26%；水生种类 7 种，约占总种数的 3%。[1]

1 由于一种苔藓植物可能存在多种生境，各生境物种数百分比之和可能超过 100%。

Bryophytes are widely distributed in such environments as trunks, branches, rotten wood, ground surface, bushes, exposed rocks, roadsides and houses in the forests of Jiuzhaigou. In addition, some like species are also distributed in waters such as the Pearl Shoal and the Wuhua Lake.

The altitudinal distribution diversity of bryophytes here has no obvious difference, but there is a change in the species composition, that is, with the increase of altitude, the species of temperate components gradually increase, while those of tropical components gradually decrease. The composition of bryophyte groups in different vegetation types is significantly different and there are fewer bryophyte species in warm coniferous forests, especially pine forests. At the same altitude, the species and populations of bryophytes in forests and shrubs near the water source are higher than those off the water area and there are fewer species in the screes and exposed rocky areas.

The bryophyte habitats here can be roughly divided into five types: epiphytic, land (including stratified litter), stone, fallen/rotten/rotted wood and aquatic. Among them, there are 78 epiphytic species, accounting for about 36% of the total; 54 species of land (including stratified litter) species, accounting for 25% of the total; 45 species of stone, accounting for about 21% of the total species; there are 55 species of fallen/rotten/rotted wood species, accounting for about 26% of the total species; 7 species of aquatic species, accounting for about 3% of the total species.[1]

1 Owing to bryophytes' possible variety of habitats, the total percentage of species in each may exceed 100%.

表 2　2021 年九寨沟中国特有苔藓植物表
Table 2 Bryophytes of Jiuzhaigou Endemic to China in 2021

科名 Family name	属名 Genus name	种名 Species name
烟杆藓科 Buxbaumiaceae	烟杆藓属 *Buxbaumia*	花斑烟杆藓 *Buxbaumia punctata*
金发藓科 Polytrichaceae	异蒴藓属 *Lyellia*	宽果异蒴藓 *Lyellia platycarpa*
木灵藓科 Orthotrichaceae	木灵藓属 *Orthotrichum*	球蒴木灵藓 *Orthotrichum leiolecythis*
提灯藓科 Mniaceae	匐灯藓属 *Plagiomnium*	九寨沟匐灯藓 *Plagiomnium jiuzhaigouense*
提灯藓科 Mniaceae	丝瓜藓属 *Pohlia*	明齿丝瓜藓 *Pohlia hyaloperistoma*
青藓科 Brachytheciaceae	青藓属 *Brachythecium*	曲枝青藓 *Brachythecium dicranoides*
灰藓科 Hypnaceae	粗枝藓属 *Gollania.*	中华粗枝藓 *Gollania sinensis*
金灰藓科 Pylaisiaceae	毛灰藓属 *Homomallium*	云南毛灰藓 *Homomallium yuennanense Broth.*
绢藓科 Entodontaceae	绢藓属 *Entodon*	云南绢藓 *Entodon yunnanensis*
牛舌藓科 Anomodontaceae	牛舌藓属 *Anomodon*	带叶牛舌藓 *Anomodon perlingulatus*
光萼苔科 Porellaceae	光萼苔属 *Porella*	截叶光萼苔 *Porella truncata*

表 3　2021 年九寨沟苔藓植物生境概况
Table 3 Overview of Bryophyte Habitats in Jiuzhaigou in 2021

生境类型 Type of habitat	种数 Species	占总种数百分比（%） Percentage of total species
水生 Aquatic	7	3
土生 Land	54	25
石生 Stone	45	21
树附生 Epiphytic	78	36
倒 / 腐 / 朽木生 Fallen/Rotten/Rotted wood	55	26

花斑烟杆藓

属烟杆藓科，中国特有物种，极危（CR）。多生长于人迹罕至的高山林地，常以腐木作为生长基质，零星散生。配子体极度退化，外形似烟杆。

密枝灰藓

属灰藓科，濒危（EN）。

带叶牛舌藓

属牛舌藓科，易危（VU）。

平齿平藓

属平藓科，易危（VU）。

暗色蛇苔

属蛇苔科。

耳坠苔

属光萼苔科。

注：本书所列动植物的濒危等级时间均为 2021 年。

1	2	3	4	5	6

1　花斑烟杆藓（2019 年，叶文 摄）
2　密枝灰藓（2019 年，夏红霞 摄）
3　带叶牛舌藓（2019 年，九寨沟管理局 供图）
4　平齿平藓（2019 年，夏红霞 摄）
5　暗色蛇苔（2019 年，夏红霞 摄）
6　耳坠苔（2019 年，叶文 摄）

Buxbaumia Punctata

It is in the family Buxbaumiaceae, a species endemic to China and critically endangered, mostly grows in inaccessible alpine woodlands, often with rotting wood as the growth substrate and grows sporadically. Its gametophyte is extremely degenerated and looks like a tobacco pipe stem.

Hypnum Densirameum

It is in the family Hypnaceae and is endangered now.

Anomodon Perlingulatus

It is in the family Anomodontaceae, which is now vulnerable.

Neckera Laevidens

It is in the family Neckeraceae, which is vulnerable now.

Conocephalum Salebrosum

It is in the family Conocephalaceae.

Ascidiota Blepharophylla

It is in the family Porellaceae.

Explanatory note: All plants and animals listed in this book are listed as endangered in 2021.

1 *Buxbaumia punctata* (photo by Ye Wen, 2019)
2 *Hypnum densirameum* (photo by Xia Hongxia, 2019)
3 *Anomodon perlingulatus* (photo by courtesy of Jiuzhaigou Management Bureau, 2019)
4 *Neckera laevidens* (photo by Xia Hongxia, 2019)
5 *Conocephalum salebrosum* (photo by Xia Hongxia, 2019)
6 *Ascidiota blepharophylla* (photo by Ye Wen, 2019)

藻类植物
Phycophyta

2015 年 6 月，研究团队对九寨沟藻类进行实地取样（肖维阳 供图）

In June 2015, a research team took field sampling of algae in Jiuzhaigou (photo by Xiao Weiyang)

水彩画《九寨之水》，19.5cm×14cm（2023 年，成都市龙江路小学：周婧涵 作品，指导老师：余文兰）

The Water of Jiuzhai, watercolor, 19.5cm×14cm (by Zhou Jinghan, under the instruction of Yu Wenlan from Longjiang Road Primary School, Chengdu, 2023)

九寨沟的水域类型多样，为藻类的生长提供有利的环境，而种类繁多的藻类不仅为水生环境中浮游动物供给食物，还为净化水体和消除污染作出卓越贡献，藻类的种类和数量变化还能够指示水污染程度的变化。

刚毛藻群落、淡水红毛藻群落、双生双楔藻群落、箱形桥弯藻群落、水树藻群落、膝接藻—转板藻群落是九寨沟水域 6 个主要的附生藻类群落。绿藻是九寨沟数量最多的藻类，而蓝藻和硅藻则在种类上占据优势。

生长在水生世界的藻类，使九寨沟的水体景观变得更加多彩多姿。有着各种藻类生存的五花海，在不同的季节，由于藻类生长繁衍，湖水的色彩亦随之变幻。阳光照在水面，水藻潜在湖底，再加上湖底大量堆积的钙华物，经过散射、反射和吸收作用，一眼看去，五花海绚烂多彩，成为九寨沟最精彩的景点之一。

The various types of water in Jiuzhaigou provide a favorable environment for the growth and wide variety of algae, not only providing food for zooplankton in the aquatic environment, but also greatly purifying water bodies and eliminating pollution. Its changes in types and quantities can indicate levels in water pollution.

In Jiuzhaigou's waters, there lie six such main epiphytic algae communities as those of *Cladophora*, *Bangia atro-purpurea*, *Didymosphenia geminata*, *Cymbella cistula*, *Hydrurus foetidus* and *Zygogonium-mougeotia*. Green alga *(Scenedesmus obliquus)* is the most abundant algae here, while blue-green algae *(Cyanobacteria)* and *Diatom* dominate in species.

The algae that grow in the aquatic world make Jiuzhaigou's waterscape more colorful. The water in the Wuhua Lake, where live all kinds of algae, changes its colors in different seasons, due to the growth and reproduction of algae. The lake, with algae and large amounts of travertine accumulated at its bottom, upon the receipt of scattering, reflection and absorption of sunshine on its surface, looks gorgeous and colorful, hence one of the most exciting scenic spots in Jiuzhaigou.

2017 年九寨沟藻类物种多样性一览表

List of Algae Species Diversity in Jiuzhaigou in 2017

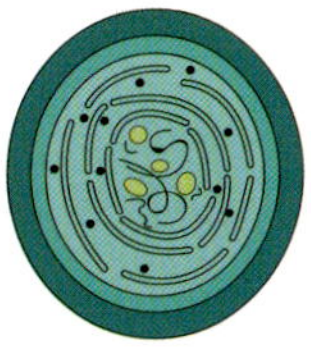

蓝藻门
属数：16
种数：37
变种：1

Cyanophyta
Number of genera: 16
Number of species: 37
Number of varieties: 1

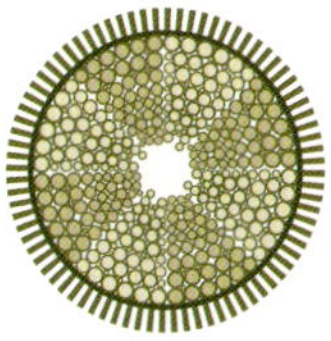

硅藻门
属数：54
种数：160
变种：16

Bacillariophyta
Number of genera: 54
Number of species: 160
Number of varieties: 16

隐藻门
属数：2
种数：2
变种：0

Cryptophyta
Number of genera: 2
Number of species: 2
Number of varieties: 0

裸藻门
属数：2
种数：11
变种：1

Euglenophyta
Number of genera: 2
Number of species: 11
Number of varieties: 1

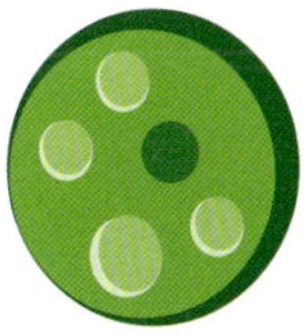

绿藻门
属数：24
种数：36
变种：3

Chlorophyta
Number of genera: 24
Number of species: 36
Number of varieties: 3

轮藻门
属数：1
种数：2
变种：1

Charophyta
Number of genera: 1
Number of species: 2
Number of variety: 1

甲藻门
属数：3
种数：3
变种：0

Pyrrhophyta
Number of genera: 3
Number of species: 3
Number of varieties: 0

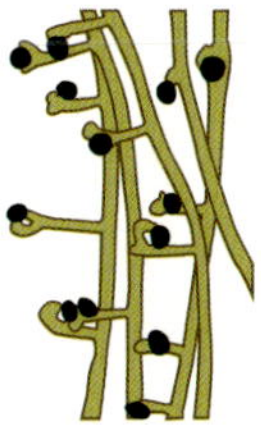

黄藻门
属数：3
种数：4
变种：0

Xanthophyta
Number of genera: 3
Number of species: 4
Number of varieties: 0

金藻门
属数：4
种数：5
变种：0

Chrysophyta
Number of genera: 4
Number of species: 5
Number of varieties: 0

总计
属数：109
种数：260
变种：22

Total
Number of genera: 109
Number of species: 260
Number of varieties: 22

资料来源：王全喜、邓贵平主编《九寨沟自然保护区常见藻类图集》，科学出版社，2017 年

Source: *Atlas of Algae in Jiuzhaigou Nature Reserve*, compiled by Wang Quanxi and Deng Guiping, Science Press, 2017

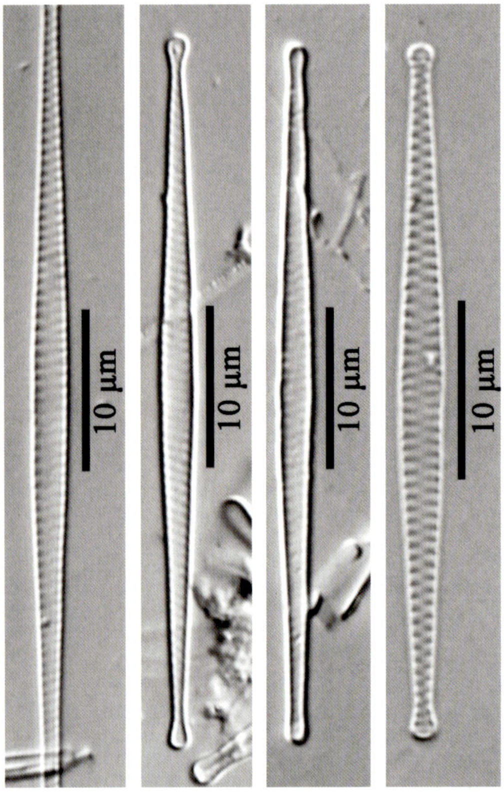

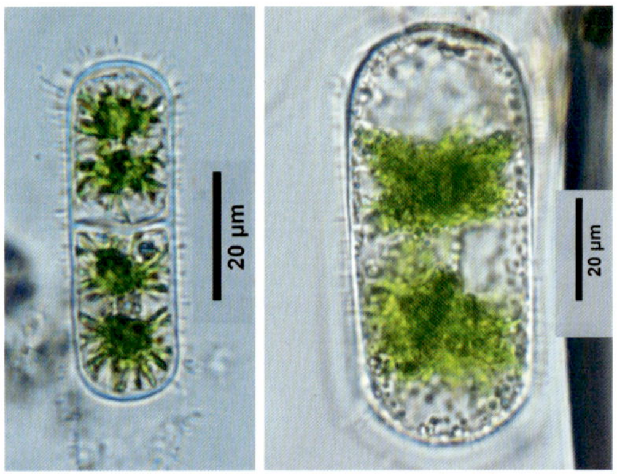

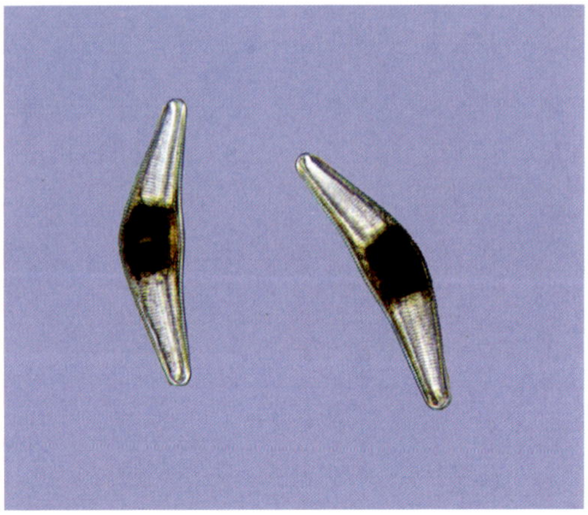

针杆藻

属脆杆藻科。

双星藻

属双星藻科。

桥弯藻

属桥弯藻科。

Synedra

It is in the family Fragilariaceae.

Zygnema

It is in the family Zygnemataceae.

Cymbella

It is in the family Rhizoctoniaceae.

1

2

3

1 针杆藻（2014 年，庞婉婷 摄）
2 双星藻（2014 年，庞婉婷 摄）
3 桥弯藻（2014 年，肖维阳 摄）
1 *Synedra* (photo by Pang Wanting, 2014)
2 *Zygnema* (photo by Pang Wanting, 2014)
3 *Cymbella* (photo by Xiao Weiyang, 2014)

小环藻

属冠盘藻科。

脆杆藻

属脆杆藻科。

舟形藻

属舟形藻科。

Cyclotella

It is in the family Stephanodiscaceae.

Fragilaria

It is in the family Fragilaceae.

Navicula

It is in the family Naviculaceae.

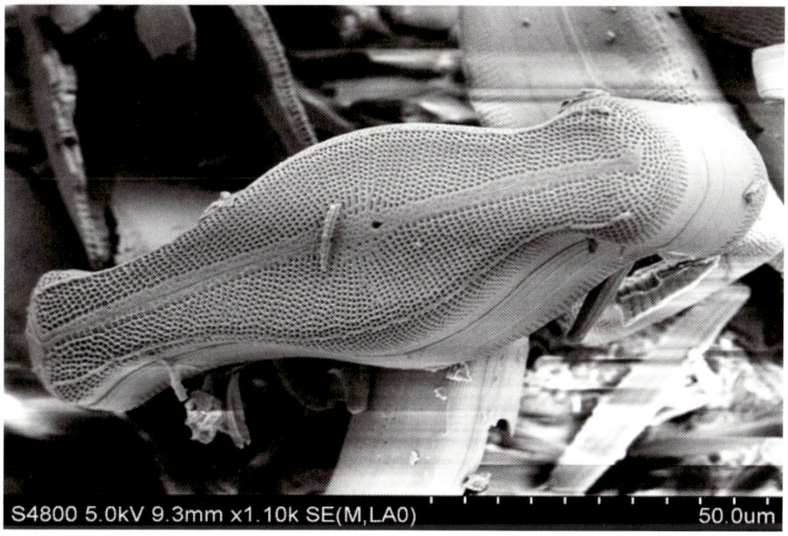

1

2

3

1　小环藻（2023 年，唐亚 供图）
2　脆杆藻（2023 年，唐亚 供图）
3　舟形藻（2023 年，唐亚 供图）
1　*Cyclotella* (photo by courtesy of Tang Ya, 2023)
2　*Fragilaria* (photo by courtesy of Tang Ya, 2023)
3　*Navicula* (photo by courtesy of Tang Ya, 2023)

平截棒瑚菌（2009 年，肖维阳 摄）

神奇真菌

Magic Fungi

Clavariadelphus truncatus (photo by Xiao Weiyang, 2009)

真菌是一种微生物，虽然不是植物，却与许多植物有千丝万缕的联系。它们分解腐木和枯枝，消化其中的有机物，让矿物质返回土壤，让二氧化碳回归大气。

绝大多数真菌无法被肉眼看到，大型真菌却是例外。木腐菌和菌根菌是九寨沟内常见的两类大型真菌。其中，云芝、漏斗大孔菌等木腐菌不仅在九寨沟生态系统物质循环中发挥着重要作用，也是药用真菌的主要来源；松塔牛肝菌、金黄柄牛肝菌和松乳菇等菌根菌共生于植物根系，在植物细胞间编织出紧密的网络，为共生植物提供营养，促进其生长发育。

除可食用的大型真菌外，九寨沟也生长着臭黄菇、黄丝盖伞、毛头乳菇等有毒的大型真菌，不是专业人士极难辨别，一旦误食，严重时可能会危及生命。

Fungi, microorganisms inextricably related to many plants, break down rotting wood and dead branches, digesting their organic matter and return minerals to the soil and carbon dioxide to the atmosphere.

The vast majority of fungi cannot be seen with the naked eye unless they are large enough. Wood-decay fungi and mycorrhizal fungi are two types of large fungi commonly found in Jiuzhaigou. Among them, wood-decay fungi such as *Coriolus versicolor* and *Favolus arcularius,* not only play an important role in the material cycle of the Jiuzhaigou ecosystem, but are also the main source of medicinal fungi; *strobilomyces strobilaceus* and *Boletus auripes* and *Lactarius deliciosus* occur symbiotically in plant roots, weave a tight network between plant cells, provide nutrients for symbiotic plants and promote their growth and development.

In addition to edible large fungi, there grow poisonous large fungi such as *Russula fotens*, *Inocybe fastigiata* and *Lactarius torminosus* in Jiuzhaigou. It is extremely difficult for non-professionals to identify them. Once ingested by mistake, they will be life-threatening.

冬虫夏草

属虫草科。国家二级保护大型真菌。青藏高原特有大型真菌，主要分布在青藏高原和喜马拉雅山脉。贵重药材。寄主为鳞翅目蝙蝠蛾科昆虫的幼虫，冬季菌丝侵入蛰居于土中的幼虫体内，使虫体充满菌丝而死亡。夏季长出子座。

Ophiocordyceps Sinensis

It is in the family Cordycipitaceae, large fungi under national second-level protection, mainly distributed in the Qinghai-Xizang Plateau and the Himalayas. They are valuable herbs. Their host is the larvae of Lepidoptera bat moths. In winter, the mycelium invades the body of the larvae hibernating in the soil, causing the body to be filled with mycelium and die; in summer it gives birth to sub-constellations.

冬虫夏草（2023 年，祝红梅 摄）
Ophiocordyceps sinensis (photo by Zhu Hongmei, 2023)

云芝（2022 年，谢大军 摄）
Coriolus versicolor (photo by Xie Dajun, 2022)

云芝

属多孔菌科。可食用，药用价值极高。常覆瓦状叠生，往往左右相连，群生于多种阔叶树的朽木上。

Coriolus Versicolor

Edible and with high medicinal value, it is in the family Polyporaceae and often grows in tile-like stacks and connected left and right in groups on the dead wood of various broad-leaved trees.

漏斗大孔菌

属多孔菌科。可食用，兼具药用价值。夏秋季生多种倒木及枯树上。

Favolus Arcularius

Being in the family Polyporaceae, edible and of medicinal value, it grows on a variety of fallen and dead trees in summer and autumn.

松杉灵芝

属灵芝科。可食用，兼具药用价值。生于落叶松的树干基部。

光滑环锈伞

属球盖菇科。可食用，兼具药用价值。秋季丛生或群生于针阔混交林或阔叶林中倒木和树桩上。

黄拟口蘑

属白蘑科。可食用。夏秋季群生、丛生或单生于针阔混交林和阔叶林中腐木上。

网纹牛肝菌

属牛肝菌科。可食用，兼具药用价值。夏秋季单生或散生于阔叶林或混交林中地上。

羊肚菌

属羊肚菌科。珍贵的食用菌和药用菌。因表面有似羊肚状的凹坑而得名。春季主要单生或群生于阔叶林中地上及草丛中。

洁小菇

属白蘑科。可食用，兼具药用价值。夏秋季丛生、群生或单生于阔叶林、灌草丛地上或腐木上。

Ganoderma Tsugae

Growing at the base of the trunk of larch, it is in the family Ganoderma lucidum, edible and of medicinal value.

Pholiota Nameko

It is in the family Strophariaceae, edible and of medicinal value. In autumn, it grows in clusters or groups on fallen logs and stumps in mixed coniferous and broad-leaved forests or broad-leaved forests.

Tricholomopsis Decora

It is in the family Tricholomataceae, edible. In summer and autumn, it grows in groups, clusters or solitarily on rotting wood in mixed coniferous and broad-leaved forests.

Boletus reticulatus

It is in the family Boletaceae, edible and of medicinal value and solitary or scattered on the ground in broad-leaved forests or mixed forests in summer and autumn.

Morchella Esculenta

It is in the family Morchellaceae, a precious edible and medicinal fungus, named after a pit on the surface that looks like a sheep's belly. In spring, it mainly grows solitarily or in groups on the ground and grass in broad-leaved forests.

Mycena Prua

It is in the family Tricholomataceae, edible and of medicinal value. In summer and autumn, it grows in clusters, groups or solitarily in broad-leaved forests or shrubs and grasses and on rotting wood.

1	2
3	

1　网纹牛肝菌（2022 年，雷开明　摄）
2　羊肚菌（2005 年，肖维阳　摄）
3　洁小菇（2004 年，肖维阳　摄）

1　*Boletus reticulatus* (photo by Lei Kaiming, 2022)
2　*Morchella esculenta* (photo by Xiao Weiyang, 2005)
3　*Mycena prua* (photo by Xiao Weiyang, 2004)

假灰杯伞

属白蘑科。可食用，兼具药用价值。夏秋季散生或群生于针阔混交林中地上或腐朽的倒木上。

Pseudoclitocybe Cyathiformis

Being in the family Tricholomataceae, edible and of medicinal value, it grows sporadically or in groups in summer and autumn in mixed coniferous and broad-leaved forests or on decaying fallen logs.

硫磺菌

属革盖菌科。可食用，兼具药用价值。生于针叶林或针阔混交林中活木或枯木上。

Laetiporus Sulphureus

Being in the family Coriolus, edible and of medicinal value, it grows on living or dead wood in coniferous forests or mixed coniferous and broad-leaved forests.

白刺马勃

属伞菌科。可食用，兼具药用价值。夏秋季生于针叶林中地上，偶生腐木上。

Lycoperdon Wrightii

Being in the family Agaricaceae, it is edible and of medicinal value, growing on the ground in coniferous forests in summer and autumn, occasionally on rotting wood.

1 硫磺菌（2022 年，雷开明 摄）
2 白刺马勃（2022 年，雷开明 摄）
3 焰耳（2003 年，肖维阳 摄）
1 *Laetiporus sulphureus* (photo by Lei Kaiming, 2022)
2 *Lycoperdon wrightii* (photo by Lei Kaiming, 2022)
3 *Phlogiotis helvelloides* (photo by Xiao Weiyang, 2003)

焰耳

属银耳科。秋季在针阔混交林中地上散生或单生，有时近丛生。

Phlogiotis Helvelloides

Being in the family Tremellaceae, it grows scattered or solitarily in autumn on the ground in mixed coniferous and broad-leaved forests, sometimes in clusters.

平截棒瑚菌

属珊瑚菌科。可食用。夏秋季单生或群生于云杉等针叶林及混交林地上。

Clavariadelphus Truncatus

Being in the family Clavariaceae, edible, it grows alone or in groups in coniferous forests such as spruce and mixed forests in summer and autumn.

猴头菇

属齿菌科。可食用，兼具药用价值。秋季多分布于栎树林等阔叶林中的立木或腐木上。

Hericium Erinaceus

It is in the family Hydnaceae, edible and of medicinal value. In autumn, it is mostly distributed on standing or rotted trees in broad-leaved forests such as an oak one.

1　平截棒瑚菌（2022 年，雷开明 摄）
2　猴头菇（2022 年，雷开明 摄）
1　*Clavariadelphus truncatus* (photo by Lei Kaiming, 2022)
2　*Hericium erinaceus* (photo by Lei Kaiming, 2022)

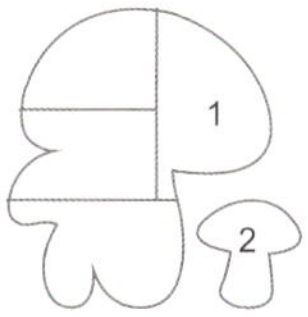

动物宝库

A Treasure House of Fauna

大熊猫缓缓走来（2007 年，周孟棋 摄）

稀有兽类

Rare Beasts

A giant panda in its leisurely gait (photo by Zhou Mengqi, 2007)

九寨沟是动物的宝库。根据《九寨沟国家级自然保护区综合科学考察报告（2021）》，九寨沟共有小型兽类 4 目、15 科、36 属、52 种，大中型兽类 13 科、25 属、29 种。其中，国家一级重点保护兽类 7 种，国家二级重点保护兽类 15 种。扎如沟是九寨沟兽类多样性最丰富的区域。

作为中国岷山大熊猫栖息地的重要组成部分，九寨沟也是大熊猫保护的重点地区之一。区别于秦岭大熊猫，四川大熊猫头部大，胸部斑块为黑色，腹侧皮毛为白色；秦岭大熊猫头部小，胸部斑块为深棕色，腹侧皮毛为棕色。

除野生大熊猫外，九寨沟还有很多珍稀动物，垂直分布在不同的生活环境和海拔高度。其中，小熊猫、豹猫等中国重点保护的珍稀野生动物主要分布在海拔 2000 ～ 3500 米的针阔混交林和亚高山针叶林带；海拔 3500 米以上的亚高山灌丛草甸、高山草甸、流石滩植被地带，也有岩羊、白唇鹿、羚牛等珍稀野生动物出没。

According to the *Report on Jiuzhaigou National Nature Reserve Comprehensive Scientific Investigation (2021)*, in Jiuzhaigou–a treasure house of animals–there are 52 species of small mammals in 4 orders, 15 families, 36 genera and 29 species of large and medium-sized mammals in 13 families and 25 genera. Among them, there are 7 species of mammals under national first-level key protection and 15 species of mammals under national second-level key protection. Zharu Gully contains the richest diversity of mammals.

As an important part of habitat for the giant panda *(Ailuropoda melanoleuca)* in China's Minshan Mountains, Jiuzhaigou is also one of the key areas for their protection. Different from those in the Qinling Mountains with small heads, dark brown chest patches and brown ventral fur, Sichuan giant pandas have large heads, black chest patches and white ventral fur.

In addition to wild giant pandas, there are many rare animals in Jiuzhaigou, which are vertically distributed in different habitats and altitudes. Among them, red panda (*Ailurus fulgens*), leopard cat (*Prionailurus bengalensis*), and others under China's key protection are mainly distributed in coniferous and broad-leaved mixed forests and subalpine coniferous forest belts at an altitude of 2,000~3,500 meters. Rare wild animals such as bharal *(Pseudois nayaur)*, white-lipped deer *(Przewalskium albirostris)* and Sichuan Takin *(Budorcas taxicolor)* also occur in the subalpine shrub meadows, alpine meadows and vegetation areas of screes above 3,500 meters above sea level.

1

2

1　大熊猫（2016 年，周孟棋 摄）

2　油画《九寨之子》，80cm×100cm（2023 年，谢纲骅 作品）

1　Giant panda (*Ailuropoda melanoleuca*) (photo by Zhou Mengqi, 2016)

2　*The Baby of Jiuzhai*, oil painting, 80cm×100cm (by Xie Ganghua, 2023)

大熊猫

属熊科，国家一级保护动物，易危（VU）。体肥胖，形似熊而略小，头躯长 160 ～ 180 厘米，尾较短，长 10 ～ 15 厘米，毛色黑白相间。生活在高山有竹丛的树林中，喜食竹类植物。能泅水，会爬树。非群居。每胎产一仔或两仔。已知的大熊猫毛色共有 3 种，除了常见的黑白色外，还有棕白色和白色。九寨沟是岷山山系大熊猫 A 种群的重要分布区，野生大熊猫分布于黑角寨、克泽沟和信扎等区域。

Giant Panda *(Ailuropoda melanoleuca)*

It is in the family Ursidae, vulnerable (VU) and under national first-level protection. Its body is obese, bear-like but slightly smaller, the head and body are 160~180 cm long, with a tail as short as about 10~15 cm long and black and white fur. It roams in forests in high mountains and feeds on bamboo plants. Nongregarious, it is good at wading water and climbing trees, giving birth to one or two per litter. There are three fur colors in giant pandas known to the world (black and white, brown and white and white). In Jiuzhaigou, an important area of Population A in the Minshan Mountains, wild giant pandas are distributed in Heijiao Village, the Keze Gully, Xinzha and other areas.

川金丝猴

属猴科，国家一级保护动物，易危（VU）。体形中等，体长约 70 厘米，尾长约与体长相等，被当地人称为“长尾巴猴”。鼻头前翘，金毛蓝面，颊部及颈侧棕红。群居，有丰富的社群行为。以野果、树叶、嫩芽、竹笋等植物性食物为主食，常栖息于海拔 1500 ～ 3300 米的云杉或冷杉林带。九寨沟的川金丝猴分布于纳久坡、扎如沟、黑角寨等与白河国家级自然保护区相邻区域。

豺

属犬科，国家一级保护动物，濒危（EN）。大小似犬而小于狼，体长 85 ～ 130 厘米。吻较狼短而头较宽，额头比狼平，耳朵半圆形，四肢比狼略短。尾比狼略长，但不超过体长的一半，其毛长而密，略似狐尾。背毛红棕色，毛尖黑色，腹毛较浅淡。群居性，集体猎食，以有蹄类为主食。九寨沟的豺分布于蝙蝠洞（翻越王朗自然保护区）及原始森林附近区域。

金猫

属猫科，国家一级保护动物，极危（CR）。体形中等，雄性体长 75 ～ 105 厘米，雌性体长 66 ～ 94 厘米。体态健美，头形壮硕，眼角前内侧各有一条白纹，眼下有一白纹延伸至耳基下部，其上、下缘均具明显黑线，喉和前胸部有淡黑色横纹或花斑点。除在繁殖期成对活动外，一般独居。肉食性动物。九寨沟内有分布，数量稀少。

1 | 2 | 3

1 川金丝猴（2022 年，梁峰 摄）
2 豺（2022 年，天下志鉴 供图）
3 金猫（2022 年，天下志鉴 供图）

Golden Snub-nosed Monkey *(Rhinopithecus roxellana)*

Being in the family Cercopithecidae and vulnerable (VU) under national first-level protection, it is medium-sized, with a body length of about 70 cm and a tail about the same length, hence the name of "long-tailed monkey" by the locals. Its nose is turned forward, hair golden, face blue, cheeks and neck brownish red. They stay together with rich social behaviors, feed mainly on wild fruits, leaves, spouts, bamboo shoots and others, inhabiting spruce or fir forest belts at an altitude of 1,500~3,300 meters. Golden snub-nosed monkeys in Jiuzhaigou are distributed in the Najiu Slope, the Zharu Gully, Heijiao Village adjacent to the Baihe National Nature Reserve.

Dhole *(Cuon alpinus)*

Being in the family Canidae, national first-level protection, endangered (EN), it is as big as a dog but smaller than a wolf, with a body length of 85~130 cm. Compared with a wolf, its snout is short and head wide, forehead flat, ears semicircular, limbs short, tail long as half of the body and hair long and dense like a fox's tail. The back hair is reddish brown, black at the tip and that on the abdomen is light. It is gregarious, hunting in groups and feeding mainly on ungulates, distributed in Jiuzhaigou's Bat Cave (beyond the Wanglang Nature Reserve) and the area near the virgin forest.

Asian Golden Cat *(Pardofelis temminckii)*

It is in the family Felidae, critically endangered（CR）and under national first-level protection. Its body length is medium, the male being 75~105 cm and the female 66~94 cm. It owns a healthy body, strong head shape, white stripe on the front and inner sides of the eyes and white stripe extending to the lower part of the ear base, with obvious black lines on the upper and lower edges, light black horizontal stripes or mottled spots on the throat and front chest. Except for activities in pairs during the breeding season, it generally stays alone, carnivorous but in small number in Jiuzhaigou.

1 Golden snub-nosed monkey (*Rhinopithecus roxellana*) (photo by Liang Feng, 2022)
2 Dhole *(Cuon alpinus)* (photo by courtesy of Tianxia Zhijian, 2022)
3 Asian Golden Cat (*pardofelis temminckii*) (photo by courtesy of Tianxia Zhijian, 2022)

1	2
3	4

1 林麝（2022 年，九寨沟管理局 供图）
2 四川羚牛（2020 年，桑吉 摄）
3 小熊猫（2012 年，黄耀华 摄）
4 马麝（2019 年，九寨沟管理局 供图）

1 Forest musk deer (*Moschus berezovskii*) (photo by courtesy of Jiuzhaigou Management Bureau, 2022)
2 Sichuan takin (*Budorcas tibetanus*) (photo by Sangji, 2020)
3 Red panda (*Ailurus fulgens*) (photo by Huang Yaohua, 2012)
4 Alpine musk deer (*Moschus chrysogaster*) (photo by courtesy of Jiuzhaigou Management Bureau, 2019)

林麝

属麝科，国家一级保护动物，极危（CR）。麝属中体型最小的一种，体长 60 ～ 78 厘米。四肢细长，蹄子狭尖。毛色深棕，颈部两侧至腋下有较宽白色带纹。幼体具斑点，成体无。雌、雄均无角，雄麝有露出口外上犬齿及巨大麝腺。短尾，耳长直立。性孤独，雌雄分居。以野果、树叶、草、苔藓、地衣为主食。九寨沟内分布较广，数量稀少，2020—2021 年在鸟艾（即上季节海）及原始森林红外监测发现实体，活动于针叶林下竹林中。

Forest Musk Deer *(Moschus berezovskii)*

It is in the family Moschidae and critically endangered (CR) and under national first-level protection. As the smallest in size in the family, it has a body length of 60~78 cm, slender limbs and narrow and pointed hooves. It is dark brown, with wide white stripes from both sides of the neck to the underarms. With spots only in the young, neither the male nor the female has horns, but exposed upper canine teeth and huge musk deer glands in the former. With a short tail and long erect ears, it roams alone, male and female separate, feeds on wild fruits, leaves, grasses, mosses and lichens. It enjoys a relatively wide distribution in Jiuzhaigou but in a small number. Infrared monitoring of Niao'ai (Upper Seasonal Lake) and virgin forests from 2020 to 2021 found some living ones, moving in bamboo forests under coniferous forests.

四川羚牛

属牛科，国家一级保护动物，易危（VU）。体长 170 ～ 220 厘米，尾长 15 ～ 20 厘米。全身棕黄或深棕色，眼周黑色。雌雄均具有扭曲状短角，群栖。以青草、树枝、竹笋为主食。常栖息于海拔 1600 ～ 4000 米的山地森林中。九寨沟内分布较广，分布于中、高海拔地区。

Sichuan Takin *(Budorcas tibetanus)*

It is in the family Bovidae, vulnerable (VU) and under first-level national protection. With a 170~220 cm in body and 15~20 cm in tail, it is brown or dark brown but black around the eyes. Gregarious, both sexes have twisted short horns. With grass, branches, bamboo shoots as staple food, it often inhabits mountainous forests at an altitude of 1,600~4,000 meters. Jiuzhaigou has widely distributed middle and high-altitude areas.

小熊猫

属小熊猫科，国家二级保护动物，易危（VU）。

Red Panda *(Ailurus fulgens)*

It is in the family Ailuridae, vulnerable (VU) under national second-level protection.

马麝

属麝科，国家一级保护动物，极危（CR）。麝属中体型最大的一种，体长 80 ～ 89 厘米。臀部与背部毛色几乎一致，通体毛色较淡呈沙黄褐色，后部棕橘色较浓，颈被有较宽的暗褐色斑块，其上有 4 ～ 6 个排成两行的棕色斑。雌、雄均无角，雄麝有露出口外上犬齿及巨大麝腺。性敏感多疑。喜食草、嫩枝、树叶、野果、苔藓。常栖息在海拔 2500 ～ 5000 米的针叶林和高山灌丛里。九寨沟内有分布，但数量不多。

Alpine Musk Deer *(Moschus chrysogaster)*

It is in the family Moschidae, critically endangered (CR) and under national first-level protection. It is the largest of its genus, with a body length of 80~89 cm. The fur of its buttocks and back is almost the same, whole body is light and sandy-yellow, rear part is thick in brown-orange and its neck has a wide dark brown patch, on which there are 4~6 brown spots arranged in two rows. Sensitive and suspicious, neither sex has any horns, a male has exposed upper canine teeth and huge glands. Fond of grass, twigs, leaves, wild fruits and moss, it often inhabits coniferous forests and alpine shrubs at an altitude of 2,500~5,000 meters. It is distributed in Jiuzhaigou, but the quantity is not much.

赤狐
Red Fox

赤狐

属犬科，国家二级保护动物。

Red Fox *(Vulpes vulpes)*

It is in the family Canidae under national second-level protection.

赤狐（2020 年，九寨沟管理局 供图）

Red fox *(Vulpes vulpes)* (photo by courtesy of Jiuzhaigou Management Bureau, 2020)

藏狐
Tibetan Fox

藏狐

属犬科，国家二级保护动物。

Tibetan Fox *(Vulpes ferrilata)*

It is in the family Canidae under national second-level protection.

藏狐（2020 年，九寨沟管理局 供图）

Tibetan fox (*Vulpes ferrilata*) (photo by courtesy of Jiuzhaigou Management Bureau, 2020)

水獭
Eurasian Otter

水獭

属鼬科。国家二级保护动物，濒危 (EN)。

Eurasian Otter *(Lutra lutra)*

It is in the family Mustelidae, endangered (EN) under national second-level protection.

水獭（2021 年，肖维阳 摄）

Eurasian Otter (*Lutra lutra*) (photo by Xiao Weiyang, 2021)

毛冠鹿

属鹿科。国家二级保护动物，易危（VU）。

Tufted Deer *(Elaphodus cephalophus)*

It is in the family Cervidae, vulnerable (VU) under national second-level protection.

毛冠鹿（2022 年，九寨沟管理局 供图）

Tufted deer (*Elaphodus cephalophus*) (photo by courtesy of Jiuzhaigou Management Bureau, 2022)

中华鬣羚

属牛科。国家二级保护动物，易危（VU）。

Chinese Serow *(Capricornis milneedwardsii)*

It is in the family Bovidae, vulnerable (VU) under national second-level protection.

中华鬣羚（2020 年，来源于《四川省志・九寨沟志》）

Chinese Serow (*Capricornis milneedwardsii*) (photo from *Sichuan Provincial Records–Jiuzhaigou Records*, 2020)

中华斑羚

属牛科。国家二级保护动物，易危（VU）。

Chinese Goral *(Naemorhedus griseus)*

It is in the family Bovidae, vulnerable (VU) under national second-level protection.

中华斑羚（2011 年，肖维阳 摄）

Chinese Goral *(Naemorhedus griseus)* (by Xiao Weiyang, 2011)

嘉陵裸裂尻鱼（2010 年，周正强 摄）

水中生灵

Aquatic Creatures

Schizopygopsis kialingensis (photo by Zhou Zhengqiang, 2010)

2021 年底，九寨沟已经发现的鱼类土著种有嘉陵裸裂尻鱼和粗壮高原鳅，外来种有虹鳟和美洲红点鲑。其中，嘉陵裸裂尻鱼分布于树正沟、日则沟和则查洼沟，在长海、树正群海、犀牛海、芦苇海、箭竹海、熊猫海、五花海、金铃海、镜海、盆景滩和诺日朗群海的种群数量大，在五彩池、老虎海、卧龙海、双龙海、天鹅海的种群数量小，在上季节海、中季节海、下季节海、芳草海、珍珠滩、珍珠滩瀑布至镜海未见分布；粗壮高原鳅分布于扎如沟，且种群数量很小。

九寨沟的两栖动物区系组成受到横断山区系的较大影响，高山环境对该地两栖动物的分布有较为明显的制约，区域内两栖动物以东洋界喜马拉雅—横断山区型的种类占优势。九寨沟发现的两栖动物有 2 目、5 科、5 种，可分为穴居静水繁殖型、林栖静水繁殖型、林栖流水繁殖型和水栖型 4 类。

水彩画《五彩九寨》，29.6cm×42cm（2023 年，曹若宸作品，指导老师：唐艺月）

Colorful Jiuzhai, watercolor, 29.6cm×42cm (by Cao Ruochen, under the instruction of Tang Yiyue, 2023)

At the end of 2021, native species of fish found in Jiuzhaigou include *Schizopygopsis kialingensis* and *Triplophysa robusta* and exotic species rainbow trout *(Oncorhynchus mykiss)* and *Salvelinus fontinalis*. Among them, *Schizopygopsis kialingensis* is distributed in the Shuzheng, Rize and Zezhawa Gullies. It is highly populated in the Long Lake, Shuzheng Lake Cluster, Rhinoceros Lake, Reed Lake, Arrow Bamboo Lake, Panda Lake, Wuhua Lake, Jinling Lake, Mirror Lakes, Bonsai Shoal, and Nuorilang Lake Cluster, yet not quite so in the Wucai Pool, Tiger Lake, Wolong Lake, Shuanglong Lake and Swan Lakes, but not from the Upper, Middle, Lower Seasonal Lakes, the Fragrant Grass Lake, the Pearl Shoal and the Pearl Shoal waterfall to the Mirror Lake; and *Triplophysa robusta* is distributed in the Zharu Gully but in very a small population.

The composition of the amphibian fauna in Jiuzhaigou is greatly influenced by the Hengduan Mountains, where the alpine environment obviously restricts the distribution of amphibians, in which the amphibians are dominated by the type species of the Himalayan-Hengduan Mountains. At present, there are 2 orders, 5 families and 5 species of amphibians found in Jiuzhaigou, which can be divided into 4 types: cave-dwelling still-water breeding, forest-dwelling still-water breeding, forest-dwelling running-water breeding and aquatic-dwelling.

表 4　2021 年九寨沟国家级自然保护区内两栖类各目、科物种组成表

Table 4 Species Composition of Various Orders, Families and Species of Amphibians in Jiuzhaigou National Nature Reserve in 2021

目 Order	科 Family	种 Species	占总种数的百分比（%） Total Amount (%)	合计百分比（%） Total (%)
有尾目 Caudata	小鲵科 Hynobiidae	1	20.0	20.0
无尾目 Anura	角蟾科 Megophryidae	1	20.0	80.0
	蟾蜍科 Bufonidae	1	20.0	
	蛙科 Ranidae	2	40.0	

嘉陵裸裂尻鱼

属鲤科，中国特有鱼类，长江上游特有鱼类，四川省重点保护鱼类。长纺锤形，侧扁。全身几乎裸露无鳞，仅在肩部有 3～5 行不规则的鳞片。体侧和背部呈绿灰或青灰色，有黑色小斑点，腹部为白色。栖息于河流、湖泊中，以水生无脊椎动物和藻类为食。

Shizopygopsis Kialingensis

It is in the family Cyprinidae, endemic to China's upper reaches of the Yangtze River under key protection in Sichuan. Laterally flattened with the shape of a long spindle, it is almost naked without scales, except for 3~5 rows of irregular scales on the shoulders. Its side and back are green-gray or blue-gray with small black spots, while its abdomen is white. It inhabits rivers and lakes and lives on aquatic invertebrates and algae.

粗壮高原鳅

属鳅科，中国特有鱼类，长江上游特有鱼类。呈长条形，前躯近圆筒形，后躯侧扁，尾柄高度向尾鳍基方向不变。体侧和背部呈褐黄色或绿黄色，腹部为白色。栖息在海拔 1800～2900 米的山区河流中。主食水生无脊椎动物，也食藻类和植物碎屑。

Triplophysa Robusta

Being in the family cobitidae and endemic to China's upper reaches of the Yangtze River, it is long and strip-shaped, its forequarters are nearly cylindrical, hindquarters laterally flat and height of caudal peduncle being unchanged toward base of caudal fin. Its side and back is brownish- or greenish-yellow and belly white. It inhabits in mountainous rivers at an altitude of 1,800~2,900 meters, foraging mainly on aquatic invertebrates, algae and plant debris.

嘉陵裸裂尻鱼（2016 年，肖维阳 摄）

Schizopygopsis kialingensis (photo by Xiao Weiyang, 2016)

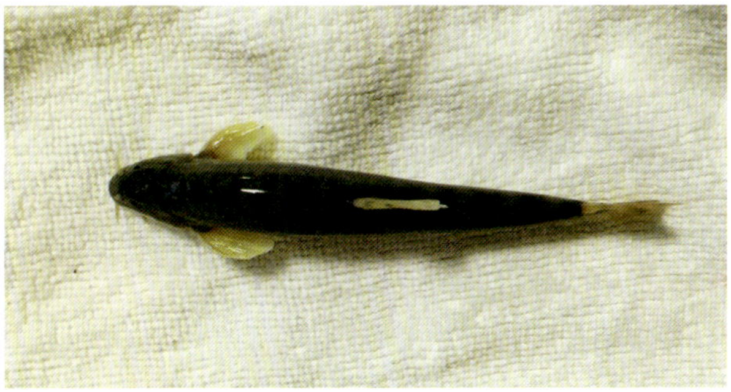

粗壮高原鳅（2018 年，九寨沟管理局 供图）

Triplophysa robusta (photo by courtesy of Jiuzhaigou Management Bureau, 2018)

西藏山溪鲵

属小鲵科。国家二级保护动物。两栖动物。中国特有物种。生活于海拔 1500 ～ 4300 米的山区或高原流溪内，多栖息于小型山溪内或泉水沟石块下，石块较多的溪段数量较多。九寨沟内分布于长海、五彩池、上季节海、卧龙海、黑角寨、扎如沟、芳草海等地，种群数量较大。

西藏齿突蟾

属角蟾科。中国特有物种。林栖静水繁殖型两栖动物。生活于海拔 3300 ～ 5100 米的高山或高原的小山溪、泉水石滩地或古冰川湖边。九寨沟内分布于长海、五彩池、上季节海、芳草海、天鹅海、扎如沟等地，种群数量较小。

Alpine Stream Salamander *(Batrachuperus tibetanus)*

As an amphibian endemic to China, it is in the family Hynobiidae under national second-level protection. Occurring in mountainous areas or plateau streams at an altitude of 1,500~4,300 meters, it mostly inhabits hilly streams or under rocks in spring ditches or streams with more rocks. It is largely distributed in Jiuzhaigou's Long Lake, Wucai Pool, Upper Seasonal Lake, Fragrant Grass Lake, Heijiao Village, Zharu Gully, Fragrant Grass Lake and so on.

Xizang Alpine Toad *(Scutiger boulengeri)*

As a forest-dwelling still-water breeding amphibian, it is in the family Megophryidae, endemic to China. It occurs in hilly streams, spring water rocky shoals or ancient glacial lakes in high mountains or plateaus at an altitude of 3,300~5,100 meters. It is distributed in Jiuzhaigou's Long Lake, Wucai Pool, Upper Seasonal Lake, Fragrant Grass Lake, Swan Lake, Zharu Gully and so on, but in a small population.

1
2
3

1 西藏山溪鲵（2020 年，九寨沟管理局 供图）
2 西藏齿突蟾（2020 年，九寨沟管理局 供图）
3 中华蟾蜍（2004 年，蹇代君 供图）

1 Alpine stream salamander (*Batrachuperus tibetanus*) (photo by courtesy of Jiuzhaigou Management Bureau, 2020)
2 Xizang alpine toad (*Scutiger boulengeri*) (photo by courtesy of Jiuzhaigou Management Bureau, 2020)
3 Zhou-shan toad (*Bufo gargarizans*) (photo by courtesy of Jian Daijun, 2004)

中华蟾蜍

属蟾蜍科。穴居静水繁殖型两栖动物。生活于海拔 120 ～ 4300 米的多种生态环境中。除冬眠和繁殖期栖息于水中外，多在陆地草丛、地边、山坡石下或土穴等潮湿环境中栖息。九寨沟内分布于树正群海、五花海、黑角寨、荷叶寨、扎如沟等多数沟内，种群数量较大。

1
2

1　高原林蛙（2020 年，九寨沟管理局 供图）
2　四川湍蛙（2020 年，九寨沟管理局 供图）

1　Plateau brown frog (*Rana kukunoris*) (photo by courtesy of Jiuzhaigou Management Bureau, 2020)
2　*Amolops mantzorum* (photo by courtesy of Jiuzhaigou Management Bureau, 2020)

Zhou-shan Toad *(Bufo gargarizans)*

It is in the family Bufonidae as a cave-dwelling still-water breeding amphibian, surviving in a variety of ecological environments at an altitude of 120~4,300 meters. In addition to inhabiting water during hibernation and breeding, it mostly inhabits humid environments such as terrestrial grass, fields, under rocks on hillsides, or in soil caves. In Jiuzhaigou, it is distributed in the Shuzheng Lake Cluster, Wuhua Lake, Heijiao Village, Heye Village, Zharu Gully and others in a relatively large number.

高原林蛙

属蛙科。中国特有物种。林栖静水繁殖型两栖动物。生活于海拔 3000 ～ 4500 米的草地、灌丛及森林边缘地带，多栖息在各种静水域边及其他潮湿环境中。九寨沟内的优势种，分布于长海、上季节海、树正群海、芦苇海、五花海、扎如沟等地，种群数量大。

四川湍蛙

属蛙科。中国特有物种。林栖流水繁殖型两栖动物。生活于海拔 1000 ～ 3800 米的大型山溪、河流两侧或瀑布较多的溪段内。白天常栖息于溪河岸边的石头下，夜间出外活动，多蹲在溪内或岸边的石头上，常常头向溪内。九寨沟内仅发现于扎如沟，种群数量较小。

Plateau Brown Frog *(Rana kukunoris)*

It is in the family Ranidae, a species endemic to China as forest-dwelling still-water breeding amphibian, living in grasslands, shrubs and forest edges at an altitude of 3,000~4,500 meters and mostly staying in various still waters and other humid environments. The dominant species in Jiuzhaigou are distributed in the Long Lake, the Upper Seasonal Lake, the Shuzheng Lake Cluster, the Reed Lake, the Wuhua Lake, the Zharu Gully and the like in a large population.

Amolops Mantzorum

A species endemic to China, it is in the family Ranidae as a forest-dwelling running-water breeding amphibian, occurs in large mountainous streams at an altitude of 1,000~3,800 meters and on both sides of rivers or streams with many waterfalls. During the day, it often stays under the rocks on the banks of streams and squats at night in the streams or on the rocks on the banks, with its head facing inwards. It is only found in Jiuzhaigou's Zharu Gully only in a small number.

黄腿渔鸮（2013 年，桑吉 摄）

多姿禽鸟

Birds of Various Kinds

Tawnyfish owl *(Ketupa flavipes)* (photo by Sangji, 2013)

九寨沟的鸟类资源非常丰富，其中不乏珍稀鸟类。根据科学调查，九寨沟有鸟类 17 目、53 科、269 种。其中，国家级及四川省级重点保护鸟类 59 种，约占保护区内所有分布鸟类总数的 22%；国家一级、二级保护鸟类 49 种，约占保护区鸟类总数的 18%。

此外，九寨沟还有斑尾榛鸡、红喉雉鹑、绿尾虹雉、蓝马鸡、红腹锦鸡、四川林鸮、黑头噪鸦、红腹山雀、川褐头山雀、银脸长尾山雀、银喉长尾山雀、凤头雀莺、白眶鸦雀、黑额山噪鹛、斑背噪鹛、橙翅噪鹛、大噪鹛、中华雀鹛、四川旋木雀、白脸䴓、宝兴歌鸫、蓝鹀 22 种中国特有鸟类，约占中国特有鸟类的 24%。

九寨沟鸟类以留鸟和夏候鸟为主，同时冬候鸟和旅鸟也占一定比例，在九寨沟的 269 种鸟类中，有 161 种留鸟、74 种夏候鸟、26 种旅鸟、7 种冬候鸟、1 种迷鸟。区内鸟类种类呈现一定程度的季节性动态变化。

随着保护程度的日益提升，越来越多的鸟类被九寨沟优良生态环境所吸引，来此繁衍生息，其中不乏区内新发现的鸟类。2005 年 5 月 21 日，九寨沟管理局科研工作者在火花海进行常规水位监测时，首次发现 2 只白冠燕尾。

Jiuzhaigou is rich in bird resources, some being rare ones. According to scientific surveys, it boasts 269 species of birds in 17 orders and 53 families. Among them, 59 species are under national and provincial-level key protection, accounting for about 22% of the total and 49 species under national first-level and second-level protection, accounting for about 18% of the total in the reserve.

In addition, it has 22 kinds endemic to China: Chinese hazel grouse (*Bonasa sewerzowi*), chestnut-throated monal partridge (*Tetraophasis obscurus*), Chinese monal pheasant (*Lophophorus lhuysii*), blue eared pheasant (*Crossoptilon auritum*), golden pheasant (*Chrysolophus pictus*), Sichuan wood owl (*Strix davidi*), Sichuan jay (*Perisoreus internigrans*), rusty-breasted tit (*Parus davidi*), willow tit (*Poecile montanus*), white-necklaced tit(*Aegithalos fuliginosus*), long-tailed tit *(Aegithalos caudatus)*, crested tit warbler (*Leptopoecile elegans*), spectacled parrotbill (*Paradoxornis conspicillatus*), black-fronted laughingthrush (*Garrulax sukatschewi*), barred laughingthrush (*Garrulax lunulatus*), Elliot's laughingthrush (*Garrulax elliotii*), giant laughingthrush (*Garrulax maximus*), Chinese fulvetta (*Alcippe striaticollis*), Sichuan creeper (*Certhia tianquanensis*), Przevalski's Nuthatch (*Sitta leucopsis*), Chinese thrush (*Turdus mupinensis*) and slaty bunting (*Latoucheornis siemsseni*), accounting for about 24% of the total across the country.

In Jiuzhaigou, the resident and summer migratory birds are the majority, while winter migratory and traveling birds account for a certain proportion. Among its 269 species, there are 161 of resident birds, 74 of summer migratory birds, 26 of traveling birds, 7 of winter migratory birds and one of stray birds, all of which show a certain degree of seasonal dynamic changes.

With the daily increase of protection, more and more birds (including newly discovered ones), attracted by the excellent ecological environment, come to multiply and flourish here. On May 21, 2005, researchers from the Jiuzhaigou Management Bureau discovered two white-crowned forktail (*Enicurus leschenaultia*) for the first time while conducting routine water-level monitoring in the Sparkling Lake.

九寨沟山中精灵（2023 年，梁峰 摄）
Mountain elves in Jiuzhaigou (photo by Liang Feng, 2023)

表 5　2021 年九寨沟鸟类组成及保护等级
Table 5 Composition and Protection Grade of Birds in Jiuzhaigou in 2021

目 Order	科 Family	种 Species	保护级别 Protection grade		
			I	II	四川省重点 Key protection species in Sichuan
鸡形目 Galliformes	1	11	3	6	
雁形目 Anseriformes	1	12		2	
䴙䴘目 Podicipediformes	1	2		1	1
鸽形目 Columibformes	1	5			
夜鹰目 Caprimulgiformes	2	2			1
鹃形目 Cuculiformes	1	7			2
鹤形目 Gruiformes	1	4			2
鸻形目 Charadriiformes	3	5			1
鲣鸟目 Suliformes	1	1			1
鹈形目 Pelecaniformes	1	6			2
鹰形目 Accipitriformes	1	14	2	12	
鸮形目 Strigiformes	1	5	1	4	
犀鸟目 Bucerotiformes	1	1			
佛法僧目 Coraciiformes	1	3			
啄木鸟目 Piciformes	1	9		2	
隼形目 Falconiformes	1	2	1	1	
雀形目 Passeriformes	34	180	3	11	
合计 Total	53	269	10	39	10

表 6　2021 年九寨沟内被列入《世界自然保护联盟濒危物种红色名录》的鸟类

Table 6 Birds of Jiuzhaigou Listed in *IUCN Red List of Threatened Species* in 2021

濒危等级 Endangerment category	鸟类名称 Name
濒危 (EN)	棕头歌鸲、猎隼 Rufous-headed robin *(Luscinia ruficeps)*, Saker falcon *(Falco cherrug)*
易危 (VU)	绿尾虹雉、黑头噪鸦、白颈鸦、黑额山噪鹛、白喉林鹟 Chinese monal pheasant *(Lophophorus lhuysii)*, Sichuan jay *(Perisoreus internigrans)*, Collared crow *(Corvus torquatus)*, Black-fronted laughingthrush *(Garrulax sukatschewi)*, White-gorgetted jungle flycatcher *(Rhinomyias brunneata)*
近危 (NT)	斑尾榛鸡、白眼潜鸭、胡兀鹫、高山兀鹫 Chinese hazel grouse *(Bonasa sewerzowi)*, White-eyed pochard *(Aythya nyroca)*, Bearded vulture *(Gypaetus barbatus)*, Grifon vulture *(Gyps himalayensis)*

表 7　2021 年九寨沟内被列入《中国生物多样性红色名录》的鸟类

Table 7 Birds of Jiuzhaigou Included in *China Biodiversity Red List* in 2021

濒危等级 Endangerment category	鸟类名称 Name
濒危 (EN)	黄腿渔鸮、绿尾虹雉、棕头歌鸲、猎隼 Tawnyfish owl *(Ketupa flavipes)*, Chinese monal pheasant *(Lophophorus lhuysii)*, Rufous-headed robin *(Luscinia ruficeps)*, Saker falcon *(Falco cherrug)*
易危 (VU)	红喉雉鹑、金雕、大鵟、黑头噪鸦、四川林鸮、四川旋木雀、黑额山噪鹛、白喉林鹟 Chestnut-throated monal partridge *(Tetraophasis obscurus)*, Golden eagle *(Aquila chrysaetos)*, Upland buzzard *(Buteo hemilasius)*, Sichuan jay *(Perisoreus internigrans)*, Sichuan woodowl *(Strix davidi)*, Sichuan creeper *(Certhia tianquanensis)*, Black-fronted laughingthrush *(Garrulax sukatschewi)*, White-gorgetted jungle flycatcher *(Rhinomyias brunneata)*
近危 (NT)	斑尾榛鸡、雪鹑、藏雪鸡、血雉、红腹角雉、蓝马鸡、红腹锦鸡、大天鹅、鸳鸯、白眼潜鸭、红胸田鸡、胡兀鹫、凤头蜂鹰、高山兀鹫、凤头鹰、苍鹰、白尾鹞、鹊鹞、灰林鸮、淡绿鵙鹛、白颈鸦、川褐头山雀、华西柳莺、凤头雀莺、白眶鸦雀、黑头鳾、藏黄雀 Chinese hazel grouse *(Bonasa sewerzowi)*, Snow partridge *(Lerwa lerwa)*, Tibetan snow cock *(Tetraogallus tibetanus)*, Blood pheasant *(Ithaginis cruentus)*, Chinese tragopan *(Tragopan temminckii)*, Blue eared pheasant *(Crossoptilon auritum)*, Golden pheasant *(Chrysolophus pictus)*, Whooper swan *(Cygnus cygnus)*, Mandarin duck *(Aix galericulata)*, White-eyed pochard *(Aythya nyroca)*, Ruddy-breasted crake *(Porzana fusca)*, Bearded vulture *(Gypaetus barbatus)*, Honey buzzard *(Pernis ptilorhynchus)*, Grifon vulture *(Gyps himalayensis)*, Crested goshawk *(Accipiter trivirgatus)*, Northern goshawk *(Accipiter gentilis)*, Northern harrier *(Circus cyaneus)*, Piedharrier *(Circus melanoleucos)*, Tawny woodowl *(Strix aluco)*, Green shrike babbler *(Pteruthius xanthochlorus obscurus)*, Collared crow *(Corvus torquatus)*, Willow tit *(Poecile montanus)*, *Phylloscopus occisinensis*, Crested tit warbler *(Leptopoecile elegans)*, Spectacled parrotbill *(Paradoxornis conspicillatus)*, Snowy-browed nuthatch *(Sitta villosa)*, *Tibetan serin (Carduelis thibetana)*

1 Chinese hazel grouse (*Bonasa sewerzowi*) (photo by courtesy of Jiuzhaigou Management Bureau, 2020)

2 Chestnut-throated monal partridge (*Tetraophasis obscurus*) (photo by courtesy of Jiuzhaigou Management Bureau, 2020)

1 | 2

1 斑尾榛鸡（2020 年，九寨沟管理局 供图）

2 红喉雉鹑（2020 年，九寨沟管理局 供图）

斑尾榛鸡

属松鸡科，国家一级保护动物。中国特有物种。中型鸟类，体长约 30 厘米。上体多褐色横斑而带黑，下体胸部棕色，及至臀部渐白，并密布黑色横斑。雌鸟色暗，喉部有白色细纹，下体多皮黄色，外侧尾羽近端黑而远端白。主要栖息于海拔 3000 ～ 4000 米的山地森林草原和散生有少许针叶树的金露梅、山柳和杜鹃灌丛地区，也出现于云杉林和赤杨林及其林缘灌丛地带。九寨沟内见于原始森林、五彩池、黑角寨的针叶林下。

Chinese Hazel Grouse *(Bonasa sewerzowi)*

It is in the family Tetraonidae and under national first-level protection, a species endemic to China, medium-sized bird about 30 cm long. Its upper body is mostly brown with black horizontal spots, lower part is brown in the chest, gradually white in the buttocks and densely covered with black horizontal spots. The female is dark in color, with white fine lines on the throat, yellow skin on the underparts and the proximal end of the outer tail feathers is black and the distal end white. It mainly inhabits mountainous forest steppes at an altitude of 3,000~4,000 meters and places scattered with a few coniferous trees' *potentilla fruticosa, Salix pseudotangii* and *rhododendron* shrubs, in addition to spruce forests, alder forests and forest edge shrubs. It can be found under Jiuzhaigou's coniferous forests of the vigin forest, the Wucai Pool and Heijiao Village.

红喉雉鹑

属雉科，国家一级保护动物。中国特有物种。中型鸟类，体长约 48 厘米。胸灰色，具黑色细纹。眼周裸皮为猩红色。雌、雄两性相似。体羽以褐色为主，翅缘有白色和淡棕色端斑。颏至前颈及尾下覆羽，为红栗色。胸、腹褐灰，胸羽有黑色纵纹，腹羽则杂以淡黄和棕色。以植物的球茎、块根、草叶、花和种子为主食。喜活动于高原针叶林和针阔混交林及杜鹃灌丛中的多岩地区。九寨沟内见于扎如沟和黑角寨。

Chestnut-throated Monal Partridge *(Tetraophasis obscurus)*

It is in the family Phasianidae, a species endemic to China under national first-level protection. Medium-sized (similar in both sexes) with a body length of about 48 cm, it has a breast gray with black fine lines, scarlet skin around the eyes. It is mainly brown in feathers, white and light brown end spots in wings, red chestnut from chin to front neck and under tail coverts, brownish gray in chest and abdomen with black longitudinal stripes in breast feathers and light yellow and brown in belly feathers. Feeding on bulbs, roots, grass leaves, flowers and seeds of plants, it is active in rocky areas in plateau coniferous forests, mixed coniferous and broad-leaved forests and rhododendron bushes. In Jiuzhaigou, it can be found in the Zharu Gully and Heijiao Village.

绿尾虹雉

属雉科，国家一级保护动物。中国特有物种。大型鸟类，体长约 80 厘米。雄鸟头顶有一簇青铜色至红铜色羽冠，上体羽毛多呈紫铜、蓝绿等色，下体黑色，尾羽蓝绿色。雌鸟体羽暗褐色，背白色，尾羽具褐色横斑。植食性，以植物的根、地下茎、球茎等为主食。一般栖息于海拔 4000 米左右的草甸灌丛或裸岩地带，或亚高山针叶林上缘及林线以上的高山灌丛。九寨沟内主要分布在扎如沟高海拔的针叶林和高山草甸带。

胡兀鹫

属鹰科，国家一级保护动物。大型猛禽，体长 1～1.4 米。全身羽色大致为黑褐色，头黄白色，有黑色贯眼纹，向前延伸与颏部的须状羽相连，枕部、颈、胸和上腹红褐色。一般雌鸟比雄鸟体型稍大。性情机警凶猛，常单独或成对活动，很少与其他猛禽混群。食性独特，喜食新鲜的尸体和骨头，90% 的食物来源为骨髓，是世界上唯一嗜食骨头的鸟类。栖息于多裸岩石山地和高原。九寨沟内 4000 米高海拔的生境中有分布。

Chinese Monal Pheasant *(Lophophorus lhuysii)*

It is in the family Phasianidae, a species endemic to China under first-level national protection. As a large bird with a body length of about 80 cm, it has a tuft of bronze to copper-colored crest, the upper body feathers being mostly copper, blue-green and so on, the lower body black and the tail feathers blue-green. A female one's body feathers are dark brown, back white, flight and tail feathers covered with brown horizontal spots. Herbivorous, with plant roots, underground stems, bulbs and others as staple food, it generally inhabits meadow shrubs or bare rock areas at an altitude of about 4,000 meters, or alpine shrubs on the upper edge of subalpine coniferous forests and above the tree line. It is mainly distributed in the high-altitude coniferous forests and alpine meadow belt of Jiuzhaigou's Zharu Gully.

Bearded Vulture *(Gypaetus barbatus)*

It is in the family Accipitridae, a large raptor with a body length of 1~1.4 meters under national first-level protection. The plumage color of its whole body is roughly dark brown, the head is yellowish white with black eye lines extending forward and connecting with the beard feathers of its chin and reddish brown in the occipital, neck, chest and upper abdomen. A female is generally slightly larger than a male. Vigilant and ferocious, it often moves alone or in pairs, rarely mixed with other raptors. It has a unique feeding habit and likes to consume fresh carcasses and bones and 90% of its food source is bone marrow. It is the only bird in the world that prefers to consume bones. Inhabiting bare rugged mountains and plateaus, it is distributed in the habitat at an altitude of 4,000 meters in Jiuzhaigou.

1 | 2

1 绿尾虹雉（2020 年，九寨沟管理局 供图）
2 胡兀鹫（2020 年，九寨沟管理局 供图）

1 Chinese monal pheasant (*Lophophorus lhuysii*) (photo by courtesy of Jiuzhaigou Management Bureau, 2020)
2 Bearded vulture (*Gypaetus barbatus*) (photo by courtesy of Jiuzhaigou Management Bureau, 2020)

1 | 2

1　金雕（2020 年，九寨沟管理局 供图）
2　四川林鸮（2022 年，梁峰 摄）

1　Golden eagle *(Aquila chrysaetos)* (photo by courtesy of Jiuzhaigou Management Bureau, 2020)
2　Sichuan wood owl (*Strix davidi*) (photo by Liang Feng, 2022)

金雕

属鹰科，国家一级保护动物。大型猛禽，雕中最大的一种，体长约 85 厘米。头颈上具有金色的羽冠，嘴巨大，头顶暗褐色，尖羽色较浅。尾长而圆，两翼呈 V 形。以大型鸟类或小型兽类为主食。常栖息于高山草原、荒漠、河谷和森林地带，活动的最高海拔超过 4000 米。于九寨沟内圆海子的高山草甸有分布，营巢于高海拔的陡岩峭壁之上。

四川林鸮

属鸱鸮科，国家一级保护动物。中国特有物种。中大型猛禽，体型比长尾林鸮稍大。面盘灰褐色，上体褐色，背部黑色而微具白纹，下体为灰黄白色，腿覆羽，为灰黄色，有细小浅褐色横斑及斑点。性隐匿。主要以鼠、兔等动物为食，也掠食雀类、鸦、喜鹊、斑鸠等。主要栖息于亚高山至高山的针阔混交林和针叶林带。九寨沟内郁闭度较高的针叶林有见。

Golden Eagle *(Aquila chrysaetos)*

It is in the family Accipitridae, a large raptor and largest among eagles, with a body length of about 85 cm under first-level national protection. It has a golden feather crest on head and neck, a huge mouth, a dark brown head and light tip feathers, with a long and rounded tail as well as V-shaped wings. Feeding on large birds or small animals, it often inhabits alpine grasslands, deserts, river valleys and forests and the highest altitude of its activities exceeds 4,000 meters. It is distributed across the alpine meadows in the Round Lake of Jiuzhaigou, nesting on the high steep rocky cliffs.

Sichuan Wood Owl *(Strix davidi)*

A medium-to-large raptor and slightly larger than *Strix uralensis Pallas* in the family Strigidae, it is a species endemic to China under national first-level national protection. Its face is grayish brown, upper body is brown, back is black with slight white streaks, lower body is grayish yellow and white, leg coverts are grayish yellow, with small light brown horizontal spots. Good at concealment, it mainly feeds on animals such as rats and rabbits and also preys on finches, crows, magpies and turtledoves. Its main habitat is coniferous and broad-leaved mixed forests and coniferous forest belts in subalpine-to-alpine mountains and it can be in such forests with high canopy density in Jiuzhaigou.

1 Saker falcon *(Falco cherrug)* (photo by Sheng You, 2021)
2 Sichuan jay *(Perisoreus internigrans)* (photo by Sheng You, 2007)

1 | 2

1 猎隼（2021 年，沈尤 摄）
2 黑头噪鸦（2007 年，沈尤 摄）

猎隼

属隼科，国家一级保护动物。中型猛禽，体长 28 ～ 78 厘米。为体大且胸部厚实的浅色隼。颈背偏白，头顶浅褐。眼下方具不明显黑色线条，眉纹白。上体多褐色而略具横斑，下体偏白，翼尖为深褐色，翼下覆羽，有黑色细纹，尾具狭窄的白色羽端。叫声似游隼但较沙哑。常栖息于开阔的山脚平原、荒野、农田耕地等生境，尤喜在少树而多石的山丘、旷野地带活动。

Saker Falcon *(Falco cherrug)*

A medium-sized raptor with a body length of 28~78 cm, it is in the family Falconidae under national first-level protection. As a large, thick-chested light-colored falcon, it has a whitish nape and light brown top. There is inconspicuous black line under the eyes and the eyebrow lines are white.Its upper body is mostly brown with slightly horizontal spots, while the lower body is white, wingtips is dark brown, large coverts under the wings covered with black fine lines and the tail with narrow white feather tips. With a sound like a *Falco peregrinus peregrinator* but hoarser, it often inhabits the spacious plain below the mountain, wilderness, farmland and others, especially likes to move about in hills and wild areas with fewer trees but more rocks.

黑头噪鸦

属鸦科，国家一级保护动物。中国特有物种。体形似乌鸦但较小。体羽呈黑色及灰褐色，通体无鲜亮色调。尾甚短。多单个或成对活动。杂食性，主要以昆虫、昆虫幼虫和蛹为食。主要栖息于亚高山针叶林丛海拔 3050 ～ 4300 米处，活动于山地针叶林较开阔地带。在九寨沟高海拔的成熟针叶林有分布。

Sichuan Jay *(Perisoreus internigrans)*

As a species endemic to China, it is in the family Corvidae under national first-level protection. Resembling a crow but smaller, it has black and taupe body feathers without any bright hues all over and very short tail, moving about alone single or in pairs. Omnivorous, it mainly feeds on insects, insect larvae and pupae and inhabits subalpine coniferous forests from 3,050~4,300 meters above sea level where lie open areas. Sichuan Jay is distributed in the mature coniferous forests in Jiuzhaigou.

1 Black-fronted laughingthrush (*Garrulax sukatschewi*) (photo by courtesy of Jiuzhaigou Management Bureau, 2020)
2 Rufous-headed robin (*Luscinia ruficeps*) (photo by Xiao Weiyang, 2011)

1 | 2

1 黑额山噪鹛（2020 年，九寨沟管理局 供图）
2 棕头歌鸲（2011 年，肖维阳 摄）

黑额山噪鹛

属噪鹛科，国家一级保护动物。中国特有物种。中型鸟类，体长约 28 厘米。脸颊及耳羽明显为白色，上下各有黑褐色条纹与烟褐色的眼相接。外侧尾羽为混灰色，端白色。尾上覆羽，为棕色，臀为暖皮黄色。以步行甲、鳞翅目幼虫、蝇等昆虫和植物种子为食。常栖息于海拔 2000 ～ 3500 米的高山灌木林中。九寨沟内黑角寨、鸟艾均有分布。

Black-fronted Laughingthrush *(Garrulax sukatschewi)*

A species of medium size with a body length of about 28 cm and endemic to China, it is in the family Leiothrichidae under national first-level protection. Its cheeks and ear feathers are obviously white, with dark brown stripes on the upper and lower sides connecting with the smoky brown eyes. Its outer tail feathers are mixed gray and tip is white. Its tail is covered with brown feathers and buttocks are yellow. Feeding on insects such as beetles, lepidopteran larvae, flies besides plant seeds, it often inhabits alpine shrubs at an altitude of 2,000~3,500 meters, distributed in Jiuzhaigou's Heijiao Village and Niao'ai.

棕头歌鸲

属鹟科，国家一级保护动物。中型鸟类，体长 13 ～ 15 厘米。雄鸟头为橙棕色，背部为暗蓝灰色，喉部为白色。雌鸟似雌性蓝歌鸲，但头侧及颈深褐，喉具鳞状斑纹。极善鸣叫，叫声洪亮悦耳。主要栖息于海拔 2000 米以上的山地杉木林、桦树林及山杨、柳树杂木林和疏林灌丛地带。常单独或成对活动在林下灌丛中和地上。“8·8”九寨沟地震前在长海、克泽沟、丹祖沟均有分布。

Rufous-headed Robin *(Luscinia ruficeps)*

As a medium-sized bird with a body length of 13~15 cm, it is in the family Muscicapidae under first-level national protection. A male has an orange-brown head, dark blue-gray back and white throat while a female resembles a female *Luscinia cyane* but is dark brown on the sides of the head and neck and has scaly markings on the throat. Very good at chirping, loud and melodious, it mainly inhabits mountainous forests of fir, birch, aspens, willows and shrubs at an altitude of above 2,000 meters. It often moves alone or in pairs in the undergrowth and on the ground. Before the "8·8" Earthquake in Jiuzhaigou, it was distributed in the Long Lake, Keze and Danzu Gullies.

1 3
2 4

1 血雉（2022 年，王国兰 摄）
2 蓝马鸡（2023 年，松潘县林业和草原局 供图）
3 红腹锦鸡（2020 年，九寨沟管理局供图）
4 大天鹅（2020 年，九寨沟管理局供图）

1 Blood pheasant (*Ithaginis cruentus*) (photo by Wang Guolan, 2022)
2 Blue Eared Pheasant (*Crossoptilon auritum*) (photo by Songpan Forestry and Grassland Bureau, 2023)
3 Golden pheasant (*Chrysolophus pictus*) (photo by courtesy of Jiuzhaigou Management Bureau, 2020)
4 Whooper swan (*Cygnus cygnus*) (photo by courtesy of Jiuzhaigou Management Bureau, 2020)

血雉

属雉科，国家二级保护动物。中国特有物种。

蓝马鸡

属雉科，国家二级保护动物。中国特有物种。

红腹锦鸡

属雉科，国家二级保护动物。中国特有物种。

大天鹅

属鸭科，国家二级保护动物。

Blood Pheasant *(Ithaginis cruentus)*

A species endemic of China, it is in the family Phasianidae under national second-level protection. Endemic species of China.

Blue Eared Pheasant *(Crossoptilon auritum)*

A species endemic of China, it is in the family Phasianidae under national second-level protection.

Golden Pheasant *(Chrysolophus pictus)*

A species endemic of China, it is in the family Phasianidae under national second-level protection.

Whooper Swan *(Cygnus cygnus)*

It is in the family Anatidae under national second-level protection.

1	3
2	4

1　黄腿渔鸮（2014 年，桑吉 摄）
2　红腹山雀（2020 年，九寨沟管理局供图）
3　银脸长尾山雀（2020 年，九寨沟管理局 供图）
4　白眶鸦雀（2020 年，王昌大 摄）

1　Tawny fish owl *(Ketupa flavipes)* (photo by Sangji, 2014)
2　Rusty-breasted tit (*Parus davidi*) (photo by courtesy of Jiuzhaigou Management Bureau, 2020)
3　White-necklaced tit (*Aegithalos fuliginosus*) (photo by courtesy of Jiuzhaigou Management Bureau, 2020)
4　Spectacled parrotbill (*Paradoxornis conspicillatus*) (photo by Wang Changda, 2020)

黄腿渔鸮

属鸱鸮科，国家二级保护动物。

Tawny Fish Owl *(Ketupa flavipes)*

It is in the family Strigidae under national second-level protection.

红腹山雀

属山雀科，中国特有物种。

Rusty-breasted Tit *(Parus davidi)*

A species endemic to China, it is in the family Paridae.

银脸长尾山雀

属长尾山雀科，国家二级保护动物。

White-necklaced Tit *(Aegithalos fuliginosus)*

It is in the family Paridae under national second-level protection.

白眶鸦雀

属莺鹛科，国家二级保护动物。中国特有物种。

Spectacled Parrotbill *(Paradoxornis conspicillatus)*

A species endemic to China, it is in the family Sylviidae under national second-level protection.

九看九寨

Jiuzhaigou in Nine Episodes

之五

Episode Five

风情藏寨

Customs of the Zang Ethnic Villages

则查洼老寨（2017 年，骞代君 摄）

村寨村社

Villages and Communities

The former Zezhawa Village (photo by Jian Daijun, 2017)

九寨沟古称“羊峒”，又称“翠海”，系嘉陵江源头上游，因和药、则查洼、尖盘、盘亚、亚那、彭布、盘信、黑果坝、布垭9个古老传统村寨而得名，全称“三舍羊峒和药九寨”。

中华人民共和国成立后，新的区、乡、村三级行政体制建立，原属白河区塔藏乡的何药九寨改为隆康公社荷叶村、扎如村、树正村3个村。此后，九寨沟行政建置多次变化，1984年恢复乡村建置，包含白河区隆康公社荷叶、扎如、树正3个行政村。荷叶、扎如、树正3个村从开放旅游开始便停止农业和畜牧业。1994年，省委发文确定的100个小城镇试点镇中，九寨沟镇被列为重点镇之一。1995年，阿坝州计经委发出《关于下达我州扩大小城镇建设试点规模“农转非”计划指标的通知》，下达给九寨沟县2000名“农转非”人口计划指标，荷叶、树正、扎如3个村的村民先后均已“农转非”，及后成立九寨沟县漳扎镇树正社区、荷叶社区、扎如社区3个居民委员会（简称“居委会”）。九寨沟景区内建立3个居委会，由处（局）统一管理，便于开展各项工作，建议处（局）增设多种经营管理科和景区居民管理办公室，“两块牌子、一套人马”，其主要职责是管理景区居民的经营活动和行政事务。

荷叶社区居委会包括荷叶寨、盘亚寨和亚拉寨，扎如社区居委会包括尖盘寨、热西寨和郭都寨，树正社区居委会包括树正寨、则查洼寨和黑角寨。

如今，树正寨、则查洼寨、尖盘寨、盘亚寨、热西寨、荷叶寨为居民居住点。黑角寨、亚拉寨、郭都寨居民分别搬迁至基础设施更完善、交通更便利的树正寨、荷叶寨及热西寨居住。

随着旅游业发展和对外交往通道拓宽，九寨沟形成由3个圈层构成的周边社区。距离九寨沟最近的圈层是九寨沟沟口沿白河上下两岸的旅游服务区，主要涉及沟口上游的彭丰村和沟口下游的隆康村；次一级为漳扎镇，包括漳扎旅游镇和其管辖范围内其他与旅游服务相关的发展区域，范围以白河流域为限；最外围是九寨沟县，既为九寨沟旅游发展提供支撑，又受益于九寨沟旅游的发展，旅游业成为县域支柱产业。

扎如村（1991年，九寨沟县档案馆 供图）
Zharu Village (photo by courtesy of Jiuzhaigou County Archives, 1991)

Jiuzhaigou was once called "Yangdong", also known as "Blue Lake". It is the upper reaches on the source of the Jialing River. It is named after such 9 traditional villages as Heyao, Zezhawa, Jianpan, Panya, Yana, Pengbu, Panxin, Heiguoba, Buya, and is fully named "Sanshe Yangdong and Heyao Nine Villages".

After the founding of the People's Republic of China (PRC) in 1949, a new three-level administrative system of districts, townships and villages was established. The "Heyao Nine Villages", originally under Tazang Town, Baihe District, changed into three villages named Heye, Zharu and Shuzheng in Longkang Commune. Since then, the administrative structure here has changed many times. In 1984, the rural structure was restored, including the three administrative villages of Heye, Zharu and Shuzheng in Baihe District. Along with the opening of tourism, these three villages discontinued their farming and animal husbandry activities. In 1994, Jiuzhaogou Town was listed among the 100 pilot towns of small town determined by the Provincial Party Committee. Jiuzhaigou Town was listed among the key ones. In 1995, Aba Prefecture Planning and Economic Commission issued *Notice on Issuing the Plan Targets of "Converting Farmers to Non-farmers" for Expanding the Experimental Scale of Small Town Construction in the Prefecture*, and assigned to Jiuzhaigou County a plan target of 2,000 persons for the conversion. Then the villagers of Heye, Shuzheng and Zharu had all been converted as members of the three neighborhood committees of the villages of Heye, Shuzheng, and Zharu respectively before neighborhood committees were established in the communities of Shuzheng, Heye and Zharu under Jiuzhaigou County. The three neighborhood committees established in Jiuzhaigou Scenic Area were brought under the unified management of a certain division (bureau) in order to carry out various tasks. It was recommended to set up a management department for diversified economy and a management office for residents in the scenic area, "one team under tow names", which were tasked with main responsibilities to manage the business activities and administrative affairs for the residents in the scenic area.

Neighborhood Committee of Heye Community includes villages of Heye, Panya and Yala, that of Zharu Community includes those of Jianpan, Rexi and Guodu, and that of Shuzheng Community includes those of Shuzheng, Zezhawa and Heijiao.

Today, villages of Shuzheng, Zezhawa, Jianpan, Panya, Rexi and Heye are residential areas. Residents of Heijiao, Yala and Guodu villages have moved into Shuzheng, Heye and Rexi, with better infrastructure and more convenient transportation.

With the development of tourism and widening of roads to the outside, Jiuzhaigou has formed a three-circle surrounding communities: the closest one is the tourism service area along the upper and lower banks of the Baihe River at the entrance to Jiuzhaigou, mainly involving Pengfeng Village on the upper reaches of the entrance to Jiuzhaigou and Longkang Village in the downstream of the entrace to Jiuzhaigou; the second is Zhangzha Town, including Zhangzha Tourist Town and other development areas under its jurisdiction related to tourism services within the Baihe River Basin; and the outermost is Jiuzhaigou County, which not only provides support for the development of Jiuzhaigou tourism, but also benefits from its development. Tourism has therefore become its pillar industry.

1 2021 年的荷叶寨（肖维阳 摄）

2 1991 年的荷叶村（九寨沟县档案馆 供图）

1 Heye Village in 2021 (photo by Xiao Weiyang)

2 Heye Village in 1991 (photo by courtesy of Jiuzhaigou County Archives)

荷叶寨

"荷叶"为藏语的汉语译音"沃若"的讹变，清代和民国文献写作"和药"或"和约"，意为爱认死理，主观意识强，不易接受不同主张。一说"和药"有"奶桶（藏族打奶的桶）"之意。由于所在山谷土地较多且肥沃，荷叶寨成为九寨沟最富庶、规模最大的一个寨子，也是过去管辖九寨沟的土司所在的村寨。

Heye Village

"Heye" is a variant of the Chinese transliteration "Woruo" in Zang language. It was written as "Heyao" or "Heyue" in the literature of the Qing Dynasty and the Republic of China, which means stubbornness, strong subjectivity and hardness to accept different opinions. It is also said that "Heyao" means "milk bucket" or "leglin". Owing to its large and fertile land, where the chieftain who used to govern Jiuzhaigou, Heye has become the richest and largest village.

盘亚寨（2006 年，杨青霞 摄）
Panya Village (photo by Yang Qingxia, 2000)

盘亚寨

“盘亚”为藏语的汉语译音，又作“盘牙”。“盘”为协助、帮助达到好的结果之意，“亚”意为牦牛。一说为“好看的山坡”的意思。盘亚寨地处接近山顶的高坡，是九寨沟内最早的聚落。过去为抗击邻近的平武一带的匪患，寨内男性子嗣成年后只能分配土地而不能分开居住，以集中居住的方式团结力量形成族群，对抗外部袭扰。

Panya Village

“Panya” is the Chinese transliteration of Zang language. “Pan” means to assist or help to achieve good results and “ya” means yak. One more explanation assumes that it means “beautiful hillside”. Panya Village, located on a slope close to the top of the mountain, was the earliest settlement in Jiuzhaigou. In the past, in order to resist the banditry in the neighboring Pingwu area, the male grown heirs in the village could only be allocated land and be forbidden to live separately, with united forces to form ethnic groups in the way of concentrated living to resist external harassment.

亚拉寨遗址（2005 年，九寨沟管理局 供图）
Yala Village ruins (photo by courtesy of Jiuzhaigou Management Bureau, 2005)

热西寨（2006 年，杨青霞 摄）
Rexi Village (photo by Yang Qingxia, 2006)

亚拉寨

“亚拉”为藏语的汉语译音，意为黑色的手，得名于村寨居民的服饰。生活在这里的居民，用羊毛纺织藏服（藏语称“亚阿”）时，袖口总是用黑色羊毛纺织，这种服饰渐渐成为这个寨子及其居民的标志。亚拉寨上方约 100 米处的林间有亚拉寺遗迹，原为当地居民举行祭祀活动的场所。

热西寨（扎如寨）

“热西”为藏语的汉语译音，意为好得像一面镜子。一说是“山脚”之意。热西寨是扎如沟最后形成的一个村寨，四面环山，气候较为湿润，土壤肥沃，地势平坦，用水便利。寨内聚集有老扎如寨和郭都寨的搬迁居民，也因此形成扎如沟集中的居民驻地。

尖盘寨

“尖盘”为藏语的汉语译音。藏语中，“尖”意为“辩论”“挑战”，“盘”意为“高超”“厉害”。据说，以前九寨沟内各村寨的人会在春天播种后的空闲时间聚集起来跳“夏嫫”。村寨间各自为阵，由能唱会道的人领唱，一问一答、边唱边跳，无形中成为一种暗中较劲的比赛。当时有位男子经常在比赛中拔得头筹，其所在村寨也因此得名“尖盘”。

Yala Village

“Yala” is a Chinese transliteration of Zang language, meaning black hands, owing to the costumes of the villagers. Local residents always weave the cuffs of Zang clothes (called “Ya'a” in Zang language) with black wool. This kind of clothing has gradually become the symbol of the village and its residents. In the forest about 100 meters above the village, there lies the remains of Yala Temple, a place originally for local residents to hold sacrificial activities.

Rexi (Zharu) Village

“Rexi” is the Chinese transliteration of Zang language, which means “as good as a mirror”. One more explanation assumes that it means “foot of the mountain”. It was the last village formed in Zharu Gully, surrounded by mountains, where the climate is relatively humid, the soil fertile, the terrain flat and the water is easy to get. In it are relocated residents from former Zharu and Guodu Villages, hence a concentrated residential area in the Gully.

Jianpan Village

“Jianpan” is the Chinese transliteration of Zang language, in which “Jian” means “debate” “challenge” and “pan” means “superior” or “powerful”. It was said that people from various villages in Jiuzhaigou would gather to dance “Xiamo” in their free time after planting seeds in spring. Each one formed a group led by those who could sing well, asking questions for the other to answer while singing and dancing, hence a kind of secret competition. At that time, there is a man who frequently won the first place in the contests, so his village named as “Jianpan” for this reason.

尖盘寨（1991 年，九寨沟县档案馆 供图）
Jianpan Village (photo by courtesy of Jiuzhaigou County Archives, 1991)

郭都寨（2017 年，肖维阳 摄）
Guodu Village (photo by Xiao Weiyang, 2017)

郭都寨

“郭都”为藏语的汉语译音，意为从四面八方聚在一起。据说，100 多年前郭都只有两三户人家，尖盘、盘亚、亚拉等寨子的人到扎如沟开荒置地，后举家搬迁到郭都定居下来。大约在 20 世纪 50 年代后，郭都形成村落。20 世纪 80 年代后，郭都寨的村民陆续搬迁到热西寨。

Guodu Village

“Guodu” is the Chinese transliteration of Zang language, which means gathering together from all directions. Only two or three families were said to be living here over 100 years ago. Then villagers from Jianpan, Panya, Yala and so on who came to open up wasteland in Zharu Gully had all their families settled. Around the 1950s, Guodu turned into a village. After the 1980s, the villagers of Guodu moved to Rexi in succession.

树正寨

“树正”为藏语的汉语译音“许季”的讹变。藏语中，“许季”意为这里的人做事、说话、辩论时点子特别多。景区内旅游公路经过树正寨旁，交通便利，更易于发展旅游业。1984 年，树正寨一名村民建起九寨沟第一个家庭旅馆，此后当地居民主要从事旅游服务，如出售旅游纪念品等工作。

Shuzheng Village

“Shuzheng” is a variant of the Chinese transliteration of “Xuji” in the Zang language, which means to the effect that people here are full of ideas when they do things, talk, speak and debate. The tourist road in the scenic area passes by Shuzheng, which helps to the development of tourism. In 1984, one of its villagers had the first family hotel built. Since then, most local residents have been engaged in tourism services, selling tourist souvenirs, for example.

1 | 2

1　1982 年的树正群海沟的藏族村寨（彭小岷　摄，牟薇　供图）
2　树正寨（2011 年，周正强　摄）
1　Zang village around Shuzheng Lake Cluster in 1982 (photo by Peng Xiaomin, by courtesy of Mou Wei)
2　Shuzheng village (photo by Zhou Zhengqiang, 2011)

1 1 则查洼老寨（2017 年，蹇代君 摄）

2 2 1982 年的则查洼村（彭小岷 摄，牟薇 供图）

1 The old Zezhawa Village (photo by Jian Daijun, 2017)

2 The Zezhawa Village in 1982 (photo by Peng Xiaomin, by courtesy of Mou Wei)

则查洼寨

“则查洼”为藏语的汉语译音“孜嚓诺”的讹变，意为在角落里。据说，生活在此寨的人性格腼腆，聚会时总是躲在角落，加之寨子的地理位置相对偏僻，因而得名。则查洼寨位于则查洼沟口的诺日朗游客服务中心旁，是到九寨沟长海、五彩池旅游的必经之地。

Zezhawa Village

“Zezhawa” is a variant of the Chinese transliteration of “Zichanuo” in Zang language, which means “in the corner”. It was said that the people living in this village were shy and always hide in the corner during gatherings. In addition, its location was relatively remote, hence came the name. It is located next to the Nuorilang Tourist Service Center at the entrance to the Zezhawa gully, which is the only place where tourists must pass on the way to the Long Lake and the Wucai Pool.

黑角寨

“黑角”为藏语的汉语译音，意为欢乐、高兴。位于黑角沟，寨子里的人是从当时南坪县城（今九寨沟县）附近的黑角村迁过来的。九寨沟旅游开发后，为方便从事旅游服务和环境保护工作，黑角寨居民搬迁到树正寨，原黑角寨 11 座年久失修的房屋处于半废弃状态。

Heijiao Village

“Heijiao”, the Chinese transliteration of Zang language, which means joy and happiness, is located in the Heijiao Gully and all its residents are from Heijiao near Nanping (now Jiuzhaigou) County. Since the tourism development of Jiuzhaigou, all these residents have been settled in Shuzheng Village for the sake of tourist services and environmental protection. And the 11 original dilapidated houses have been left unattended.

黑角寨（2017 年，肖维阳 摄）
Heijiao Village (photo by Xiao Weiyang, 2017)

扎依扎嘎山（2020 年，九寨沟管理局 供图）

宗教文化
Religious Culture

Zhayi Zhaga Mountain (photo by courtesy of Jiuzhaigou Management Bureau, 2020)

重彩《圣水》，80cm×80cm（2006 年，王庆九 作品）
Holy Water, heavy color painting, 80cm×80cm (by Wang Qingjiu, 2006)

九寨沟藏族同胞信仰苯教。如今，相信万物有灵的宗教信仰已映射到当地群众生产生活的方方面面。他们会在自家墙壁、门框、房梁等处画上各式各样的保护神画，经济宽裕的家庭，还会在家里修建佛堂、经轮、佛龛。同时还会举行撒龙达、转经、请山神等活动。

在九寨沟，人们把扎依扎嘎山视为圣山，定期到此朝圣、转山；把达戈山和沃洛色嫫山奉为神山、“守护神”。在每年定期举办的良美都卿、嘛孜珍卿等各种宗教庆典上，人们通过庆祝活动，祈求远离灾祸，让平安吉祥降临。

Compatriots of the Zang nationality in Jiuzhaigou believe in Bonpo in which the belief in animism has been reflected in all aspects of the local production and life. People will get all kinds of paintings of patron saints painted on their walls, door frames, beams, etc. Some well-off families will have Buddhist halls, prayer-wheels and Buddhist niches built at home, in addition to such rites as tossing Longda, turning the prayer-wheel and bringing back mountain gods.

People in Jiuzhaigou hold Zhayi Zhaga Mountain in reverence as regular pilgrimage and circumambulating mountains. They also regard Dage Mountain and Woluosemo Mountain as holy mountains and “guardian gods”. Every year, people hold religious celebrations such as Liangmeiduqing and Mazizhenqing regularly, through which to avoid disasters and welcome in peace and auspiciousness.

苯教

苯教信众坚持多神崇拜，崇拜对象包括日、月、星辰、山川、河流、湖泊、飞禽走兽等，相信万物有灵。其中，神山信仰表现最为突出，信众不能在神山上乱扔脏物、杀生等。宗教信仰活动则有转山、转经、煨桑、插经幡等。

Bon

Believers of Bonpo insist on polytheistic worship, including the sun, the moon, stars, mountains, rivers, lakes, birds and animals, etc. They believe that all things have anima. Among them, the belief in the holy mountain is the most prominent. Bonpo insists that no believer is allowed to throw dirt or kill life there. Religious rites include circumambulate mountains, turning the prayer-wheel, burning incense and hanging prayer flags.

念经祈祷 (2005 年，杨青霞 摄)
Chanting and praying (photo by Yang Qingxia, 2005)

转经祝福（2009 年，桑吉 摄）
Prayer-wheel turning for blessings (photo by Sangji, 2009)

转经

藏族同胞中普及程度最高的信仰习俗之一。九寨沟的转经形式多样，有水转经、风转经和手转经等。除此之外，信众还可绕神山、圣水、佛塔、寺院等转圈。与其他教派不同，苯教的转经方向为逆时针。转经所用转经筒里藏有经卷，转经筒有大有小，大的一般固定在寺庙的转经道上，小的则可手持。

Prayer-wheel Turning

It is one of the most popular religious customs in various forms among the Zang people in Jiuzhaigou, such as prayer-wheel turning by means of water, wind and hand. In addition, believers can also circumambulate around the holy mountain, holy water, pagodas, and temples, etc. Unlike the practice of other sects, Bonpo does it counterclockwise. There are prayer scrolls of varied sizes stored in the wheels to be turned. Large wheels are generally fixed on the prayer-wheel-turning paths of temples, while small ones can be turned in one hand.

良美都卿

九寨沟每年都会在农历正月初三到初六，举行为期 4 天的良美都卿佛事活动。其间，九寨沟僧人会在寺庙里吃斋念经，表达对活佛的崇敬和思念。苯教信徒也会带上香、酥油和哈达到寺庙转经、念八字真言祭奠活佛。

Liangmei Duqing

Jiuzhaigou holds a four-day Buddhist event every year from the third day to the sixth day of the first month of the lunar calendar. During this period, the monks here will practise abstinence from meat and recite scriptures in the temple to express their respect and yearning for the Living Buddha. Bon believers will arrive with incense, ghee and hada to turn prayer-wheels and recite the eight-character mantra to pay their homage to the Living Buddha.

扎如寺（2005 年，杨青霞 摄）
Zharu Temple (photo by Yang Qingxia, 2005)

扎如寺（1989 年，九寨沟县档案馆 供图）
Zharu Temple (photo by courtesy of Jiuzhaigou County Archives, 1989)

扎如寺

位于扎如沟口海拔 2026 米处，是九寨沟内唯一经政府依法批准开放的宗教活动场所，也是苯教信仰者的圣地。相传为明万历元年(1573 年)，在西藏尕让尼玛活佛指点下，由日格、奔卡、盘兴 3 座小庙 (拉康) 合建而成。历经 2 次翻修，现占地面积约 6.67 万平方米，为综合藏汉建筑艺术的寺院建筑群。

Zharu Temple

As a holy place for Bonpo believers located at the entrance to Zharu Gully at an altitude of 2,026 meters, it is the only place in Jiuzhaigou that has been approved by the government to open to religious rites according to law. As legend goes: it was built together with the three small temples (Lakang) of Rige, Benka and Panxing in the first year of Wanli reign in the Ming Dynasty (1573), under the guidance of the Living Buddha Garang Nima from Xizang. After two renovations, it is now a monastery complex on an area of 66,667 square meters that integrates Zang and Han architectural styles.

撒龙达

龙达是纸制或布制的印有图案和经文的宗教仪式用品，用以祭祀神灵，以祈求平安吉祥，远离灾祸。祭祀时，将纸制的龙达随风撒放，将布制的龙达穿在绳索上悬挂在桥梁、神山、牙则等地，这种祈祷形式被称为撒龙达。因龙达被抛撒后随风飞舞的样子像乘风飞腾的骏马，故龙达又被称为风马，撒龙达也被称为放风马。

Longda Tossing

Longda, as a religious ritual item, is made of paper or cloth printed with patterns and scriptures, to be sacrificed to gods for peace and auspiciousness and avoidance of disasters. During the rite, the paper-made Longda is scattered in the wind and the cloth-made Longda hung with a rope on the bridge, holy mountain, Yaze and so on. As Longda flies in the wind when scattered like a horse riding, it is also called a wind horse, so Longgda Tossing is also called a loose horse.

撒龙达（2013 年，钟彦 摄）
Longda tossing (photo by Zheng Yan, 2013)

撒龙达（2010 年，桑吉 摄）
Longda tossing (photo by Sangji, 2010)

煨桑上香（2013年，九寨沟管理局 供图）
Aromatic plant burning (photo by courtesy of Jiuzhaigou Management Bureau, 2013)

桑烟

也叫熏香，是藏族同胞在煨桑时所产生的烟雾。藏族同胞认为，燃烧柏树枝产生的香气可净化空气，祛除异味，从而愉悦天上诸神，让他们保佑世间之人事事顺心如意，平安、喜乐、幸福。

Incense Burning

Also calls aromatic plant burning, it refers to the smoke from the incense burned by the Zang people. They believe that the aroma produced by burning cypress branches can purify the air and remove any peculiar smells. By that, they can please the heavenly gods, who will bless the people in the world with good luck, peace, joy and happiness.

请山神

九寨沟每年农历正月十五会举行“请山神”活动。这是一种请山神告知新的一年吉凶祸福的信仰活动，可在白天举行，也可在晚上举行，反映当地居民对风调雨顺、五谷丰登的祈愿，是农耕生活方式留下的印记。

Inviting Mountain God

Every year on the fifteenth day of the first lunar month in Jiuzhaigou, the rite of “Inviting Mountain God” is to be held either during the day or at night, which enables the residents to know the good and bad luck of the new year. As the mark left in the farming way of life, it reflects the local residents' wishes for good weather and abundant grains.

牙则

在九寨沟的路旁、湖边、村寨入口等处常可见到一堆堆刻着佛像、经文、吉祥图案的石头，这就是九寨沟的牙则。它是涉藏地区常见的祈福形式之一，每个经过牙则的藏族同胞，都会停下脚步合掌行礼，并往石堆上添加一块小石头，以消灾免祸，赐福延年。所以，牙则的每一颗石头都凝聚着祈愿与祝福。

Yaze

A stone pile engraved with Buddha statues, scriptures and auspicious patterns can often be seen beside the road, lake and village entrance in Jiuzhaigou. This is Yaze in Jiuzhaigou. As one of the common forms of blessing in Zang-related areas, each and every Zang people who passes by it will stop and salute with his or her palms put together and then add a small stone on it for fend off disasters and prolonging life. Therefore, every stone on it embodies prayers and blessings.

喇嘛石

位于距离九寨沟扎如寺约 2000 米处，是一块被当地居民赋予神性的大石头。各地前往扎依扎嘎山朝拜的人都会到此煨桑、撒龙达，以示虔诚。

Lama Stone

Located about 2,000 meters away from Zharu Temple in Jiuzhaigou, it is a large stone endowed with divinity by the local residents. People from all quarters to worship at Zhayi Zhaga Mountain will stay here to burn incense and toss Longda as a sign of piety.

佛塔

亦称宝塔，一般建在寺院或各村寨人口较少的地方。佛塔原色必须为白色，塔名则根据塔内存放经文、法器类别、塔身造型及装饰特点等来决定。如果是塔群，则根据主体佛塔内的经文内容和名称合并命名。

Pagoda

It is generally built in a temple or a village with thin population. The original color of a pagoda must be white and its name is determined according to what scriptures is stored as well as the type of musical instruments, its shape and the decorative features. If it is a tower group, it will be named according to the content and name of the scriptures in the main one.

佛塔（2006 年，桑吉 摄）
Pagoda (photo by Sangji, 2006)

日桑文化节敬山神（2013 年，桑吉 摄）
Mountain god worshipping on Risang Cultural Festival (photo by Sangji, 2013)

牙则（2008 年，桑吉 摄）
Yaze (photo by Sangji, 2008)

1 嘛智节（1989 年，九寨沟县档案馆 供图）
2 社区居民参加嘛智节（2012 年，泽仁珠 摄）
1 Mazhi Festival (photo by courtesy of Jiuzhaigou County Archives, 1989)
2 Community participants in the Mazhi Festival (photo by Zeren Zhu, 2012)

首届日桑文化节期间，高僧大德讲经说法（2012 年，苏杰 摄）
Sermons by venerable monks during the First Risang Cultural Festival (photo by Su Jie, 2012)

嘛智节

九寨沟扎如寺每年农历四月初七至十六日举行的大型宗教文化活动，有转经、灌顶仪式、法舞仪式、庆功仪式等流程。活动期间，九寨沟周边群众会身穿节日盛装，带着龙达、香烛、唐卡参加活动，游客也可参与其中。

Mazhi Festival

Zharu Temple in the valley holds a large-scale religious and cultural event every year from the seventh to sixteenth day of the fourth month of the lunar calendar, including prayer-wheel turning, Abhiseca, Dharma dance and celebration ceremony. During the event, participants around Jiuzhaigou will arrive in festive costumes, bringing with them longda, joss sticks and thangkas. Tourists can also join in it.

日桑文化节

九寨沟藏族祭拜神山、神水的传统节日。每年藏历四月（公历 6 月）由九寨沟管理局、大九旅集团九旅分公司主办，景区 3 个社区居委会，漳扎村、彭丰村、中查村村委会承办，为期 5 天。藏族同胞会带着装满吉祥如意物件的精美宝瓶参加节庆，听高僧大德讲经说法。文化节结束当天，高僧会放置宝瓶以祈福。此外，文化节上还有射箭、押加（围脖拔河）等藏族传统体育竞技活动。

Risang Cultural Festival

It is a 5-day-long traditional festival for Zang people to worship the holy mountain and water every April in the Zang people calendar (June in the Gregorian calendar) hosted by the Jiuzhaigou Management Bureau and the Jiuzhaigou Tourism Branch of Dajiu Tourism & Travel Group, and organized by the three communities in the scenic area and village committees of Zhangzha, Pengfeng, Zhongcha. Zang people participants will come with exquisite vases filled with auspicious objects and listen to the sermons of some venerable monk, who will place vases to pray for blessings at the end of the festival. In addition, there are traditional Zang ethnic sports such as archery and Yajia (neck-supported tug-of-war).

树正民俗表演舞长龙（2009 年，苏杰 摄）

多彩文艺

Colorful Literature and Art

Dragon dance: Shuzheng folklore performance (photo by Su Jie, 2009)

受汉、回、羌等民族文化影响，九寨沟的文化艺术在保留原始色彩浓郁的藏民族文化特色的同时，具有多元融合特征。

唐卡、各种护法神兽、建筑装饰画、壁画是九寨沟藏民族绘画艺术的主要形式。宝伞、胜利幢、金法轮、双鱼、宝瓶、白海螺、吉祥花、吉祥结（八宝吉祥图）是九寨沟藏画的基调。藏族雕塑的工匠多为民间艺人和寺庙僧人，主要形式有泥塑、石刻、木雕、酥油花和藏戏面具等。

九寨沟的藏族同胞能歌善舞，在节日及劳作、喝酒、祈神等场合都会唱歌、跳舞。信仰苯教的九寨沟人根据每个地方的神灵决定所跳的舞蹈，如尖盘只能跳“狮子舞”，盘亚只能跳“牦牛舞”等。九寨沟藏民族最流行的舞蹈是“夏嫫锅庄”，这是一种地域特征明显的传统舞蹈，多在春种秋收时表演。藏戏也是九寨沟典型的舞蹈，与“坝坝舞”类似，主要形式为说唱，表演内容多为历史、宗教故事。

九寨沟藏民族文学主要体现在以苯教文化为主的民间传说与故事中，包括《九寨沟格萨尔王传说》《达戈、色嫫斗雪山王》《九寨沟海子的传说》《魔鬼岩的传说》等。

Influenced by Han, Hui, Qiang and other ethnic cultures, the culture and art of Jiuzhaigou has the characteristics of multiple fusion while retaining the original rich Zang ethnic cultural characteristics.

Thangkas, various guardian gods and animals, architectural decorative paintings and murals are the main forms of Zang painting art in Jiuzhaigou. Precious Umbrella, Dhvaja (Victory Banner), Golden Falun, Pisces, Aquarius, White Conch, Auspicious Flowers, Auspicious Knot (Eight Treasures) are the keynotes of Jiuzhaigou Zang paintings. The artisans of Zang sculpture are mostly folk artists and temple monks. The main forms include clay sculpture, stone carving, wood carving, ghee flower and Zang opera masks.

The Zang people in Jiuzhaigou are so good at singing and dancing that they would do so on such occasions as working, drinking, praying to gods and festivals. Those who believe in Bonpo will decide what they dance according to the gods they worship locally. For example, the “lion dance” only in Jianpan and the “yak dance” only in Panya. The most popular dance by the Zang people in Jiuzhaigou is “Xiamo Guozhuang”, a traditional one with obvious regional characteristics, mostly performing during spring planting and autumn harvest period. So is the “Zang Opera” typical dance of Jiuzhaigou (similar to the “Plaza Dance”), its main form being talking and singing about historical and religious stories.

Zang national literature of Jiuzhaigou is mainly reflected in folk legends and stories based on Bonpo culture, including *Jiuzhaigou Legend of King Gesar*, *Dage and Semo Fight Against Snow Mountain King*, *Legend of Lakes in Jiuzhaigou* and *Legend of the Devil Rock*.

擦擦（2020 年，祝红梅 摄）
Tsatsa (photo by Zhu Hongmei, 2020)

酥油花（2017 年，祝红梅 摄）
Ghee flower (photo by Zhu Hongmei, 2017)

擦擦

一是指一种用凹形模具压制成浮雕的模制泥塑技术，这种技术因藏民族聚居区广泛供奉各种泥塑佛像、菩萨像，对泥塑雕像有广泛需求而产生。二是指用这种技术制成的雕像。每个擦擦都须经过僧人的开光仪式才能够最终完成。藏族村寨中普遍设立有专门存放擦擦的地方，被称为“擦锅”。

Tsatsa

It refers to a sculpture technique created for pressing clay into relief sculpture with a concave mold on account of a wide demand of various clay statues of Buddhas and Bodhisattvas widely worshiped in Zang areas. It also stands for statues made with this technique. Each tsatsa needs to go through the consecration ceremony by monks before it can be finally completed. In every Zang people village, there is generally a place dedicated to storing the tsatsa that is called “Caguo”.

酥油花

指藏族寺庙特有的以酥油为原料，塑造各种人物、飞禽走兽等的雕塑艺术，是中国国家级非物质文化遗产代表项目中的一种。用酥油雕塑而成的工艺品也被称为酥油花，现在发展为雕塑各种吉祥喜庆主题的工艺品以祈愿供佛，展示信众的虔诚。

Ghee Flower

It refers to the unique sculpture art of Zang temples that shape various characters, stories, birds and animals with ghee as the raw material. It is one of the representative items of China’s national intangible cultural heritage. The handicrafts made of ghee sculpture are also called ghee flowers, nowadays they developed into sculptures of various auspicious and festive themes, offering prayers to the Buddha shows the devotion of believers.

藏戏面具（2012 年，桑吉 摄）
Zang Opera Mask (photo by Sangji, 2012)

藏戏面具

一种用于藏戏表演的面部化妆工具，主要有泥塑面具、布制面具和铜制面具。其诞生与原始苯教仪式中的“拟兽图腾舞”有密切关系，后由宗教仪式走入藏戏中，得以深入民间，得到更多民众的认可。藏戏面具以宗教中的神佛、动物、妖魔鬼怪和藏戏中的角色为主要题材，用白、黄、蓝、绿等不同色彩来表现不同的角色特征，头戴面具演绎的㑇舞、熊猫舞为国家级非物质文化遗产。

Zang Opera Mask

A facial makeup tool used in Zang opera performances, mainly including masks of clay, cloth and copper. Its birth was closely related to the imitation animal zang potem dance in the original Bonpo ceremony, was later introduced into Zang operas and won a general approval among people. Zang opera masks take gods and Buddhas, animals, demons and ghosts in religion and characters in Zang opera as the main themes and use various colors such as white, yellow, blue and green to symbolize different characteristics of the roles, zhou dance and panda dance performed by it are both national intangible cultural heritages.

劳动歌

劳动歌是九寨沟人在长期生产劳动过程中产生的民歌，主要有《春耕与除草曲》《秋收与打粮曲》《劳动曲》等歌曲。以歌唱劳动为主题，讲述春播、秋收等劳动内容，记录九寨沟人的农耕时令，是农耕生活的一种体现，表达了九寨沟人勤劳、积极向上的美好品质与生活态度。

Labor Song

Labor songs are sung by the people of Jiuzhaigou in their long-term production and labor processes, mainly including *Spring Plowing and Weeding Song*, *Autumn Harvest and Thrashing Grain Song*, *Labor Song* and so on. The theme of singing about labor centers on spring sowing and autumn harvest and records the farming seasons of the hardworking locals, which expresses their progressive qualities and postive attitude toward life.

1 | 2

1　绰夜绰嫫（2011 年，桑吉 摄）
2　法舞（2014 年，桑吉 摄）

1　Chuoye Chuomo (photo by Sangji, 2011)
2　Dharma Dance (photo by Sangji, 2014)

绰夜绰嫫

九寨沟藏族民间流行的在农历正月初一至十五表演的一种藏戏。由一男一女头戴面具，佩戴各种饰品，扮演夫妻或恋人进行对话或对唱，有铙钹、锣、鼓伴奏。以妇女为主的群众也会参与到节目中。这种表演会进入到村寨中的每家每户，为他们驱祟祈福，受到群众热烈欢迎。

Chuoye Chuomo

A popular Zang opera in Jiuzhaigou performed from the first to fifteenth day of the first month of the lunar calendar. A man and a woman wear masks and various ornaments, acting as husband and wife or lovers to have a dialogue or duet, accompanied by cymbals, gongs and drums. The masses, mainly women, can participate in the performence. It may visit every household in the village to drive away evil spirits and pray for blessings and so is warmly accepted by the masses.

法舞

祈愿法会上表演的仪式性舞蹈，有独特的面具、服饰、乐曲和舞蹈程式，被用于祭祀、祈祷、驱邪等。多以鼓、大号、唢呐、钹为伴奏乐器。舞蹈时，法舞僧人头戴面具，手拿法器，节奏缓慢，三步或四步一变，多为旋转的动作。

Dharma Dance

This ceremonial dance performed at the praying ceremony equipped with unique masks, costumes, music and dance procedures, is meant for sacrifices, prayers and exorcising evil spirits, mostly accompanied by drums, tuba, suona horn and cymbals. During the dance, the monks in masks hold Buddhist instruments in their hands. Its rhythm is slow, with a change of mostly rotating movements every three or four steps.

夏嫫锅庄（舞蹈）

锅庄是青藏高原的传统歌舞，流行于九寨沟的锅庄叫“夏嫫”。“夏嫫”是九寨沟当地藏语的音译，意为“田地耕作”。音乐节奏鲜明，舞蹈动作粗犷、豪迈。歌舞进行时，九寨沟男女老少围绕篝火边唱边跳，一问一答，有时可通宵达旦。

Xiamo Guozhuang (Dance)

Guozhuang is a traditional song and dance on the Qinghai-Xizang Plateau. In Jiuzhaigou, this popular dance is called “Xiamo”, a transliteration of the local Zang language, which means “field farming”. With its music rhythm clear and dance moves bold and heroic, men, women, elder and children in Jiuzhaigou sing and dance around the bonfire all night long (sometimes), asking and answering questions.

达戈与沃洛色嫫的故事

九寨沟流传已久的一系列传说故事。达戈、沃洛色嫫是一男一女两位神灵。两位神灵善良、勇敢，同情生活艰难的九寨沟居民，将九寨沟变得美丽、富饶，并由此相爱。九寨沟人民用达戈与沃洛色嫫的故事记录达戈山、沃洛色嫫山等地的地理环境及自身的族群历史，体现出对山神的信仰、对大自然的敬畏与热爱，以及对幸福生活的渴望。

Story of Dage and Woluosemo

Jiuzhaigou prides itself on a series of legends passed down for a long time. Dage and Woluosemo are two kind and brave gods, who sympathize with the local residents' hard lives by making the valley beautiful and better-off. The people here, through the stories of the two lovers, have recorded their geographical environment and their own history, which reflects the belief in mountain gods, awe and their love for nature and yearning for a happy life.

格萨尔王传说

藏族民间史诗，勾勒出人间妖魔鬼怪横行、残害百姓的特殊环境，在这种水深火热的危难之中，格萨尔王投生下界，作黑头凡人（苯教中尊贵的藏族人，因为他们的祖先是神）的君长，留下许多传说故事。受格萨尔说唱艺术影响和方言差异，九寨沟人称格萨尔王为“阿尼·格萨”，称以格萨尔为君王的众神为“阿岭措”，流传有格萨尔王除蛇妖、格萨尔王除恶魔等格萨尔民间传说故事。

Legend of King Gesar

Zang folk epics outline the special environment in which demons and ghosts run amok and harm the people. In this dire crisis, King Gesar was reborn in the mortal and became the ruler of the black-headed mortals (noble Zang people in Bonpo because their ancestors were gods), leaving many legends and stories. Influenced by Gesar's art of rapping and dialect differences, people in Jiuzhaigou called King Gesar “Ani Gesa” and the gods who took Gesar as their king “Alingcuo”. There are Gesar folklore stories such as his elimination of the snake demons.

1 | 2 | 3

1 水彩画《伯舞“闷墩儿”在五彩九寨》，42cm×29.6cm（2023年，陈品言 作品，指导老师：张媛）

2 九寨沟夏嫫锅庄舞蹈表演（2016年，杨青霞 摄）

3 格萨尔王藏戏（2022年，四川省非物质文化遗产保护中心 供图）

1 *Zhou Dance “Menduner” in Colorful Jiuzhai*, watercolor, 42cm×29.6cm (by Chen Pinyan, under the instruction of Zhang Yuan, 2023)

2 Xiamo Guozhuang dance performance in Jiuzhaigou (photo by Yang Qingxia, 2016)

3 King Gesar's Zang Opera (photo by courtesy of Sichuan Intangible Cultural Heritage Protection Center, 2022)

独特民俗

Unique Folk Customs

九寨沟夏娱锅庄舞蹈表演（2016 年，杨青霞 摄）

Xiamo Guozhuang dance performance in Jiuzhaigou (photo by Yang Qingxia, 2016)

九寨沟独特的自然地理环境和气候，孕育出具有浓厚地域色彩的服饰、饮食、建筑等习俗。

九寨沟藏族同胞的传统服饰与自然环境、气候条件息息相关，且色彩搭配和构图大胆而精巧，具有鲜明的藏文化特色。九寨沟的藏族服装主要由藏袍和藏式衬衫组成，羔皮帽、礼帽、毡帽、皮靴、腰带（金、银）、藏刀、藏式耳环、奶钩、土枪、佛珠、珊瑚项链等也是其典型服饰。

九寨沟藏族同胞饮食种类丰富，且具有鲜明的藏族特色，加之地理位置靠近甘肃，也受到甘肃饮食文化的明显影响。常见的饮食有糌粑、洋芋糍粑、酸菜面块、血肠、奶酪、奶渣、酸奶、酥油茶、青稞酒等。后来各地美食随着交通发展和旅游开发等进入九寨沟，使这里形成以本地饮食为代表，兼具各色菜系和异域风情的饮食结构。

九寨沟的藏寨民居具有浓郁的宗教文化色彩，在修建中既坚持就地取材原则，又注重宗教信仰的融入与展现，如在房梁、门框、墙壁等处绘制象征平安、吉祥的保护神画，在厨房正前方修建神龛等。在建筑习俗上，九寨沟的藏寨建筑与西藏地区有明显差异，融入披顶、翘屋角、垂花柱等汉式建筑元素，并在女儿墙转角、门楣、窗楣等处放置白石，与汶川、茂县等地的羌族一样拥有“白石崇拜”，表现出多民族融合的特征。

Jiuzhaigou's unique physical geographical environment and climate have given birth to customs such as clothing, food and architecture with strong regional styles.

The traditional costumes of the Zang ethnic compatriots here are closely related to the natural environment and climatic conditions, the color matching and composition are bold and exquisite, with distinct characteristics of Zang culture. Their clothing mainly consists of robes and shirts, lambskin hats, top hats, felt hats, leather boots, belts (gold and silver) , Zang knives, Zang earrings, milk hooks, pipe guns, prayer beads, coral necklaces, are some typical trappings.

They have a rich variety of diets with distinct Zang characteristics. They live close to Gansu and are therefore obviously influenced by its diet culture. Their common foods include tsampa, glutinous potato cake, sauerkraut dough piece, blood sausage, cheese, milk dregs, yogurt, buttered tea and highland barley wine. Later, with the development of transportation and tourism, delicacies from all over the world entered Jiuzhaigou, forming a diet structure and habits represented by local diets with various cuisines.

The Zang dwellings here have a strong religious and cultural flavor. In construction, they adhere to the use of local materials, but not to the neglect of the integration and display of religious beliefs. For example, they paint protective gods symbolizing peace and auspiciousness on beams, door frames, walls and build a shrine right in front of the kitchen. In architectural customs, the Zang buildings here differ a lot from those in Xizang. They incorporate Han-style architectural elements such as draped roofs, upturned corner, vertical flower columns and place white stones at the corner of parapet, door lintel and window lintel, having the same "white stone worship" as the Qiang people in the counties of Wenchuan and Maoxian, which is a sign of characteristics of multi-ethnic integration.

血肠

一种以牛羊猪血为主料的加工食品，习惯在入冬以后制作，被视为上等食物。制作时将小肠清洗干净后灌入搅拌均匀的血汁、牦牛肉（或猪肉）和香料的混合物，分节，煮熟，即可食用。

Blood Sausage

It is regarded as a first-class food customarily made from blood of cattle, sheep or pig, after winter. To make it, the small intestine is cleaned for a mixture of evenly stirred blood, yak meat (or pork) and spices to be put in one segment after another. It can be consumed only after cooked.

糌粑

当地藏族的一种主要日常食品。将青稞晒干炒熟，磨成细面，即为待食的糌粑。食用时加入少量酥油茶和奶渣、糖等揉捏成团即可食用，也可直接加水揉捏食用。

Tsampa

A local staple food among the Zang ethnic villagers. The process of making tsampa is to dry and fry highland barley and then grind it into fine flour. Before eaten, it is kneaded into a ball with a small amount of buttered tea, milk dreg and sugar or with water only.

酥油茶

藏族的一种传统日常饮食。制作时，先将马茶熬成浓汁备用，在陶瓷碗中放入糌粑、奶渣、酥油、盐、油炸面粒等，然后倒入茶水反复搅拌成浓汤状，即可食用。

Buttered Tea

A traditional daily Zang diet. To make it, Macha (horse tea) is first boiled into thick juice for later use, tsampa, milk dreg, ghee, salt and fried flour pellets are put into a ceramic bowl and then poured in the tea water to be stirred repeatedly to form a thick soup before consumption.

血肠（2022 年，梁峰　摄）

Blood sausage (photo by Liang Feng, 2022)

酥油茶 (2012 年，九寨沟管理局 供图)

Buttered tea (photo by courtesy of Jiuzhaigou Management Bureau, 2012)

糌粑（2023 年，杨保长　摄）

Tsampa (photo by Yang Baochang, 2023)

戴着羔皮帽和藏式耳环的藏族妇女（2017 年，泽仁珠 摄）
Women in lambskin hats and Zang earrings (photo by Zeren Zhu, 2017)

水彩《九寨姑娘》，29.6cm×42cm
（2023 年，任泊语 作品，指导老师：张媛）
Jiuzhai Girl, watercolor, 29.6cm×42cm (by Ren Boyu, under the instruction of Zhang Yuan, 2023)

羔皮帽

妇女专用。一般为 3 层，以羊毛毡子为芯，内置白布，外以毛卷而白的羔皮做 10 厘米的镶边，用桃红、粉红或藏红色的布折叠、收圆盖顶，美观而得体。

Lambskin Hat

For women only, it generally has 3 layers, with wool felt as the center, white cloth inside and 10-cm curly white lambskin as the border and peach, pink, or saffron cloth is folded and closed to cover the top, which is beautiful and decent.

藏式耳环

材质一般为金、银和各类宝石，环形较大。有的耳环上镶嵌珠宝，有的耳环拧成麻花形状。

Zang Earrings

Generally made of gold and silver inlaid with various gemstones, such earrings are relatively large, some with jewels and some in a twisted shape.

藏袍

藏装的基本款式，是一种直筒服装，基本特点是腰肥、袖长、襟大，怀中可容纳糌粑、酥油、茶叶等大量物品，还可根据冷热程度穿脱右袖，多以白色、黄色、红色为主要颜色。

Zang Robe

The primary style of Zang clothing is a kind of straight clothes, which is characterizaed by loose waist, long sleeves, large collars that can hold many items such as tsampa, ghee, and tea. One can also put on and take off the right sleeve according to the temperature. Zang clothing is mainly colored in white, yellow and red.

藏族服饰（2008 年，桑吉 摄）

Zang ethnic costumes (photo by Sangji, 2008)

榻板屋顶

九寨沟传统民居中最具特色的是用榻板盖成的房顶。榻板通常用杉木制成，为防风掀，一般用石块压住。榻板面有一条条自然形成的年轮沟，下雨时雨水很容易排出，太阳出来，榻板又会很快晒干，经风吹雨打日晒，到木板腐烂方换。

Couch Roof

The most distinctive feature of traditional folk houses in Jiuzhaigou is the couch roof usually made of firwood, which is pressed down with stones against wind. It has a groove of natural annual ring on the surface, which makes rainwater easily discharged and quickly dried in the sun, the wooden board undergoes wind, rain and sun exposure and can only be replaced when it decays.

荷叶老寨榻板屋顶（2005 年，九寨沟管理局 供图）

Couch roof of old Heye Village (photo by courtesy of Jiuzhaigou Management Bureau, 2005)

1 树正寨水磨房（2010 年，桑吉 摄）
2 1982 年的磨房（彭小岷 摄，牟薇 供图）

1 Water mill at Shuzheng Village (photo by Sangji, 2010)
2 Mill in 1982 (photo by Peng Xiaomin, by courtesy of Mou Wei)

水磨房

为水磨搭建的木板房，简称磨房。九寨沟过去每个村寨都有几座水磨房。房子为吊脚楼，由 4 根粗大的圆木撑起，临空而筑，立于水上。木柱上架梁，梁上铺木板，中间挖个大洞安放水磨。退耕还林后，九寨沟人主要从事旅游服务，沟内水磨房闲置，年久失修，保存最为完好的是位于树正沟树正寨旁的水磨房群。

Water Mill

It is a wooden house built for water mill, shortened as a mill. Jiuzhaigou used to have several such houses in every village. It is a stilted building, propped up by four thick logs and stands above water. Beams are erected on wooden pillars with planks on them and a large hole is dug in the middle for the placement of the water mill. Since farmland was returned to forest, the locals have been mainly engaged in tourism services, which have long left such mills out of repair. The best-preserved ones are the water mill cluster close to Shuzheng Village.

晒架

九寨沟各村寨晒场都建有晒架，用于晾晒青稞、小麦等。晒架由木头搭建，高 6 米左右，顺应晒场的地形和走势成排分布。

Sunning Rack

Every village in the valley has such a rack for drying highland barley, wheat ect. Made of wood about 6 meters high, it is distributed in rows along the terrain and trend of the drying yard.

1 1982 年的晒架（牟航远 摄，牟薇 供图）

2 2007 年的晒架（王燕 摄）

1 Sunning Rack in 1982 (photo by Mou Hangyuan, by courtesy of Mou Wei)

2 Sunning Rack in 2007 (photo by Wang Yan)

九看
Jiuzhaigou in
Nine Episodes
九寨

之六
Episode Six

科考当先

A Pioneer in Scientific Research

2009 年 5 月，扎如生态科考游（桑吉 摄）

发现之旅

Journey to Discovery

An ecological research tour of Zharu in May 2009 (photo by Sangji)

九寨沟的科研活动始于20世纪70年代。1970年8月，中国科学院成都生物研究所主持的薯蓣（山药）调查队来到九寨沟，重点调查区域内的薯蓣资源。这是国家科研单位在九寨沟范围内开展的第一项科研课题。

在九寨沟被正式划为保护区后，区域内进行了申遗考察、生态保护考察、旅游考察与调研、生物多样性监测等角度多样的考察调研活动。2002年4月，四川省林业科学研究院受九寨沟管理局邀请，启动对九寨沟国家级自然保护区的野外调查工作，先后进行6次野外调查，2004年完成九寨沟首次综合科学考察，形成《四川九寨沟国家级自然保护区综合科学考察报告》。

2019年10月，四川省林业科学研究院受九寨沟管理局委托，启动对九寨沟国家级自然保护区的野外调查工作，先后进行8次野外调查，2021年完成九寨沟第二次综合科学考察，形成《四川九寨沟国家级自然保护区综合科学考察报告》。报告在第一次资源调查的基础上，总结保护区内的物种变化情况，完成物种种类的新增、修订和删除工作，提出具体的生物多样性保护建议。

从第一次薯蓣资源调查至今，九寨沟境内进行了数次科学考察调研活动，摸排了区域内生物多样性现状、景观生态体系现状、潜在可利用资源状况以及潜在威胁等，为九寨沟生物多样性研究、生态环境保护与旅游资源开发提供了方向。

The scientific research activities in Jiuzhaigou began in the 1970s. In August 1970, an investigation team from Chengdu Institute of Biology, Chinese Academy of Sciences focused on yam resources in Jiuzhaigou, the first ever project carried out by a national scientific research institute.

Since Jiuzhaigou was officially made a protected area, investigations from such perspectives as application for world heritage, ecological protection, tourism and biodiversity monitoring, have been carried out. In April 2002, Sichuan Academy of Forestry Sciences, at the invitation of Jiuzhaigou Management Bureau, conducted 6 field surveys and completed the first comprehensive scientific survey called *Comprehensive Scientific Investigation Report of Jiuzhaigou National Nature Reserve* in 2004.

In October 2019, entrusted by the Management Bureau, the Sichuan Academy of Forestry Sciences started a second field investigation of the National Nature Reserve and conducted 8 field investigations. This comprehensive investigation was completed in 2021 and the results were named *Comprehensive Scientific Investigation Report of Sichuan Jiuzhaigou National Nature Reserve*. Building on the first resource survey, this report summarized the species changes in the Reserve, completed, added, revised, deleted the species together with specific proposals on biodiversity conservation.

From the first survey of yam resources up to now, times of scientific surveys and research activities have been carried out and the status quo of biodiversity, landscape ecosystem, potential resources and potential threats in the region sorted out, providing a basis for the study of biodiversity in Jiuzhaigou and development direction of its ecological environment protection and tourism resource.

1
2

1　2008 年 4 月 20 日，九寨沟国家级自然保护区保护处生物多样性监测站工作人员在黑角沟发现大熊猫粪便痕迹（九寨沟管理局 供图）

2　水彩《苇海精灵》，53cm×38cm（2019 年，王庆九 作品）

1　On April 20, 2008, staff of the biodiversity monitoring station of Jiuzhaigou National Nature Reserve found giant panda feces in Heijiao Gully (photo by courtesy of Jiuzhaigou Management Bureau)

2　*Reed Lake Elf,* watercolor, 53cm×38cm (by Wang Qingjiu, 2019)

大熊猫调查

1974 年 6 月至 1977 年 10 月，开展全国第一次大熊猫调查工作，拉开九寨沟大熊猫调查的序幕。经过这次调查，人们对九寨沟的野生大熊猫数量、活动范围等情况形成基本认识。1985 年 10 月至 1988 年，开展全国第二次大熊猫调查工作，调查显示九寨沟保护区内有 7 只野生大熊猫。1999—2002 年，开展全国第三次大熊猫调查工作，调查显示九寨沟保护区内有 2 只野生大熊猫。2011—2013 年，开展全国第四次大熊猫调查工作，调查显示九寨沟保护区内有 3 只野生大熊猫。

Survey of Giant Pandas

From June 1974 to October 1977, the first national giant panda survey was carried out, which has provided a basic understanding of their number and range of activities in Jiuzhaigou. From October 1985 to 1988, the second national survey found seven wild giant pandas in its Nature Reserve. From 1999 to 2002, the third national survey showed that there were two wild giant pandas. From 2011 to 2013, the fourth survey found three.

鹰雕（2021 年，九寨沟管理局 供图）
Mountain hawk eagle *(Spizaetus nipalensis)* (photo by courtesy of Jiuzhaigou Management Bureau, 2021)

分布新记录物种——红胸田鸡

2020 年 10 月 23 日，由四川省林业科学研究院和九寨沟管理局组成的秋季调查队在圆海子首次发现分布新记录物种红胸田鸡。这是一种秧鸡科四川省重点保护鸟类，嘴粗短、性胆小，善奔跑和藏匿。

New Record Species: Ruddy-breasted Crake (*Porzana fusca*)

On October 23, 2020, an autumnal survey team composed of Sichuan Provincial Academy of Forestry Sciences and Jiuzhaigou Management Bureau discovered for the first time the ruddy-breasted crake, a new record species in Round Lake. With a thick and short beaked, timid and good at running and hiding, it is a kind of Rallidae under Sichuan's key protection.

分布新记录物种——鹰雕

2022 年 5 月 20 日，九寨沟管理局在正常进行的生物多样性红外相机监测工作中首次发现分布新记录物种鹰雕。这是一种鹰科国家二级保护鸟类，体形偏大，翅形宽阔，常在阔叶林和混交林中活动。

New Record Species: Mountain Hawk Eagle *(Spizaetus nipalensis)*

First found by the Jiuzhaigou Management Bureau during a normal infrared camera monitoring of biodiversity on May 20, 2022, it is one of the Accipitridae family under the second-level national protection with a large body and broad wings, moving about in the broad-leaved and mixed forests.

九寨沟国家级自然保护区第一次综合科学考察（2002—2004 年）
The First Comprehensive Scientific Expedition to Jiuzhaigou National Nature Reserve (2002~2004)

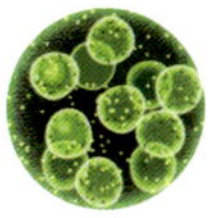

藻类 419 种

419 species of algae

菌类 203 种

203 species of fungi

高等植物有 2375 种

包括苔藓植物 213 种，蕨类植物 81 种，裸子植物 30 种，被子植物 2051 种

2,375 species of higher plants

including 213 species of bryophytes, 81 species of ferns, 30 species of gymnosperms and 2051 species of angiosperms

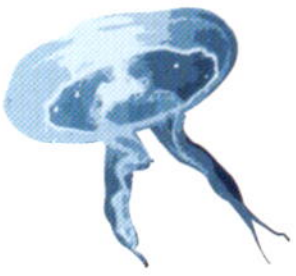

无脊椎动物有 693 种

包括浮游动物 71 种，底栖无脊椎动物 45 种，昆虫 539 种，非昆虫陆生无脊椎动物 38 种

693 species of invertebrates

including 71 species of zooplankton, 45 species of benthic invertebrates, 539 species of insects and 38 species of non-insect terrestrial invertebrates

脊椎动物 310 种

鱼类 2 种，两栖类 6 种，爬行类 4 种，鸟类 222 种，兽类 76 种

310 species of vertebrates

2 species of fishes, 6 species of amphibians, 4 species of reptiles, 222 species of birds and 76 species of beasts

九寨沟国家级自然保护区第二次综合科学考察（2019—2021 年）
The Second Comprehensive Scientific Expedition of Jiuzhaigou National Nature Reserve (2019~2021)

大型真菌14目48科118属284种

Macrofungus, 14 orders, 48 families, 118 genera, 284 species

苔藓植物55科105属213种

Bryophytes, 55 families, 105 genera, 213 species

蕨类植物19科33属81种

Ferns, 19 families, 33 genera, 81 species

裸子植物6科13属30种

Gymnosperms, 6 families, 13 genera, 30 species

被子植物129科611属2051种

Angiosperms, 129 families, 611 genera, 2051 species

昆虫14目89科322属445种

Insects, 14 orders, 89 families, 322 genera, 445 species

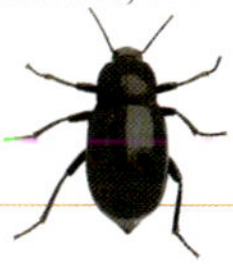

鱼类1目2科2属2种

Fishes, 1 orders, 2 families, 2 genera, 2 species

两栖类2目4科5种

Amphibians, 2 orders, 4 families, 5 species

爬行动物1目6科7种

Reptiles, 1 order, 6 families, 7 species

鸟类17目53科269种

Birds, 17 orders, 53 families, 269 species

小型兽类4目15科36属52种

Small beasts, 4 orders, 15 families, 36 genera, 52 species

大中型兽类3目12科24属29种

Large and medium-sized beasts, 3 orders, 12 families, 24 genera, 29 species

荷叶寨遗址

2005 年 11—12 月，阿坝州文物管理所与九寨沟县文化体育局联合组成的考古调查组，在位于荷叶寨西北侧的荷叶、尖盘、盘亚 3 个自然村发现荷叶寨遗址。考古调查组在该遗址采集了大量泥质陶器和夹砂陶器，并根据陶质、陶色及纹饰判断其年代最迟为汉代。

阿梢垴遗址出土彩陶片（2008 年，杨青霞 供图）

Pottery fragment unearthrf from Ashaonao Site (photo by courtesy of Yang Qingxia, 2008)

阿梢垴遗址

2007 年 6 月上旬，九寨沟管理局、四川大学、华盛顿大学三方组成的“九寨沟文化资源”研究小组，在位于尖盘寨东侧的黄土台地发现阿梢垴遗址。这是目前考古发现的九寨沟境内年代最早的考古遗址，遗址内发现房屋建筑、陶器、铁器、竹制用具、动物骨骼等丰富遗物遗迹，将九寨沟的人类历史上溯至距今 2000 年左右的汉代，而且还可能上溯至 5000 年前的马家窑文化时期。

Heye Village Ruins

From November to December 2005, an archaeological survey team jointly formed by Aba Prefecture Cultural Relics Management Institute and Jiuzhaigou County Culture and Sports Bureau discovered the ruins of Heye Village in three natural villages of Heye, Jianpan and Panya, located in its northwest, where the large numbers of argillaceous and sandy pottery colleted were made no later than the Han Dynasty, according to the quality, color and ornamentation of the pottery.

Ashaonao Site

In early June 2007, the research team of “Jiuzhaigou Cultural Resources” composed of Jiuzhaigou Management Bureau, Sichuan University and University of Washington discovered the Ashaonao Site on the loess tableland to the east of Jianpan Village, the earliest archaeological site in Jiuzhaigou discovered so far. Houses, pottery, ironware, bamboo utensils, animal bones and other rich relics have been found here, which traces the human history of the valley back to the Han Dynasty about 2000 years ago. And it may also be traced back to the Majiayao culture period 5000 years ago.

阿梢垴遗址出土珠饰（2008 年，杨青霞 供图）

Beadwork unearthed from Ashaonao Site (photo by courtesy of Yang Qingxia, 2008)

阿梢垴遗址考古研究（2011 年，九寨沟管理局 供图）

Archaeological research on Ashaonao Site (photo by courtesy of Jiuzhaigou Management Bureau, 2011)

九寨沟生态环境与可持续发展国际联合实验室现场调查熊猫海湖泊沉积（2015 年，Steb Fisher 摄，唐亚 供图）

Field investigation on lake sedimentation of Panda Lake by the Jiuzhaigou International Laboratory for Ecology, Environment and Sustainability (photo by Steb Fisher, courtesy of Tang Ya, 2015)

以九寨沟为对象展开的深入研究课题，从早期发展至今可大致分为两个阶段。第一个阶段主要围绕灾害治理、环境与生态调查展开；第二个阶段一方面向地学研究深入发展，另一方面向旅游业发展、管理科学、信息技术、历史文化等多学科领域扩散。

多年来，九寨沟管理局以科技为支撑，建成九寨沟国家国际科技合作基地、九寨沟生态环境与可持续发展国际联合实验室、九寨沟博士后科研工作站等实体性科研平台，成功申报执行国家高技术研究发展计划（“863”计划）、国家科技支撑计划项目、国家国际科技合作项目等系列课题，多次荣获四川省科技进步奖、阿坝州科技进步奖等。

九寨沟管理局还分别和华盛顿大学、加利福尼亚大学、优山美地国家公园、世界自然保护联盟（IUCN）、世界自然基金会（WWF）等科研机构与非政府组织开展生物多样性、环境保护等方面的合作，使九寨沟的保护与管理水平处于世界前沿。

The in-depth research topic on Jiuzhaigou can be roughly divided into two stages from its early development to the present: the first mainly revolves around disaster management, environment and ecological investigation; and the second focuses on in-depth development of geoscience research on the one hand and spreads to multidisciplinary fields such as tourism development, management science, information technology and history and culture on the other.

Over the years, propped by science and technology, the Jiuzhaigou Management Bureau has built physical scientific research platforms such as National International Science and Technology Cooperation Base, International Laboratory for Jiuzhaigou Ecological Environmental and Sustainable Development Research and Post-doctor Research Workstation and applied for the implementation of the The National High Technology Research and Development Program of China (863 Program), Program for National Science and Technology Support Plan, National International Science and Technology Cooperation Project and so on and won for times Sichuan Science and Technology Progress Award and Aba Prefecture Science and Technology Progress Award.

The Jiuzhaigou Management Bureau also cooperates with University of Washington and University of California, Yosemite National Park, International Union for Conservation of Nature (IUCN), World Wide Fund for Nature (WWF) and other scientific research institutions and non-governmental organizations to carry out projects on biodiversity and environmental protection, which makes its protection and management at the forefront of the world.

1 树正群海磨房旁木栈道（2019 年，梁峰 摄）

2 20 世纪 80 年代，树正群海磨房旁木栈道（九寨沟管理局 供图）

1 Wood Plank Road near the mill, Shuzheng Lake Cluster (photo by Liang Feng, 2019)

2 Wood Plank Road near the milll, Shuzheng Lake Cluster in the 1980s (photo by courtesy of Jiuzhaigou Management Bureau)

九寨沟木栈道环境影响研究

2002 年，九寨沟管理局与北京大学环境管理学院联合完成“九寨沟木栈道环境影响研究”课题。该课题就九寨沟木栈道工程对九寨沟的生态和环境影响进行评估与分析。研究认为，九寨沟木栈道建设为九寨沟生态环境保护和旅游持续发展奠定了良好基础。

Study on Environmental Impact of Wood Plank Road in Jiuzhaigou

In 2002, Jiuzhaigou Management Bureau and College of Environmental Management of Peking University jointly completed the project mentioned above. This project evaluated and analyzed how the wood plank road project affected the local ecology and environment. According to the study, the construction of wood plank road has laid a good foundation for the valley's ecological environment protection and sustainable development of tourism.

世界自然遗产九寨沟泥石流综合治理研究

1983—2003 年，九寨沟管理局与中国科学院·水利部成都山地灾害与环境研究所联合完成“世界自然遗产九寨沟泥石流综合治理研究”课题。课题研究了九寨沟泥石流发育条件及分布规律、泥石流危害特点与成灾规律、灾情评估、泥石流形成机理、泥石流防治技术、风景区泥石流综合防治模式、减灾管理以及防治效益分析等，形成一套较完整的风景区泥石流防治理论与技术体系。在研究成果基础上发表的《世界自然遗产九寨沟泥石流综合治理研究》，荣获 2003 年度四川省科技进步一等奖。

Research on Comprehensive Treatment of Debris Flow in Jiuzhaigou, a World Natural Heritage Site

From 1983 to 2003, Jiuzhaigou Management Bureau and Institute of Mountain Hazards and Environment, CAS jointly completed the project above-mentioned. They studied the development conditions and distribution rules of debris flow in Jiuzhaigou, the hazard characteristics of debris flow and the law of disaster, disaster assessment, formation mechanism of debris flow, debris flow prevention technology, comprehensive prevention and control mode of debris flow in the scenic area, disaster reduction management and prevention and control benefit analysis, forming a relatively complete set of the theory and technical system of its debris flow prevention and control. *Research and Prevention of Debris Flow in Scenic Areas* published on the basis of the research results won the first prize of the Science and Technology Progress Award from the Sichuan in 2003.

1	2
3	4

1 克泽沟格栅坝现场讨论（1991 年，九寨沟管理局 供图）
2 国外学者参观九寨沟泥石流防治工程（1991 年，九寨沟管理局 供图）
3 克泽沟泥石流格栅坝现场讨论（1997 年，九寨沟管理局 供图）
4 丹祖沟泥石流现场调查（2007 年，朱忠福 摄）

1 On-site discussion at Keze Gully grid dam (photo by courtesy of Jiuzhaigou Management Bureau,1991)

2 International scholars on visit to the prevention and control project on Jiuzhaigou debris flow (photo by courtesy of Jiuzhaigou Management Bureau, 1991)

3 On-site discussion at Keze Gully debris flow grid dam (photo by courtesy of Jiuzhaigou Management Bureau, 1997)

4 On-site investigation of mudslides in Danzu Gully (photo by courtesy of Zhu Zhongfu, 2007)

九寨—黄龙核心景区水资源及生态地质环境可持续发展综合应用研究

2004 年立项，2007 年成果入库，为四川省“十五”重大应用科技攻关项目，荣获四川省科技进步一等奖。

研究工作以“水”为核心，建立景观水系统及转化模型，揭示景观水系统对景观形成演化的作用，构建生态地质环境评价体系，从水循环角度得出景观总体稳定和稳定性较好的结论，同时建立景区监测系统和景区水循环及生态地质环境数据库与空间信息系统。采用地学、生态学和环境科学等多学科、跨领域的理论和多种先进技术方法对景区景观联合攻关、综合研究，其中，地球物理勘探方法和高分辨率遥感技术在景区的应用在国际国内尚属首次。

获 奖 项 目：九寨—黄龙核心景区水资源及生态地质环境可持续发展综合应用研究

获 奖 单 位：九寨沟风景名胜区管理局

奖 励 等 级：一 等

奖 励 日 期：二 0 0 七年

证 书 号：国-01-01-09

四川省人民政府

2007 年，九寨—黄龙核心景区水资源及生态地质环境可持续发展综合应用研究项目荣获四川省科技进步一等奖（九寨沟管理局 供图）

Comprehensive Application Research Project on Sustainable Development of Water Resource and Ecological Geological Environment in Jiuzhai-Huanglong Core Scenic Spot in 2007 won the first prize of Sichuan Science and Technology Progress Award (photo by courtesy of Jiuzhaigou Management Bureau)

Comprehensive Application Research on Sustainable Development of Water Resource and Ecological Geological Environment in Jiuzhai-Huanglong Core Scenic Spot

The project was established in 2004 and its result put into the database in 2007 as a major applied science and technology research project in Sichuan's "Tenth Five-Year Plan" and won the first prize of Science and Technology Progress Award in the Province.

This research work centered on "water", established a waterscape system and transformation model, revealed the role of waterscape sysem in the Formation and evolution of landscape, built the ecological geological environment evaluation system, drew the conclusion that the landscape was generally stable and relatively stable from the perspective of water cycle and established the scenic spot monitoring system and scenic water cycle, ecological geological environment database and spatial information system. Its use of multidisciplinary and cross-field theories such as geosciences, ecology and environmental science and various advanced technical methods to jointly tackle key problems and comprehensive research on scenic spots and landscapes, especially the application of geophysical exploration methods and high-resolution remote sensing technology in scenic spots has for the first time gained international and domestic popularity.

1

2

1 九寨沟“三水”（大气降水、地表水、地下水）循环示意图（2022 年，云何视觉 制图）

资料来源：“九寨—黄龙核心景区水资源及生态地质环境可持续发展综合应用研究课题”成果

2 2005 年 10 月 12 日，阿坝州政府、九寨沟管理局、加利福尼亚大学、四川大学科研合作研讨会在九寨沟管理局召开（苏杰 摄）

1 Hydrologic cycle of precipitation, surface runoff and groundwater in Jiuzhaigou (by Yunhe Vision, 2022)

Source: Achievements of the "Comprehensive Application Research Project on Sustainable Development of Water Resource and Ecological Geological Environment in Jiuzhai-Huanglong Core Scenic Spot"

2 On October 12, 2005, Aba Prefecture Government, Jiuzhaigou Administration, University of California and Sichuan University jointly held a Seminar on Academic Collaborations at the bureau (photo by Su Jie)

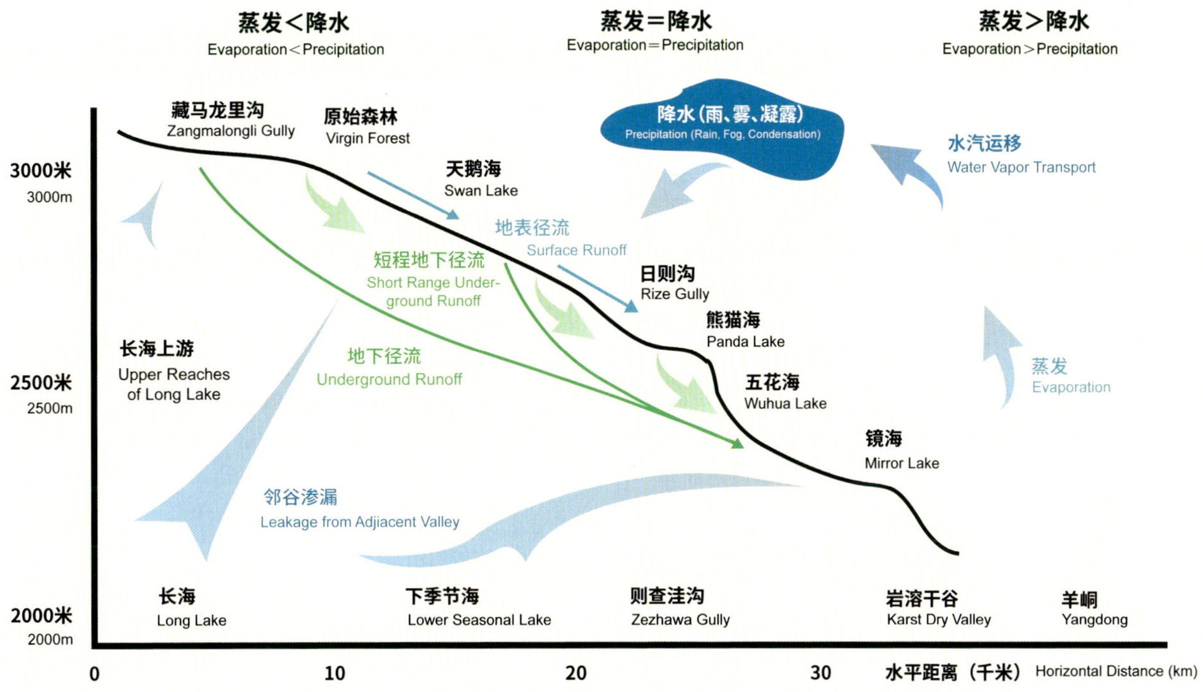

蒸发<降水
Evaporation<Precipitation
蒸发=降水
Evaporation=Precipitation
蒸发>降水
Evaporation>Precipitation
降水(雨、雾、凝露)
Precipitation (Rain, Fog, Condensation)
水汽运移
Water Vapor Transport
藏马龙里沟
Zangmalongli Gully
原始森林
Virgin Forest
天鹅海
Swan Lake
地表径流
Surface Runoff
短程地下径流
Short Range Under-ground Runoff
日则沟
Rize Gully
熊猫海
Panda Lake
长海上游
Upper Reaches of Long Lake
地下径流
Underground Runoff
五花海
Wuhua Lake
蒸发
Evaporation
镜海
Mirror Lake
邻谷渗漏
Leakage from Adjiacent Valley
3000米
3000m
2500米
2500m
2000米
2000m
长海
Long Lake
下季节海
Lower Seasonal Lake
则查洼沟
Zezhawa Gully
岩溶干谷
Karst Dry Valley
羊峒
Yangdong
0
10
20
30
水平距离（千米） Horizontal Distance (km)

阿坝州政府、九寨沟管理局、美国加州大学、四川大学
科研合作研讨会
Seminar on Academic Collaborations
Government, Jiuzhaigou Administration,University of California, USA, and Sichua
地点：中国四川九寨沟 Jiuzhaigou, Sichuan, China
时间：2005年10月12日 Oct
李 川
马 刚
Peter Preuss

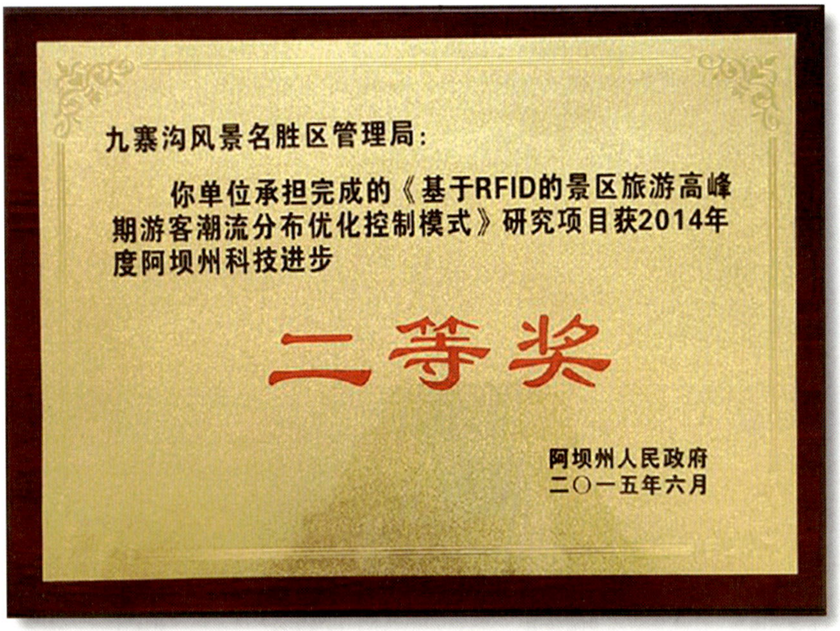

2015 年，九寨沟风景名胜区管理局《基于 RFID 的景区旅游高峰期游客潮流分布优化控制模式》研究项目获 2014 年度阿坝州科技进步二等奖（九寨沟管理局 供图）

Research project on *Optimization and Control Model of Tourist Flow Distribution in Scenic Areas During Peak Tourism Period Based on RFID* by Jiuzhaigou Scenic and Historic Area Management Bureau won second prize of Aba Prefecture Science and Technology Progress Award for 2014, in 2015 (photo by courtesy of Jiuzhaigou Management Bureau)

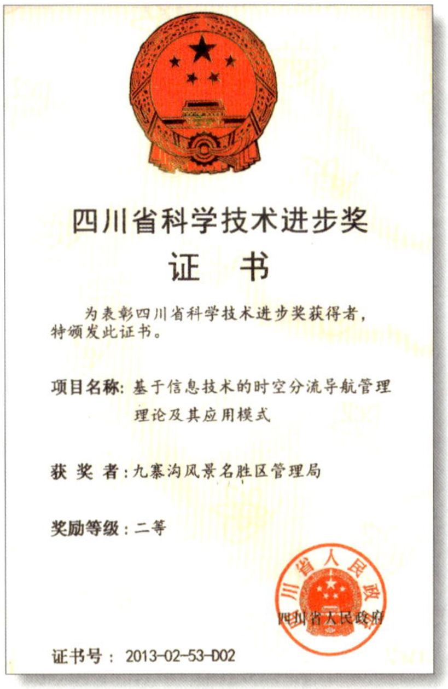

《基于信息技术的时空分流导航管理理论及其应用模式》获四川省科学技术进步奖二等奖（2013 年，九寨沟管理局 供图）

Information Technology-based Space-time Diversion Navigation Management Theory and Its Application Model won second prize of Sichuan Science and Technology Progress Award (photo by courtesy of Jiuzhaigou Management Bureau, 2013)

九寨沟景区容量研究

2005 年，九寨沟管理局完成景区容量研究项目。参照九寨沟的地形、交通、餐饮条件，自然环境对旅游影响的可接受程度，游客在九寨沟景区内的心理和行为特征等，建立起适合九寨沟旅游环境的旅游容量计算指标和模型。项目确定了九寨沟的旅游容量，可指导景区开展管理、进行环境保护、打造基础建设和设计营销策略。

Capacity Research of Jiuzhaigou Scenic Area

In 2005, Jiuzhaigou Management Bureau completed the capacity research project of the scenic area. With reference to Jiuzhaigou's topographical conditions, traffic conditions, catering conditions, acceptability of the natural environment's impact on tourism and psychological and behavioral characteristics of tourists in the scenic spots, the tourism capacity calculation indicators and models suitable for its tourism environment were established. The project determined Jiuzhaigou's tourism capacity, which provided an opportunity for scenic spot to improve management, protect enviroment, build infrastructure and desigh marketing strategies.

2006 年 8 月 30 日，九寨沟生态环境与可持续发展国际联合实验室挂牌成立（2006 年，温勇 摄）

International Laboratory for Jiuzhaigou Ecological Environmental and Sustainable Development Research was established on August 30, 2006 (photo by Wen Yong, 2006)

九寨沟生态环境与可持续发展国际联合实验室

2006 年 8 月，四川大学、九寨沟管理局和美国加利福尼亚大学、华盛顿大学联合组建“九寨沟生态环境与可持续发展国际联合实验室”，面向国内外开放，开展自然、文化和经济等跨学科综合研究，探索解决西部与山地资源开发与环境保护、民族地区经济发展与社会进步、自然保护与旅游发展之间的矛盾，从而促进九寨沟的生态恢复和环境保护。

International Laboratory for Jiuzhaigou Ecological Environmental and Sustainable Development Research

In August 2006, the international laboratory mentioned above established jointly by Sichuan University, Jiuzhaigou Management Bureau, University of California and University of Washington was opened domestically and abroad for conducting interdisciplinary comprehensive research on nature, culture and economy so as to explore and solve the contradictions between the development of West China's mountainous resources and environmental protection, economic development and social progress in ethnic areas and natural protection and tourism development, promote Jiuzhaigou's ecological restoration and environmental protection.

九寨沟水资源与生态安全保护关键技术合作研究（2014 年，肖维阳 摄）
Collaborative research on keytechnologies for water resource and eco-security protection in Jiuzhaigou (photo by Xiao Weiyang, 2014)

九寨沟水资源与生态安全保护关键技术合作研究

2013 年，九寨沟景区作为首个国家国际科技合作基地科研国际合作项目启动，历时 3 年，以优秀等次通过国家技术验收。项目为解决增长型旅游压力下高山湖泊景观维持技术问题，通过与俄罗斯、克罗地亚等国高校和科研机构的合作，形成“水环境生物监测和水质生物评估技术”等 3 项相关技术，获得 2 项专利，发表 19 篇论文（其中 SCI 8 篇），出版 4 部专著。

Collaborative Research on Key Technologies for Water Resources and Eco-security Protection in Jiuzhaigou

In 2013, Jiuzhaigou Scenic Area was launched as the first international scientific research cooperation project since the National International Cooperation Base, for Science and Technology established which lasted for 3 years and passed the national technical acceptance with excellence. In order to solve the technical problems of mountain lakescape maintenance under the pressure of growing tourism, the project formed 3 related technologies including “Water Environment Biological Monitoring and Water Quality Biological Assessment Technology” through cooperation with universities and scientific research institutions in Russia, Croatia and other countries and won 2 patents, got 19 papers published (including 8 SCI) and 4 monographs.

"中国—克罗地亚生物多样性和生态系统服务'一带一路'联合实验室（筹）九寨沟科研基地"揭牌仪式（2021 年，桑吉 摄）
Unveiling Ceremony for China-Croatia "Belt and Road" Joint Laboratory on Biodiversity and Ecosystem Services Jiuzhaigou Research Base (photo by Sangji, 2021)

中国—克罗地亚生物多样性和生态系统服务"一带一路"联合实验室

九寨沟与克罗地亚的普利特维采湖群国家公园同为"世界遗产"，且后者也是钙华湖泊，与九寨沟景观相似。2021 年 9 月 26 日，"中国—克罗地亚生物多样性和生态系统服务'一带一路'联合实验室（筹）九寨沟科研基地"揭牌仪式在九寨沟举行。中克双方以生态保护研究为切入点，在钙华景观、水资源、可持续发展、生物多样性保护等科学研究和管理方面开展一系列科研合作。

China-Croatia "Belt and Road" Joint Laboratory on Biodiversity and Ecosystem Services

Jiuzhaigou and Croatia's Plitvice Lakes National Park are both "World Heritage Sites", the latter is a travertine lake being similar in landscape to the former. On September 26, 2021, the unveiling ceremony for "China-Croatia 'Belt and Road' Joint Laboratory on Biodiversity and Ecosystem Services Jiuzhaigou Research Base" was held. Taking ecological protection research as an entry point, the two countries carried out a series of cooperation in scientific research and management such as travertine landscape, water resources, sustainable development and biodiversity protection.

科学普及

Popularization of Science

九寨沟国家级自然保护区曲那俄沟科考活动（2011 年，肖维阳 摄）

Scientific research in Qunae Gully, Jiuzhaigou National Nature Reserve (photo by Xiao Weiyang, 2011)

纸本水墨《九寨圣景》
168cm×68cm
（2018 年，米金铭 作品）

Sacred Scenery of Jiuzhai, ink and wash on paper, 168cm×68cm (by Mi Jinming, 2018)

为实现九寨沟旅游资源开发的可持续性，九寨沟管理局等单位长期以来始终坚持科普工作，帮助大众提升自然保护意识，从而更好地保护九寨沟的生态环境。

前期大量的考察调研和研究成果成为科普材料的直接来源。借助海报、标识标牌、博物馆、图书、电视、音乐、互联网等多种渠道，人们不仅可以领略九寨沟各景点的自然风光，感受人文风情，还可以学到护林防火、动植物保护、景观资源维护等知识。

九寨沟管理局还与世界自然基金会（WWF）、大自然保护协会（TNC）等非政府组织建立长期合作关系，开展系列环境教育活动，发行科普读物，组织生态旅游项目等。国际力量的参与为九寨沟的科普工作注入新活力，使更多国内外公众体验到九寨沟的天然美景和传统文化底蕴。

In order to realize the sustainable development of tourism resources in Jiuzhaigou, Jiuzhaigou Management Bureau and other institutions concerned have long been persisting in science popularization work to help the public raise their awareness of nature protection, so as to better safeguard the local eco-environment.

Plenty of investigations and research results in the early stages have become the direct source of popular science materials. With the help of posters, signs, museums, books, TV, music, the Internet and so on, people can not only appreciate the natural scenery of various scenic spots here and feel the cultural customs, but also learn about forest protection and fire prevention, animal and plant protection and landscape resource maintenance.

The Jiuzhaigou Management Bureau has also been in long-term cooperation with non-governmental organizations such as World Wide Fund for Nature (WWF) and The Nature Conservancy (TNC), to carry out a series of environmental education activities, issue popular science books and organize eco-tourism projects. The participation of international forces has injected new vitality into the science popularization work of Jiuzhaigou, enabling more people at home and abroad to experience its natural beauty and traditional cultural heritage.

2013年6月，环境保护部、教育部向九寨沟管理局授"全国中小学环境教育社会实践基地"牌（建措 摄）

National Social Practice Base on "Environmental Education for Primary and Secondary Schools" awarded to Jiuzhaigou Management Bureau in June 2013 by the Ministry of Environmental Protection and the Ministry of Education (photo by Jiancuo)

环境教育活动

九寨沟坚持把环境教育放在重要位置，面向大众开展"4・22"世界地球日、"6・5"世界环境日等环境纪念日活动和各类环保专题研讨会、科普咨询活动，不断增强环保教育的针对性和实效性。2013年，九寨沟荣获"全国中小学环境教育社会实践基地"称号，2016年被授予"国家环保科普教育基地"荣誉称号，2021年创建为四川省首批"地学研学旅行实践基地"。

Environmental Education Activities

Jiuzhaigou, which attaches great importance to environmental education, carries out commemorative activities such as World Earth Day on April 22 and World Environment Day on June 5. In addition to seminars on environmental protection and consultations on popular science, more pertinence and effectiveness are enhanced on environmental education. In 2013, it won the title of National Social Practice Base on Environmental Education for Primary and Secondary Schools, and in 2016, it was awarded the title of National Educational Base for Environmental Science Popularization. In 2021 Jiuzhaigou became one of the members in the first batch of Geoscience Research Travel Practice Bases in Sichuan Province.

1 游客中心的地质博物馆（2004 年，蹇代君 摄）
2 游客中心的沙盘（2005 年，蹇代君 摄）
1 Geological Museum at the Visitor Center (photo by Jian Daijun, 2004)
2 Sand table at the Visitor Center (photo by Jian Daijun, 2005)

九寨沟国家地质公园博物馆

基于九寨沟沟口游人中心展陈功能，2004 年，九寨沟国家级地质公园博物馆设立，并成为首批“四川省环境教育基地”。博物馆设内有三维互动漫游系统、电子沙盘（GIS 展示园）、2 米 ×9 米环形投影屏幕、多媒体电子触摸及环境教育互动园等设施，利用声、光、电等技术，向游客、员工和园区居民进行科普宣传。

Jiuzhaigou National Geopark Museum

Based on the exhibition function of Tourist Center in Jiuzhaigou's entrance, Jiuzhaigou National Geopark Museum was established in 2004, and became the first batch of "Sichuan Environmental Education Base".This museum, equipped with facilities such as tridimensional interactive roaming system, electronic sand table (GIS display park), 2m×9m circular projection screen, multimedia electronic touch screen and interactive environmental education park, is meant for scientific popularization to tourists, employees and residents in the secenic area by means of its sound, light and other electronics.

游客中心外观（2011 年，九寨沟管理局 供图）
Appearance of the Visitor Center (photo by courtesy of Jiuzhaigou Management Bureau, 2011)

九看九寨

Jiuzhaigou in Nine Episodes

之七

Episode Seven

遗产呵护

Heritage Well Protected

俄罗斯自然科学院院士、成都理工大学生态环境学院院长、教授裴向军做题为《基于OUV的九寨沟震后地质环境调查评价与修复关键技术》的主题报告（2021年，建措 摄）

八方聚力
Joining Forces from All Sectors

Report on *Key Technologies for Jiuzhaigou Post-quake Geological Environment Investigation, Evaluation and Restoration based on OUV* by Pei Xiangjun, academician of the Russian Academy of Natural Sciences, Dean and Professor of Ecology and Environment School at Chengdu University of Technology (photo by Jiancuo, 2021)

20世纪50年代前，九寨沟鲜为人知。随着哲泽林场和日则林场的组建以及林场工人的到来，九寨沟开始进入越来越多人的视野。人们逐渐发现九寨沟的价值，开始注重保护这里的生态环境。

1973年，中国科学院学部委员吴中伦在考察九寨沟后向四川省革命委员会林业组组长韩正夫建议九寨沟内不应再采伐森林。此后，又有多位到九寨沟考察、研究的专家不约而同地提出保护九寨沟生态的建议。1975年，四川省革命委员会林业组向南坪林业局发出《关于日则、格泽沿沟200米以下禁止砍伐的通知》，九寨沟生态保护第一次有了政策依据。

1977年，四川省珍贵动物资源调查队所写的《四川省珍贵动物资源调查报告》建议，将南坪白河自然保护区的范围扩大到九寨沟。1978年，中国科学院成都生物研究所在《关于建议在四川建立几个自然保护区的报告》中提出九寨沟建立自然保护区的必要性，得到国家认可与重视。同年12月15日，国务院批转国家林业总局《关于加强大熊猫保护、驯养工作的报告》，九寨沟被正式批准建立自然保护区。

1982年，九寨沟被国务院列为第一批国家级重点风景名胜区。1983年，四川省人民政府多次召开会议，为九寨沟的保护作出指示，强调要千方百计地保护九寨沟的自然风景和珍稀动物，在此基础上有计划、有控制地开展旅游活动，并赴九寨沟当地指导工作。九寨沟独创的"保护型开发"从此拉开序幕，1984年，九寨沟景区正式对外开放。

1994年5月，四川省人民政府申报九寨沟为国家级森林和野生动物类型自然保护区。同年7月，林业部正式发文，为保护大熊猫、金丝猴等珍稀动物及其自然生态环境，将九寨沟确认为国家级自然保护区。

此后，保护力度不断加大，九寨沟原始而脆弱的生态环境得到有效保护。1995年9月，九寨沟成为"中国生物圈保护区"成员。1997年12月，九寨沟被正式纳入"世界生物圈保护区"。2003年，九寨沟管理局向国土资源部递交国家地质公园申报书，并编制《四川九寨沟岩溶国家地质公园总体规划》。2004年1月，九寨沟国家地质公园被批准建立，并于当年10月揭牌开园。八方聚力，共同呵护人间仙境九寨沟。

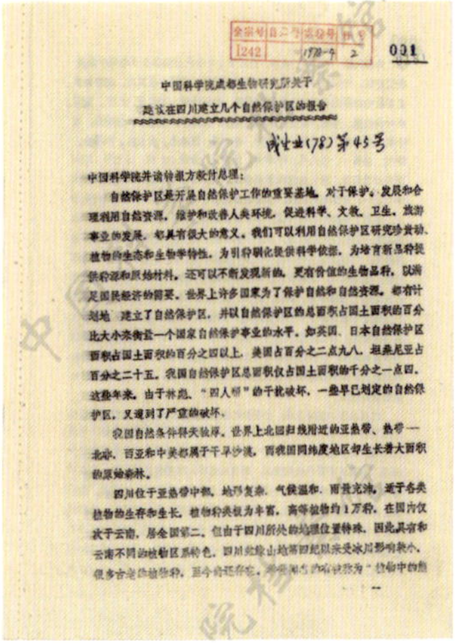

1242 1978-9 2 001

中国科学院成都生物研究所关于

建议在四川建立几个自然保护区的报告

成生业(78)第45号

中国科学院并请转报方毅付总理：

自然保护区是开展自然保护工作的重要基地。对于保护、发展和合理利用自然资源，维护和改善人类环境，促进科学、文教、卫生、旅游事业的发展，都具有很大的意义。我们可以利用自然保护区研究珍贵动、植物的生态和生物学特性，为引种驯化提供科学依据，为培育新品种提供种源和原始材料，还可以不断发现新的、更有价值的生物品种，以满足国民经济的需要。世界上许多国家为了保护自然和自然资源，都有计划地建立了自然保护区，并以自然保护区的总面积占国土面积的百分比大小来衡量一个国家自然保护事业的水平。如英国、日本自然保护区面积占国土面积的百分之四以上，美国占百分之二点九八，坦桑尼亚占百分之二十五。我国自然保护区总面积仅占国土面积的千分之一点四。这些年来，由于林彪、"四人帮"的干扰破坏，一些早已划定的自然保护区，又遭到了严重的破坏。

我国自然条件得天独厚。世界上北回归线附近的亚热带、热带——北非、西亚和中美都属于干旱沙漠，而我国同纬度地区却生长着大面积的原始森林。

四川位于亚热带中部，地形复杂，气候温和，雨量充沛，适于各类植物的生存和生长。植物种类极为丰富，高等植物约1万种，在国内仅次于云南，居全国第二。但由于四川所处的地理位置特殊，因此具有和云南不同的植物区系特色。四川北部山地第四纪以来受冰川影响较小，很多古老的植物种，至今仍还存在。[illegible]

1 九寨橡树，学名辽东栎，九寨彩林主要树种代表。在九寨沟自然保护区成立前，九寨橡树是当地居民主要薪柴树种和烧木炭主要资源（2023年，肖维阳 摄）

2 1978年，中国科学院成都生物研究所关于建立九寨沟等一批自然保护区的报告（印开蒲 供图）

1 Jiuzhai Oak (*Quercus mongolica Fischer ex Ledebour*), used to serve as firewood locally or be burned for charcoal before the establishment of Jiuzhaigou Nature Reserve, is one of the main species in Jiuzhai Colorful Forest (Photo by Xiao Weiyang, 2023)

2 Report by Chengdu Institute of Biology, Chinese Acoademy of Sciences in 1978 on the establishment of nature reserves such as Jiuzhaigou (photo by courtesy of Yin Kaipu)

Before the 1950s, Jiuzhaigou had been little known. Until the establishment of Zheze and Rize Forest Farms and the arrival of farm workers, people gradually discovered its value and began to protecting its ecological environment.

In 1973, back from his inspect of Jiuzhaigou, Wu Zhonglun, a member of the Chinese Academy of Sciences, suggested to Han Zhengfu, forestry group leader with Sichuan Provincial Revolutionary Committee, that deforestation there should be stopped. After that, many other experts to Jiuzhaigou put forward similar suggestions. In 1975, the Forestry Group above-mentioned issued to the Nanping Forestry Bureau the *Notice on the Prohibition of Logging Below 200 Meters above the valley bottom Along the Rize and Geze Gullies*, which served as the first policy basis for the ecological protection of Jiuzhaigou.

In 1977, *Investigation Report on Sichuan's Precious Animal Resources* was written by the Survey Team concerned, suggesting that Jiuzhaigou be included in the scope of Nanping Baihe Nature Reserve. In 1978, Chengdu Institute of Biology, Chinese Academy of Sciences, made known the necessity of Jiuzhaigou being a nature reserve in its *Report on Suggesting the Establishment of Several Nature Reserves in Sichuan*, which was recognized and valued by the state. On December 15 of the same year, the State Council approved and forwarded the State Forestry Administration's *Report on Strengthening the Protection and Domestication of Giant Panda* and Jiuzhaigou was officially approved as a nature reserve.

In 1982, Jiuzhaigou was listed as the first batch of national key scenic spots by the State Council. In 1983, the People's Government of Sichuan Province instructed at several meetings for the protection of Jiuzhaigou, including its natural scenery and rare animals, on this basis, carried out tourism activities in a planned and controlled manner and went to Jiuzhaigou to guide the local work. Its original "protection oriented development" thus kicked off and in 1984, this Scenic Area was officially opened to the public.

In May 1994, the People's Government of Sichuan Province applied for Jiuzhaigou as a national forest and wild animal nature reserve. In July of the same year, the Ministry of Forestry officially issued a document to recognize it as a national nature reserve for the protection of rare animals such as giant panda and golden snub-nosed monkey and its natural ecological environment.

Since then, protection efforts have been increased and the original and fragile ecological environment of Jiuzhaigou effectively protected. In September 1995, Jiuzhaigou became a member of "China Biosphere Reserve" and was in December 1997 officially included in "World Biosphere Reserve". In 2003, the Management Bureau submitted the National Geopark Application to the Ministry of Land and Resources and compiled *Master Plan for Sichuan Jiuzhaigou Karst National Geopark*. In January 2004, the National Geopark was approved and opened in October of that year. Hence the Joining Forces from All Sectors for the protection of Jiuzhaigou, a fairyland on earth.

王志强、傅春华

四川省林业局下属林业勘探工作者。1956 年，王志强和傅春华为调查森林储备量带队进入九寨沟，发现这里蕴藏着丰富的森林资源和雄伟壮观的瀑布、海子等水景。他们将所有数据整理成文，上报四川省林业厅勘察设计院，报告首次将塔藏乡扎如村、荷叶村和树正村所在的林区称为九寨沟林区，这是“九寨沟”称谓首次出现在政府文件中。

Wang Zhiqiang, Fu Chunhua

As forestry explorers of Sichuan Provincial Forestry Bureau, Wang Zhiqiang and Fu Chunhua led a team into Jiuzhaigou in 1956 for forest reserves and found rich forest resources and majestic waterfalls, lakes and other water features. They compiled all the data into a document and reported it to the Survey and Design Institute of Sichuan Povincial Department of Forestry. For the first time, the report named the forest area where Zharu, Heye and Shuzheng Villages in Tazang Township were located as the Jiuzhaigou Forest Area. This was the first time that the name “Jiuzhaigou” appeared in government documents.

王友州、泽仁珠

王友州，1978—1987 年先后担任九寨沟自然保护区管理所所长、九寨沟自然保护区管理处副主任、九寨沟管理局副局长。任职期间，多次提出保护景区生态、造福当地百姓的建议，践行“保护是第一要务、旅游是最好发展”的理念，领导建设九寨沟区内旅游基础设施及保护站保障设施等，引导原住居民转变保护和发展方式，共同参与旅游地建设。

泽仁珠，1988—1998 年先后担任九寨沟自然保护区管理处主任、九寨沟风景名胜区管理局局长。曾多次治理九寨沟泥石流灾害、规范景区经营管理，提出“保景育人”的理念。

Wang Youzhou, Zeren Zhu

Wang Youzhou, from 1978 to 1987, had been the head of Jiuzhaigou Nature Reserve Management Institute, Conservation Department and deputy director of Jiuzhaigou Management Bureau. During his tenure, he put forward many suggestions on the protection of the ecology of the scenic spot for the wellbeing of the local people, practiced the concept of “protection as first priority and tourism as best

1 | 2 | 3 | 4 | 5

1 王志强（2016 年，九寨沟管理局 供图）
2 傅春华（2016 年，九寨沟管理局 供图）
3 王友州（2023 年，九寨沟管理局 供图）
4 泽仁珠（2023 年，九寨沟管理局 供图）
5 印开蒲（2023 年，九寨沟管理局 供图）

1 Wang Zhiqiang (photo by courtesy of Jiuzhaigou Management Bureau, 2016)
2 Fu Chunhua (photo by courtesy of Jiuzhaigou Management Bureau, 2016)
3 Wang Youzhou (photo by courtesy of Jiuzhaigou Management Bureau, 2023)
4 Zeren Zhu (photo by courtesy of Jiuzhaigou Management Bureau, 2023)
5 Yin Kaipu (photo by courtesy of Jiuzhaigou Management Bureau, 2023)

development", by taking the lead in constructing tourism infrastructure and improving support facilities for the protection stations here, guided the residents concerning the way of protection and development, so they would be glad participants in the construction of tourist destinations.

Zeren Zhu, from 1988 to 1998, successively served as the head of Jiuzhaigou Nature Reserve Management Office and Scenic and Historic Area Administration. He had led repeated treatment of the local debris flow disasters, standardized the operation and management of scenic spots and put forward the concept of "preserving the scenery by educating the people".

印开蒲、胡铁卿、邓一、张国威、田树昌、泽旺秀

印开蒲，中国科学院成都生物研究所研究员、生态学家。1969—1978 年，三次考察九寨沟。1978 年，起草的关于建立九寨沟等一批自然保护区的建议被国家采纳。同年 12 月，九寨沟获批为自然保护区。

胡铁卿，四川省林业厅野生动物保护处原处长。1974 年，随大熊猫考察队进入九寨沟，并将域内生态信息反馈回省林业局。1975 年，四川省革委林业组第一次发出保护九寨沟的正式文件。1978 年，指导印开蒲起草关于建立九寨沟等一批自然保护区的建议。

邓一（1983 年 11 月至 1986 年 6 月，先后担任南坪县九寨沟自然保护区管理处主任、南坪县九寨沟风景名胜区管理局局长）、张国威（南坪林业局原职工）、田树昌（南坪县委宣传部原新闻干事）通过撰写文章、拍摄照片等多种方式，向上级部门呼吁停止砍伐森林，保护九寨沟。

泽旺秀，曾任树正村村主任、书记，阿坝州人大代表，九寨沟县人大代表、九寨沟县政协委员。带领村民以户为单位创建股份制九寨沟民俗文化村，组织编写九寨沟民俗文化村志，推进九寨沟景区实行"沟内游，沟外住"政策等。

Yin Kaipu, Hu Tieqing, Deng Yi, Zhang Guowei, Tian Shuchang, Zewang Xiu

Yin Kaipu, former researcher and ecologist at Chengdu Institute of Biology, Chinese Academy of Sciences. From 1969 to 1978, he visited Jiuzhaigou three times. In 1978, his draft proposal on establishment of nature reserves such as Jiuzhaigou was adopted by the state. In December of the same year, the valley above was approved as a nature reserve.

1 | 2 | 3 | 4 | 5

1　胡铁卿（2023 年，印开蒲　供图）
2　邓一（2023 年，九寨沟管理局　供图）
3　张国威（2023 年，九寨沟管理局　供图）
4　田树昌（2023 年，九寨沟管理局　供图）
5　泽旺秀（2023 年，九寨沟管理局　供图）

1　Hu Tieqing (photo by courtesy of Yin Kaipu, 2023)
2　Deng Yi (photo by courtesy of Jiuzhaigou Management Bureau, 2023)
3　Zhang Guowei (photo by courtesy of Jiuzhaigou Management Bureau, 2023)
4　Tian Shuchang (photo by courtesy of Jiuzhaigou Management Bureau, 2023)
5　Zewang Xiu (photo by courtesy of Jiuzhaigou Management Bureau, 2023)

Hu Tieqing, former director of the Wildlife Protection Department of the Forestry Department of Sichuan Province. In 1974, he entered Jiuzhaigou with the giant panda expedition and fed back the ecological information in the region to the Provincial Forestry Bureau. In 1975, the Forestry Group of the Revolutionary Committee of Sichuan Province issued an official document on the protection of Jiuzhaigou for the first time. In 1978, he guided Yin Kaipu to draft proposals on the establishment of a number of nature reserves such as Jiuzhaigou.

Deng Yi (from November 1983 to June 1986 as head of Management Office of Jiuzhaigou Nature Reserve and Management Bureau of Jiuzhaigou Scenic and Historic Area in Nanping County), Zhang Guowei (former employee of Nanping Forestry Bureau), Tian Shuchang (former news clerk with Publicity Department of Nanping County Party Committee) reported to the higher authorities calling for an end to deforestation and protection of Jiuzhaigou by means articles and photos.

Zewang Xiu, head and Party chief of Shuzheng Village, a deputy to the People's Congress of Aba Prefecture, of the County People's Congress and a member of the County Political Consultative Conference, led the villagers to establish a joint-stock Jiuzhaigou Folk Culture Village on a household basis, organize the compilation of jiuzhaigou folk culture village records and promote the policy of "touring in but lodging outside the valley" in the Scenic Area.

钱振越

钱振越，中华人民共和国住房和城乡建设部风景名胜区专家顾问，国家级风景名胜规划专家，注册城市规划师。曾率省规划专家组进驻九寨沟，参与《九寨沟风景名胜区总体规划》编制工作，为九寨沟提出“保护第一”的总体原则、“沟内游，沟外住”的布局原则，主持九寨沟风景名胜区申遗工作。

Qian Zhenyue

Qian Zhenyue is an expert consultant of scenic spots from the Ministry of Housing and Urban-Rural Development, national-level scenic spot planner and registered urban planner. He once led and resided in Jiuzhaigou with the provincial planning expert group, compiling *Jiuzhaigou Scenic Area Master Plan*, put forward the overall principle of "Protection First" and the layout principle of "touring in but lodging outside the valley", and presided over the application for Jiuzhaigou Scenic Area as a world heritage.

吉姆 · 桑塞尔、景峰

吉姆 • 桑塞尔，博士，加拿大人，国际自然与自然资源保护联盟高级顾问，“世界自然遗产名录”首席考察官，曾与卢卡斯

1 | 2 | 3

1　钱振越（2023 年，九寨沟管理局 供图）
2　吉姆 • 桑塞尔（2023 年，九寨沟管理局 供图）
3　景峰（2023 年，九寨沟管理局 供图）

1　Qian Zhenyue (photo by courtesy of Jiuzhaigou Management Bureau, 2023)
2　Jim Thorsell (photo by courtesy of Jiuzhaigou Management Bureau, 2023)
3　Jing Feng (photo by courtesy of Jiuzhaigou Management Bureau, 2023)

博士对九寨沟开展实地考察评估，为九寨沟题词“这是世界上最伟大的一处自然奇观”。

景峰，联合国教科文组织（UNESCO）世界遗产中心亚洲和太平洋部原主任。协理完成九寨沟世界自然遗产评估工作，多次陪同世界遗产中心负责人、IUCN 专家到九寨沟考察评估。

Jim Thorsell, Jing Feng

Dr. Jim Thorsell, Canadian, senior advisor of the International Union for Conservation of Nature and Natural Resources, chief investigator for the World Natural Heritage List, on his field investigation and evaluation of Jiuzhaigou with Dr. Lucas, left a message that reads “one of the world’s great natural wonders is found here”.

Jing Feng, former head of Asia and Pacific Department of World Heritage Center of UNESCO, assisted to complete the assessment of Jiuzhaigou World Natural Heritage and repeatedly accompanied World Heritage Center heads and IUCN experts to Jiuzhaigou for investigation and assessment.

容中尔甲、于宁

容中尔甲，民族歌手，四川省人大代表。主要作品有《神奇的九寨》《永远的九寨》《神奇九寨更迷人》等，把对九寨沟的感情写进歌里，传播九寨文化。

于宁，九寨沟风景名胜区管理局退休职工，在九寨沟“世界自然遗产”“世界人与生物圈”“国家地质公园”等的国际范本申报书中任图片主编，著有大量与九寨沟相关的画册、明信片、影像等作品宣传九寨沟。

Rongzhong Erjia, Yu Ning

Rongzhong Erjia, national singer, deputy to Sichuan Provincial People’s Congress. Main works by Rongzhong Erjia, national singer, deputy to Sichuan Provincial People’s Congress. Main works include include *Magical Jiuzhaigou*, *Perpetual Jiuzhaigou* and *May the Magical Jiuzhaigou Be More Charming*. He has writen his affections for Jiuzhaigou into songs and spread its culture.

Yu Ning, a retired employee of the Jiuzhaigou Scenic Area Administration, once the editor-in-chief of “World Natural Heritage”, “Man and Biosphere of the World” and “National Geopark” international model application forms, has helped publicize Jiuzhaigou by creating plenty of picture albums, postcards and videos.

1 | 2

1　容中尔甲（2023 年，九寨沟管理局 供图）
2　于宁（2023 年，九寨沟管理局 供图）

1　Rongzhong Erjia (photo by courtesy of Jiuzhaigou Management Bureau, 2023)
2　Yu Ning (photo by courtesy of Jiuzhaigou Management Bureau, 2023)

1992年6月，联合国教科文组织专家组代表桑塞尔博士（前排右）和卢卡斯博士（前排左），在九寨沟全面考察自然遗产状况及申报工作（于宁 摄）

申遗之路
On the Road to Apply for World Heritage

Dr. Jim Thorsell (right, front row) and Dr. Bing Lucas (left, front row), representatives from the UNESCO team, made a comprehensive investigation on the status of natural heritage and application process in Jiuzhaigou Scenic and Historic Interest Area in June 1992 (photo by Yu Ning)

1991 年 3 月 15 日，九寨沟管理局收到四川省建设委员会转建设部城市建设司文件，国务院将九寨沟列入向联合国教科文组织申报世界自然遗产的名单，文中对九寨沟给予高度评价，称其“景色秀丽奇绝，世所罕见”。

6 月 14 日，中共南坪县委、南坪县人民政府成立以县委书记为组长的世界自然遗产申报工作领导小组，并在四川省建设委员会主持下，成立世界自然遗产中国九寨沟编辑委员会（简称“九寨沟编辑委员会”），制作申报材料。历时 3 个多月，九寨沟编辑委员会按要求完成申请书、电视片、幻灯片等，共计 5 万多字、108 张照片、中英文 2 种版本的全部申报材料。

9 月，九寨沟风景名胜区申遗材料提交世界遗产委员会。此后直到 1992 年上半年，九寨沟管理局随申报工作推进，继续组织专家、学者搜集、整理、编印、呈报申遗所需补充材料。

与此同时，四川省人民政府、南坪县人民政府及各相关单位围绕申遗目标，开展九寨沟景区建设和管理提升工作。1991 年 8 月 23 日，南坪县人民政府制定《关于加强九寨沟风景名胜区管理的规定》；10 月 14—15 日，四川省风景名胜区检查团对九寨沟景区的保护和管理工作进行检查督促。年内，九寨沟管理局完成景区公路全部路面的柏油化，结束景区公路尘土飞扬的历史。

1992 年 6 月 5—6 日，联合国教科文组织派出以博士桑塞尔和博士卢卡斯为首的专家组，到九寨沟风景名胜区全面考察自然遗产状况及申报工作。九寨沟人文景观和自然风景和谐并存、经济效益与生态效益兼顾的做法赢得专家组的高度认同与赞赏。

1992 年 12 月 14 日，在联合国教科文组织世界遗产委员会（WHC）全委会第十六届大会上，九寨沟被全票通过列入《世界遗产名录》。1993 年 2 月 28 日，世界自然遗产证书颁发仪式及新闻发布会在北京人民大会堂举行，联合国教科文组织总干事马约尔向九寨沟颁发世界自然遗产证书。

纸本综合材料
《草甸——通往九寨的路》
40cm×80cm
（2022 年，米金铭 作品）

Meadow–The Road to Jiuzhai, painting on paper-based composite material, 40cm×80cm (by Mi Jinming, 2022)

On March 15, 1991, Jiuzhaigou Management Bureau received a document by the Urban Construction Department of the Ministry of Construction from Sichuan Provincial Construction Committee, which showed that the State Council had included Jiuzhaigou in the list of world natural heritages application to UNESCO, highly praising it to the effect that "The scenery is unique and unrivaled in the world".

On June 14, the CPC Nanping County Committee and the People's Government of Nanping established a leading group for the application of World Natural Heritage headed by its Party Secretary, and under the auspices of Sichuan Provincial Construction Committee, established China's Jiuzhaigou Editorial Committee of World Natural Heritage ("Jiuzhaigou Editorial Committee" for short), preparing application materials. Over three months, the Editorial Committee completed all materials necessary in both Chinese and English, including application forms, TV films, slides, etc, totaling 50,000-plus words and 108 photos.

In September, application materials for Jiuzhaigou Scenic Area were submitted to the World Heritage Committee (WHC). From then until the first half of 1992, the Management Bureau continued to have experts and scholars to collect, collate, compile, print and submit supplementary materials required.

Meanwhile, the People's Governments of Sichuan Province and Nanping County as well as its relevant agencies carried out the construction and management improvement of the Scenic Area around the goal of application. On August 23, 1991, Nanping County People's government formulated *Regulations on Strengthening the Management of Jiuzhaigou Scenic Area*; from October 14 to 15, Sichuan Scenic Area Inspection Team inspected and supervised the protection and management of the Scenic Area. Within the year, the Management Bureau completed the asphalting of all roads within the scenic area, ridding it of dusty roads.

From June 5 to 6, 1992, UNESCO sent an expert group headed by Dr. Jim Thorsell and Dr. Bing Lucas to the scenic area to investigate the status of natural heritage and the work of application. Jiuzhaigou's practice of harmonious coexistence of cultural landscape and natural scenery and taking into account both economic and ecological benefits, had won high recognition and appreciation from the expert group.

On December 14, 1992, at the 16th session of World Heritage Committee (WHC) of UNESCO, Jiuzhaigou was included in the World Heritage List by unanimous approval. On February 28, 1993, World Natural Heritage Certificate Presentation Ceremony and Press Conference were held at the Great Hall of the People, Beijing, at which Jiuzhaigou received the World Natural Heritage Certificate from UNESCO Director-General Mayor.

世界自然遗产

根据联合国教科文组织制定的《保护世界文化与自然遗产公约》，符合下列条件之一的可被列为自然遗产。一是从审美或科学角度看具有突出的普遍价值的由物质和生物结构或这类结构群组成的自然面貌；二是从科学或保护角度看具有突出的普遍价值的地质和自然地理结构，以及明确划为受威胁的动物和植物生境区；三是从科学、保存或自然美角度看具有突出的普遍价值的天然名胜或明确划分的自然区域。

World Natural Heritage

According to *Convention on the Protection of World Cultural and Natural Heritage* formulated by UNESCO, those that meet one of the following conditions can be listed as natural heritages. First, natural features consisting of physical and biological structures, or groups of such structures, of outstanding universal value from the aesthetic and scientific point of view; second, geological and physical geographical structures of outstanding universal value from the scientific or conservative point of view and clearly designated as threatened animal and plant habitats; and third, natural scenic spot or clearly demarcated natural areas with outstanding universal value from the perspective of science, conservation or natural beauty.

1 1993 年 2 月 28 日，联合国教科文组织总干事马约尔（左）在北京人民大会堂向九寨沟管理局局长泽仁珠（右）颁发世界自然遗产证书（九寨沟管理局 供图）

2 1993 年 2 月 28 日，北京人民大会堂举行“世界自然遗产证书颁发仪式暨新闻发布会”（九寨沟管理局 供图）

3 世界自然遗产证书（2005 年，九寨沟管理局 供图）

1 World Natural Heritage Certificate presented at the Great Hall of the People in Beijing to Zeren Zhu (right), Director of Jiuzhaigou Management Bureau on February 28, 1993, by Mr. Mayor (left), Director-General of UNESCO (photo by courtesy of Jiuzhaigou Management Bureau)

2 Issuing ceremony for World Natural Heritage Certificate and press conference held at the Great Hall of the People in Beijing on February 28, 1993 (photo by courtesy of Jiuzhaigou Management Bureau)

3 Certificate of World Heritage Site (photo courtesy of Jiuzhaigou Management Bureau, 2005)

桑塞尔博士重访九寨沟

2011 年 5 月 15—17 日，桑塞尔博士在时隔 20 年后，又一次来到九寨沟。在全面考察九寨沟发展现状，包括旅游基础设施和服务设施建设、景区标准化管理、智慧景区建设等后，桑塞尔对九寨沟的巨大变化、取得成就给予高度评价。

Dr. Jim Thorsell's Revisit to Jiuzhaigou

From May 15 to 17, 2011, Dr. Jim Thorsell came to Jiuzhaigou again 20 years later. After comprehensively inspecting its development status, including its tourism infrastructure and service facilities, standardized management and construction of smart scenic spots, he spoke highly of Jiuzhaigou's great changes and achievements.

1
2

1　桑塞尔博士（左）和卢卡斯博士（右）与时任九寨沟管理局局长泽仁珠（中）在犀牛海前合影（1992 年，于宁　摄）

2　2011 年 5 月，桑塞尔博士为九寨沟管理局题词："很少有外国人能像我一样，能两次来到这个地方。很幸运的是，我是龙年出生的。在完成世界自然保护联盟世界遗产评估工作后，都过去 20 年时间了，我印象最深刻的是你们所取得的进步，把这个地方建成了世界遗产地的典范。继续努力，好好干吧！"（于宁　摄）

1　A group photo of Dr. Jim Thorsell (left) and Dr. Bing Lucas (right) with Zeren Zhu (middle), then Director of Jiuzhaigou Management Bureau, standing before Rhinoceros Lake (photo by Yu Ning, 1992)

2　On May, 2011, Dr. Jim Thorsell inscribed in Jiuzhaigou Management Bureau to the effect that "Few foreigners get to visit the place two times as I have just done. Very lucky but I am from the "Year of Dragon". After 20 years since I was here for the World Heritage evaluation for IUCN. It is impressive the progress you have made in making this a model WH site. Keep up the good work!" (photo by Yu Ning)

日则保护站（2022 年，九寨沟管理局 供图）

分级分片
Gradation and Sharding

Rize Protection Station (photo by courtesy of Jiuzhaigou Management Bureau, 2022)

自开放旅游以来，九寨沟管理局始终坚持把“尊重自然、生态优先”作为行动准则和先导，走出一条独特的保护开发道路。

1985 年，《九寨沟风景名胜区总体规划（1985—2000）》制定，根据景观价值、生态地位、游览需要和管理实际对九寨沟内的景观资源实行分级保护，划分出景点景物特殊保护区、游览范围严格保护区、景观环境重点保护区和自然生态全面保护区 4 个级别。

2003 年，九寨沟管理局根据景区和自然保护区分级情况，编制完成《四川九寨沟岩溶国家地质公园总体规划》，将九寨沟地质公园划分为特级、一级、二级、三级共四级保护区，划定每个保护区的范围，明确在每个保护区内可开展的活动。

除分级保护外，有关管理部门还建立保护站点，对九寨沟进行分片保护。1990 年，建立长海、日则、树正、诺日朗、荷叶、扎如、沟口 7 个保护组。1995 年，建成扎如、荷叶、树正、诺日朗、日则 5 个保护站。1998 年，增建长海保护站，实行站长责任制。九寨沟内以保护站为支撑点进行分区管理，并逐渐调整布局，建立起完善的保护体系和保护网络。

Since the opening to tourists, Jiuzhaigou Management Bureau has always been insisting on “respect for nature, priority to ecology” as its principle of action and guide, taking a unique path of protection and development.

In 1985, *Master Plan for Jiuzhaigou Scenic Area (1985~2000)* was formulated. According to the value of landscape, ecological status, tourism needs and management practice, its resources were protected by grades and scenic spots divided into four grades: scenic spot special protection area, strict sightseeing scope protection area, key protection area of landscape environment and comprehensive protection area of natural ecology.

In 2003, according to the grading of its scenic spots and nature reserves, the Jiuzhaigou Management Bureau compiled *Master Plan for Sichuan Jiuzhaigou Karst National Geopark*, which divided the Geopark into four grades of protected areas: special, first, second and third. The scope of each protected area was defined and its activities specified the that could be carried out in it.

In addition, relevant management departments established protection sites according to their shards. In 1990, seven protection groups were set up such as Long Lake, Rize, Shuzheng, Nuorilang, Heye, Zharu and GouKou. In 1995, 5 protection stations were built in Zharu, Heye, Shuzheng, Nuorilang and Rize. In 1998, Long Lake Protection Station was added and the responsibility system of its chief was implemented. In Jiuzhaigou, the protection station serves as the bearing point for zoning management and its layout is gradually adjusted for the establishment of a complete protection system and protection network.

克泽沟核心区指示牌（2020 年，刘志祥 摄）
Sign of core area of Keze Gully (photo by Liu Zhixiang, 2020)

核心景区特级保护区

2005 年，《九寨沟风景名胜区总体规划（2006—2020）》修编完成，将《九寨沟风景名胜区总体规划（1985—2000）》中划分的四级分区合称为特级、一级和二级结构的“核心景区”。其中，原规划中的第三级和第四级保护区合并称为核心景区特级保护区，是除游览区域外的核心景区，面积计 588 平方千米。该保护区严禁与资源保护无关的各种工程建设，严格限制各类建筑物、构筑物，禁止建设各类宾馆、索道和大型人工设施，符合规划要求的建设项目须严格按照规定程序报批，手续不全不得组织实施。

地质公园特级保护区

为树正沟、日则沟、则查洼沟、扎如沟 4 条主沟两岸宽约 1000 米范围和丹祖沟、悬泉沟等 7 条支沟两岸约 500 米范围外的地带，面积 484.8 平方千米。该保护区主要保护对象为九寨沟层湖叠瀑景观形成的水流运动系统，游人不得进入，不得修建任何建筑设施，可进行少量科学考察和研究。

Premium Protected Areas in the Core Scenic Area

In 2005, *Master Plan for Jiuzhaigou Scenic Areas (1985~2000)* was revised as *Master Plan for Jiuzhaigou Scenic Areas (2006~2020)*, in which the former four-grade core scenic areas were shortened as: special, first and second. Among them, the combination of the last two grades in the original plan was called the core scenic spots for special protection, except the area for tourists, with an area of 588 square kilometers. The protected area strictly prohibits any engineering construction unrelated to resource protection, any buildings and structures and any construction of hotels, cableways and large-scale artificial facilities. Construction projects that meet the planning requirements must be submitted for approval in accordance with the prescribed procedures.

Premium Protection of Geopark

It covers an area of 484.8 square kilometers stretching from the gullies of Shuzheng, Rize, Zezhawa and Zharu with a width of about 1,000 meters on both sides to the rest area outside the range of about 500 meters on both sides of Danzu and Xuanquan Gullies. The main protection in the nature reserve is the water movement system formed by the landscape of overlapping lakes and waterfalls. No visitor is allowed to enter and no building facilities to be constructed but a few for scientific investigation and research.

扎如保护站
Zharu Protection Station

扎如保护站（2022 年，九寨沟管理局 供图）
Zharu Protection Station (photo by courtesy of Jiuzhaigou Management Bureau, 2022)

位于扎如沟进沟 2000 米处，海拔 2360 米，距九寨沟管理局驻地 5000 米。主要管护扎如沟下游汇水面积区域，管理面积 3758 公顷。

2,360 meters above sea level, it is located 2,000 meters away from the entrance to Zharu Gully and 5,000 meters away from Jiuzhaigou Management Bureau. It protects and manages the catchment area at downstream of Zharu Gully, a total area of 3,758 hectares.

诺日朗保护站
Nuorilang Protection Station

诺日朗保护站（2022 年，九寨沟管理局 供图）
Nuorilang Protection Station (photo by courtesy of Jiuzhaigou Management Bureau, 2022)

位于诺日朗，海拔 2620 米，距九寨沟管理局驻地 13000 米。主要管护黑角沟以上至克泽沟汇水面积区域，管护面积 8951 公顷。

2,620 meters above sea level, it is located in Nuorilang, 13,000 meters away from Jiuzhaigou Management Bureau. It protects and manages the catchment area from above Heijiao Gully to Keze Gully, a total area of 8,951 hectares.

荷叶保护站
Heye Protection Station

荷叶保护站（2008 年，九寨沟管理局 供图）
Heye Protection Station (photo by courtesy of Jiuzhaigou Management Bureau, 2008)

位于荷叶沟，海拔 2360 米，距九寨沟管理局驻地 4000 米。主要管护荷叶沟汇水面积区域和沟口大门至黑角桥一段，管护面积 6095 公顷。

2,360 meters above sea level and located in Heye Gully, 4,000 meters away from Jiuzhaigou Management Bureau, it protects and manages the catchment area of Heye Gully and the section from the entrance gate to Heijiao bridge, a total area of 6,095 hectares.

树正保护站
Shuzheng Protection Station

位于树正寨附近，海拔 2560 米，距九寨沟管理局驻地 8000 米。主要管护黑角沟、丹祖沟汇水面积区域，管护面积 932.6 公顷。

2,560 meters above sea level and located close to Shuzheng Village, 8,000 meters away from Jiuzhaigou Management Bureau, it protects and manages the catchment areas of Heijiao and Danzu Gullies, a total area of 932.6 hectares.

树正保护站（2008 年，九寨沟管理局 供图）
Shuzheng Protection Station (photo by courtesy of Jiuzhaigou Management Bureau, 2008)

长海保护站
Long Lake Protection Station

位于长海口，海拔 3103 米，距九寨沟管理局驻地 30000 米。主要管护克泽沟以上的则查洼沟汇水面积区域，管护面积 14305 公顷。

3,103 meters above sea level and located near Long Lake, 30,000 meters away from Jiuzhaigou Management Bureau, it protects and manages the catchment area of Zezhawa Gully above Keze Gully, a total area of 14,305 hectares.

长海保护站（2022 年，九寨沟管理局 供图）
Long Lake Protection Station (photo by courtesy of Jiuzhaigou Management Bureau, 2022)

日则保护站
Rize Protection Station

位于日则沟中部，海拔 2760 米，距九寨沟管理局驻地 21000 米。主要管护五花海至原始森林各沟系，管护面积 15333 公顷。

2,760 meters above sea level and located in the middle of Rize Gully and 21,000 meters away from Jiuzhaigou Management Bureau, it protects and manages all gullies from Wuhua Lake to the Virgin Forest, a total area of 15,333 hectares.

日则保护站（2022 年，九寨沟管理局 供图）
Rize Protection Station (photo by courtesy of Jiuzhaigou Management Bureau, 2022)

九寨沟林业有害生物中心测报站工作人员开展林业有害生物春季普查工作（2022 年，九寨沟管理局 供图）

巡查救护

Inspection and Rescue

Spring census of forestry pests conducted by the monitoring and forecasting station of Jiuzhaigou Forestry Pest Center (photo by courtesy of Jiuzhaigou Management Bureau, 2022)

1979—1984 年，在九寨沟自然保护区管理机构筹建时期，保护工作主要由管理处（所）组织沟内村寨居民共同完成。到 1988 年，形成由 20 户居民组成的治安护林巡逻队和 50 人的巡山队，分段定期巡山检查，开展护林防火、治安消防和野生动物保护等工作。

九寨沟管理局成立后，坚持走社区联防道路，动员沟内群众参与保护工作，不断调整充实护林组织和护林队伍，落实护林责任区；开展《中华人民共和国消防法》《中华人民共和国森林法》等有关法律、法规和条例的宣传活动，以支部书记、村委会主任为责任人，把护林防火与村寨群众的管理工作相结合；与九寨沟县人民政府签订景区外围保护协议，加强同周边地区的联系，协同做好外围保护区的保护工作。

From 1979 to 1984, during the preparatory period for the establishment of the management organization of Jiuzhaigou Nature Reserve, protection was mainly completed by the management office (unit) and the villagers in the valley. By 1988, a public security forest patrol team composed of 20 households and a 50-person mountain patrol team were formed to carry out regular inspections one section after another concerning fire, public security and wildlife protection.

Since its establishment, Jiuzhaigou Management Bureau has been persistent in joint prevention with communities, and mobilized the residents in the valley to take part in the protection work, constantly adjusted and enhanced the forest protection organization and protection team and implemented protection responsibility schemes in the area, and carried out *Fire Protection Law of the People's Republic of China, Forestry Law of the People's Republic of China* and the like, with the Party chief and village committee head as the responsibility takers, combined forest protection and fire prevention with villagers' management, signed an agreement with the Jiuzhaigou County People's Government on the protection of the periphery of the scenic spot and strengthened cooperation and contact with surrounding areas, collaborated on the protection of peripheral protection areas and so on.

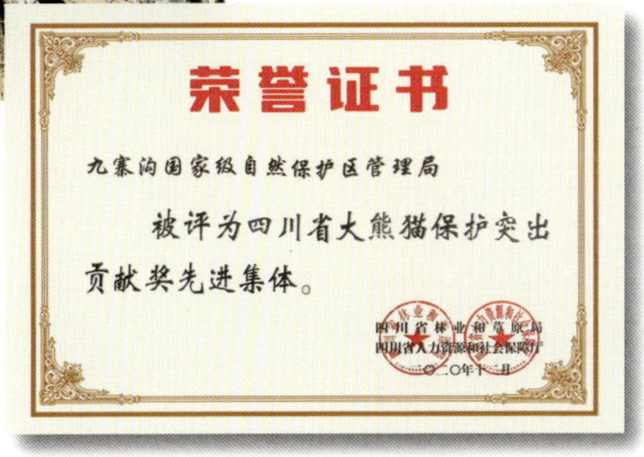

1 | 2

1　2022 年 5 月 9 日，九寨沟管理局工作人员检查、补充灭火器（九寨沟管理局 供图）

2　2020 年 12 月，九寨沟国际级自然保护区管理局获四川省大熊猫保护突出贡献奖先进集体荣誉证书（九寨沟管理局 供图）

1　Staff of Jiuzhaigou Management Bureau checking and replacing fire extinguishers on May 9, 2022 (photo provided by Jiuzhaigou Management Bureau)

2　Jiuzhaigou International Nature Reserve Management Bureau awarded the honorable title of advanced unit with remarkable contributions in protecting the giant panda in Sichuan Province in December 2020 (photo by courtesy of Jiuzhaigou Management Bureau)

社区联防

九寨沟管理局坚持护林效果与经济效益相结合的原则，通过与居民签订护林防火合同、护林防火公约、护林防火责任书等形式，落实护林责任区，动员沟内居民组成护林联防小组，负责护林防火、治安消防、野生动物保护等工作，实现政府与个人协同发力，共同做好景区保护工作。

Community Prevention

The Jiuzhaigou Management Bureau adheres to the principle of combining forest protection effects with economic benefits. By signing forest protection and fire prevention contracts, agreements and responsibility letters with residents, it implements the forest protection responsibility area and mobilizes residents in the valley to form a forest protection joint prevention team to take charge in public security and fire prevention, wildlife protection and other work and realizes the coordinated efforts of the government and individuals for the protection of the scenic spot.

保护大熊猫

九寨沟是岷山山系大熊猫 A 种群的核心地和走廊带，栖息着一定数量的大熊猫。多年来，九寨沟相关部门和单位先后发布《关于抢救大熊猫的紧急通知》《关于保护大熊猫的实施条例》等政策文件，收缴、撤除非法捕猎工具，播放保护大熊猫的电影、录像，分发相关宣传册等，增强公众对保护野生珍稀动植物重要性的认识。

Protection of Giant Pandas

Situated in the Minshan Mountains, Jiuzhaigou is the core and corridor of giant pandas, where a certain number of giant pandas occur. Over the years, relevant departments and units here have successively issued policy documents such as *Urgent Notice on the Rescue of* giant panda and *Implementation Regulations on the Protection of Giant Pandas*, confiscating and pulling apart illegal hunting tools, protecting giant panda by means of films and videos and distributing relevant brochures, so as to enhance public awareness and importance of rare wild animals and plants.

2017年7月11日，九寨沟国家级自然保护区开展巡护立牌工作（兰成君 供图）

Start of sign erecting and patrolling of Jiuzhaigou National Nature Reserve on July 11, 2017 (photo by courtesy of Lan Chengjun)

巡护立牌

九寨沟管理局始终把巡护工作作为常态化管理手段。巡护时，巡护人员会在九寨沟重要地段埋桩立牌、警示行人。巡护立牌对有关组织、团体和个人非法进入九寨沟国家级自然保护区起到很好的警示作用，同时也可保护景区的生态环境，为维护景区原真性和完整性奠定基础。

Patrol and Signboard

Jiuzhaigou Management Bureau, which keeps patrol work as a normalized management method, requires that the patrol personnel spike piles and erect signboards in its key positions to warn pedestrians. This plays a very good role against trespassers into Jiuzhaigou National Nature Reserve while protecting the ecological environment of scenic spots, hence a foundation for maintaining their authenticity and integrity.

1

2

1　1998 年，九寨沟自然保护区管理处获云杉落针病流行规律及防治技术研究三等奖（九寨沟管理局 供图）

2　1996 年 8 月，九寨沟林业有害生物中心测报站工作人员对保护区原始森林、长海人工林（云杉落针病）开展病虫害防治工作（九寨沟管理局 供图）

1　Jiuzhaigou Nature Reserve Management Office awarded the third prize for research on the prevalence and control technology of spruce needle cast in 1998 (photo by courtesy of Jiuzhaigou Management Bureau)

2　Pest control of virgin forest in the Nature Reserve and l ona l ake artif. cial forest (spruce needle cast) by the monitoring station of jJiuzhaigouForestry Pest Center in August 1996 (photo by courtesy of Jiuzhaigou Management Bureau)

治理云杉落针病

云杉落针病是一种重要叶部病害，云杉林常遇“杀手”之一，会造成云杉针叶脱落。1990 年 4 月，九寨沟长海一带大片云杉针叶林枯萎。6 月，四川省林业厅组建的专业队伍前往长海安营扎寨，对 1100 亩（约 73.33 公顷）病树进行防治。至 1992 年，云杉落针病治理取得良好效果。九寨沟成立森林病虫害监测站和生态环境监测站，定期对保护区森林病虫害进行监测。

Treatment of Spruce Needle Cast

Spruce needle cast, an important leaf disease among the spruce forest, is a killer which causes the drop of spruce needles. In April 1990, a large spruce coniferous forest in the Long Lake area withered. In June, a professional team from Sichuan Povincial Department of Forestry arrived and set up camps at Long Lake to treat about 73.33 hectares of diseased trees. By 1992, this work had achieved good results. Since then, stations for forest pest monitoring and ecological environment monitoring have been set up for regular work.

九看
Jiuzhaigou in
Nine Episodes
九寨

之八
Episode Eight

安逸畅游

Tourism in the Easy Way

机构沿革
Institutional Evolution

九寨沟管理局机构标牌(2023 年，建措 摄)

Plaques of organizations under Jiuzhaigou Management Bureau (photo by Jiancuo, 2023)

1992 年的九寨沟沟口（来源于《四川省志·九寨沟志》）

The entrance to Jiuzhaigou in 1992 (photo from *Sichuan Provincial Records–Jiuzhaigou Records*)

1980 年 1 月，四川省南坪县九寨沟自然保护区管理所正式成立。1982 年 11 月 8 日，九寨沟与黄龙寺合并列入第一批国家重点风景名胜区。

1983 年上半年，南坪县人民政府筹划建立九寨沟管理局。9 月 8 日，四川省人民政府确定将九寨沟自然保护区管理所更名为“九寨沟自然保护区管理处”，对九寨沟的自然保护区和风景名胜区进行统一管理，九寨沟管理局筹备组和九寨沟自然保护区管理处开始走向合并办公。1984 年初，九寨沟风景名胜区管理局正式挂牌，与九寨沟自然保护区管理处合并办公。

2000 年 10 月，九寨沟国家级自然保护区管理局、九寨沟风景名胜区管理局升格为阿坝州人民政府直属正县级事业单位。2006 年 7 月 28 日，九寨沟世界遗产管理局成立。2011 年 5 月，九寨沟国家地质公园管理局获批成立；7 月，九寨沟国家 AAAAA 级旅游景区管理局成立，与九寨沟风景名胜区管理局合署办公，实行“五块牌子、一套班子”的管理体制 。至 2023 年，九寨沟管理局下设办公室、科研处、旅游营销处、护林防火与自然保护处、景区居民管理办公室等 23 个部门，编制 491 个。

除九寨沟管理局外，九寨沟区域还设立有综合管理机构——九寨沟国家级风景名胜区、国家级自然保护区管理委员会、漳扎镇人民政府，治安管理机构——九寨沟公安分局、武警阿坝州支队第七中队（现为武警阿坝支队九寨沟中队）、武警九寨沟森林中队（现为九寨沟县森林消防中队），经营机构——九寨沟旅游公司、九寨沟县联合经营有限责任公司等，形成与基层行政机构协调发展格局。

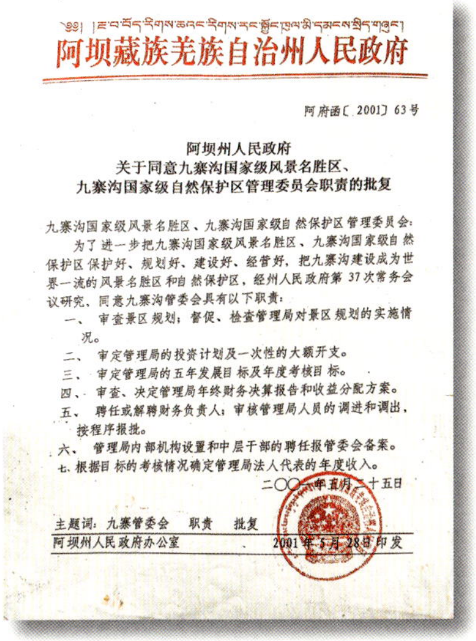

阿坝藏族羌族自治州人民政府

阿府函〔2001〕63号

阿坝州人民政府
关于同意九寨沟国家级风景名胜区、
九寨沟国家级自然保护区管理委员会职责的批复

九寨沟国家级风景名胜区、九寨沟国家级自然保护区管理委员会：

为了进一步把九寨沟国家级风景名胜区、九寨沟国家级自然保护区保护好、规划好、建设好、经营好，把九寨沟建设成为世界一流的风景名胜区和自然保护区，经州人民政府第37次常务会议研究，同意九寨沟管委会具有以下职责：

一、审查景区规划；督促、检查管理局对景区规划的实施情况。

二、审定管理局的投资计划及一次性的大额开支。

三、审定管理局的五年发展目标及年度考核目标。

四、审查、决定管理局年终财务决算报告和收益分配方案。

五、聘任或解聘财务负责人；审核管理局人员的调进和调出，按程序报批。

六、管理局内部机构设置和中层干部的聘任报管委会备案。

七、根据目标的考核情况确定管理局法人代表的年度收入。

二〇〇一年五月二十五日

主题词：九寨管委会　职责　批复

阿坝州人民政府办公室　2001年5月28日印发

《阿坝州人民政府关于同意九寨沟国家级风景名胜区、九寨沟国家级自然保护区管理委员会职责的批复》（2001年，九寨沟管理局 供图）

Reply from the People's Government of Aba Prefecture on approving of the responsibilities of Jiuzhaigou National Scenic and Historic Area and Jiuzhaigou National Nature Reserve Management Committee (photo by courtesy of Jiuzhaigou Management Bureau, 2001)

In January 1980, Jiuzhaigou Nature Reserve Management Office in Nanping County, Sichuan, was established. On November 8, 1982, Jiuzhaigou and Huanglong Temple were jointly included in the first batch of national key scenic spots.

In the first half of 1983, Nanping County People's Government planned to establish the Jiuzhaigou Management Bureau. On September 8, the People's Government of Sichuan Province decided to turn Jiuzhaigou Nature Reserve Management Bureau into Jiuzhaigou Nature Reserve Management Bureau for unified management of its natural protection and scenic spots. Early in 1984, the Bureau of Jiuzhaigou Scenic Area was established with Jiuzhaigou Nature Reserve Management Office merged in.

In October 2000, Management Bureau for Jiuzhaigou National Nature Reserve and Bureau for Jiuzhaigou Scenic Area were upgraded to county-level institutions directly under Aba Prefecture. On July 28, 2006, Management Bureau for Jiuzhaigou World Heritage was established. In May 2011, Management Bureau for Jiuzhaigou National Geological Park was established; in July, Management Bureau for Jiuzhaigou National AAAAA-level Tourist Scenic Spot was established, co-located with that for Jiuzhaigou Scenic Area, all these Management Bureaus function with one team of personnel. By 2023, there were 23 departments under Jiuzhaigou Management Bureau, including offices, scientific research department, tourism marketing department, forest fire prevention and natural protection department and scenic spot resident management office, with a staff of 491.

In addition, Jiuzhaigou has such comprehensive management organizations as Jiuzhaigou National Scenic and Historic Area, National Nature Reserve Management Committee, Zhangzha Town People's Government, public security management organization of Jiuzhaigou Public Security Bureau, Armed Police's Seventh Squadron of Aba Prefecture Detachment (now Jiuzhaigou Squadron of the Armed Police Aba Detachment) and Armed Police's Jiuzhaigou Forest Squadron (now Jiuzhaigou County Forest Fire Squadron), operating agencies such as Jiuzhaigou Tourism Company, Jiuzhaigou County Joint Operation Co., Ltd. in a coordinated development pattern with grassroots administrative agencies.

九寨沟智慧管理中心（2023 年，建措 摄）
Intelligence Management Center of Jiuzhaigou (photo by Jiancuo, 2023)

九寨沟国家级风景名胜区、国家级自然保护区管理委员会

1998 年 11 月 7 日，九寨沟国家级风景名胜区、国家级自然保护区管理委员会由阿坝州委、州政府牵头成立，以州、县领导为主要成员，简称“九寨沟管理委员会”或“九寨沟管委会”。2001 年起对九寨沟实施统一的宏观管理。

Management Committee of Jiuzhaigou National Scenic and Historic Area and National Nature Reserve

On November 7, 1998, it was established under the leadership of Aba Prefecture Party Committee and government, with prefecture and county leaders as the main members, referred to as “Jiuzhaigou Management Committee”. In 2001, unified macro-management began to be performed on Jiuzhaigou.

漳扎镇人民政府

1998 年 7 月，九寨沟镇更名为漳扎镇，成立漳扎镇人民政府。驻地在漳扎村，距九寨沟县城45000米，海拔2089米。除常设机构外，还设有综治维稳办、城市管理服务中心、村镇规划建设管理办、综合行政执法办等部分机构，管辖九寨沟旅游区内的各项事务。

Zhangzha Town People’s Government

In July 1998, Jiuzhaigou Town was renamed Zhangzha Town together with its People’s Government. It is located at Zhangzha Village, 45,000 meters away from Jiuzhaigou County, at 2,089 meters in altitude. In addition, there are also some institutions such as Comprehensive Management and Stability Maintenance Office, Urban Management Service Center, Village Planning and Construction Management Office and Integrated Administrative Law Enforcement Office in charge of various affairs within the tourist area.

公安干警和武警在景区上车点维护秩序（2005 年，九寨沟管理局 供图）
Public security police and armed police maintain order at the scenic spot boarding point (photo by courtesy of Jiuzhaigou Management Bureau, 2005)

治安管理机构

九寨沟相继组织成立一系列治安管理机构，包括九寨沟公安分局、武警阿坝州支队第七中队、武警九寨沟森林中队等，维护景区及景区周围社会治安，保障游客及国家财产安全以及为九寨沟保护管理及旅游发展创造良好社会环境。

Security Management Agency

Jiuzhaigou successively organized and established a series of public security management agencies, including its Public Security Bureau, Armed Police's Seventh Squadron of Aba Prefecture Detachment and Armed Police's Forest Squadron to maintain the public order in and around the scenic spot, ensure the safety of tourists and state property and create a good social environment for the protection, management and tourism development of Jiuzhaigou.

乐享出行
Enjoyable Tours

游人畅游孔雀河道（2019 年，梁峰 摄）

Tourists on the Peacock River (photo by Liang Feng, 2019)

1984 年 1 月，九寨沟正式对外开放，九寨沟管理局等机构陆续建设配套游览设施和基础工程，不断改善硬件设施质量，让游客在九寨沟安心畅游。

1985 年，通往九寨沟的道路包括低等级柏油路、土路和石子路 3 种，路况很差。1998 年以后，随着九环线公路建成和不断完善、九寨—黄龙机场通航，以及阿坝州通县柏油路、汶九路改造等工程顺利完成，围绕九寨沟的公路、航空、铁路交通体系正形成东西南北畅通、景区景点连接、安全舒适的交通骨架网。

九寨沟旅游开发中的服务设施建设，包括游览道路系统、游客服务场站、食宿设施和购物娱乐设施等方面。其中，游览道路系统由沟内主干公路、游览步行道、观光公交系统、停车场和休息亭、观景台、饮食服务站点、巡山房、公共卫生间等设施组成，并配有标志讲解系统；游客服务场站包括各景点游客服务站点、医疗服务站、诺日朗游客服务中心、九寨沟游人中心等；食宿设施和购物娱乐设施包括水上餐厅、九寨沟宾馆、边边街等。

九寨沟管理局坚持把信息化建设作为九寨沟保护、开发、管理的基础平台，不断优化基础设施，降低人为污染，推进智慧景区建设。

2001—2005 年，九寨沟管理局推进国家“十五”重点科技攻关项目“数字九寨沟”工程建设。2005 年 6 月，该项目通过国家验收，荣获 2006 年度四川省科技进步二等奖，并被作为“国家重点风景名胜区数字化景区”建设样板工程向全国 177 个景区推广，其技术体系构成中国景区数字化建设标准。2006—2009 年，九寨沟管理局巩固、完善“数字九寨沟”相关应用系统，从理论上探索、建设“数字九寨沟”二期工程，并在全国首次提出“智慧景区”概念。

“数字九寨沟”工程是中国第一个城市数字化示范应用工程，“数字九寨沟”体系的建立，让机器代替大部分人工，既方便游客又节约人力。

九寨沟景区第一家民营餐厅（1987 年，九寨沟管理局 供图）

The first private restaurant in Jiuzhaigou Scenic Area (photo by courtesy of Jiuzhaigou Management Bureau, 1987)

Since Jiuzhaigou officially opened to the outside world in January 1984, its Management Bureau and other institutions have successively improved necessary hardware facilities and infrastructure, so that tourists can play to their hearts' content.

In 1985, the roads leading to Jiuzhaigou included three types in poor conditions: low-grade asphalt, dirt and gravel. Since 1998, with the completion and continuous improvement of roads around Jiuzhaigou, the opening of Jiuzhai-Huanglong Airport and completion of projects such as the asphalt road to Aba Prefecture and renovation of Wenchuan-Jiuzhaigou Highway, there has formed a safe and comfortable traffic skeleton network of east-west and north-south highway, aviation and railway transportation system around the Scenic Spots.

The construction of service facilities in its tourism development includes the tour road system, tourist service stations, board and lodging, shopping and entertainment facilities, of which the sightseeing road system is composed of trunk roads in the valley, sightseeing walking trails, sightseeing bus system, parking lots and rest pavilions, observation decks, catering service stations, mountain patrol rooms, toilets and sign interpretation systems; tourist service centers include medical service stations, Nuorilang Tourist Service Center and Jiuzhaigou Tourist Center; food and accommodation facilities, shopping and entertainment facilities include floating restaurants, Jiuzhaigou Hotel and roadside eateries.

The Management Bureau insists on using IT-application construction as the basic platform for Jiuzhaigou's protection, development and management, continuously optimizes infrastructure, reduces man-made pollution and promotes the construction of smart scenic spots.

From 2001 to 2005, the Management Bureau furthered the construction of "Digital Jiuzhaigou", part of the national Key Technology Research and Development Program of China during the "the 10th Five-Year Plan". In June 2005, the project passed the national inspection and won the second prize of 2006 Sichuan Science and Technology Progress Award and was promoted to 177 scenic spots across the country as a model in the construction of "National Key Scenic Area Digital Scenic Area". Its technical system constitutes the digitalization of Chinese scenic spots construction standards. From 2006 to 2009, Jiuzhaigou Management Bureau consolidated and perfected its relevant application system of "Digital Jiuzhaigou", explored and constructed the second-phase "Digital Jiuzhaigou" in theory and put forward the concept of "Smart Scenic Area" for the first time in the country.

The "Digital Jiuzhaigou" Project is China's first urban digital demonstration application project and the establishment of its digital system makes it possible for equipment to do most of human work, which makes it convenient for tourists and saves manpower.

九寨—黄龙机场

简称“九黄机场”，位于四川省阿坝藏族羌族自治州松潘县川主寺镇东北 12000 米处，海拔 3447 米，距九寨沟沟口 88000 米。2002 年 3 月 11 日正式全面开工建设，2003 年 9 月 28 日正式通航。九黄机场通航前，游客从成都到九寨沟景区需要历经 10 个多小时的地面交通。通航后，时间缩短为 35 分钟的空中航程和 90 分钟的地面旅程。

Jiuzhai-Huanglong Airport

Short as Jiu Huang Airport, it is located at an altitude of 3,447 meters, 12,000 meters northeast of Chuanzhusi Town of Songpan County, Aba Zang and Qiang Autonomous Prefecture and about 88,000 meters from the entrance to Jiuzhaigou. On March 11, 2002, its full construction started and on September 28, 2003, it was opened to navigation. Before the Jiu Huang Airport came into use, it would take tourists over 10 hours by bus from Chengdu to the scenic spot. And now it is 35 minutes by air and 90 minutes aground away.

九环线

九寨沟旅游环线的简称，是以九寨沟景区和成都市为轴线两端，由进出九寨沟的南线（西半环）与东线南路（东半环）构成的环状旅游交通干道。以成都为起点，九寨沟景区为终点，全长 913 千米。

Jiuzhaigou Tourist Ring Road

A ring-shaped trunk road for tourist traffic in Jiuzhaigou, it is composed of the south route (west half) entering and leaving Jiuzhaigou and the south road of the east route (east half) with the scenic area and Chengdu as the two ends of the axis, which starts from Chengdu and ends at Jiuzhaigou scenic area, running a total length of 913 kilometers.

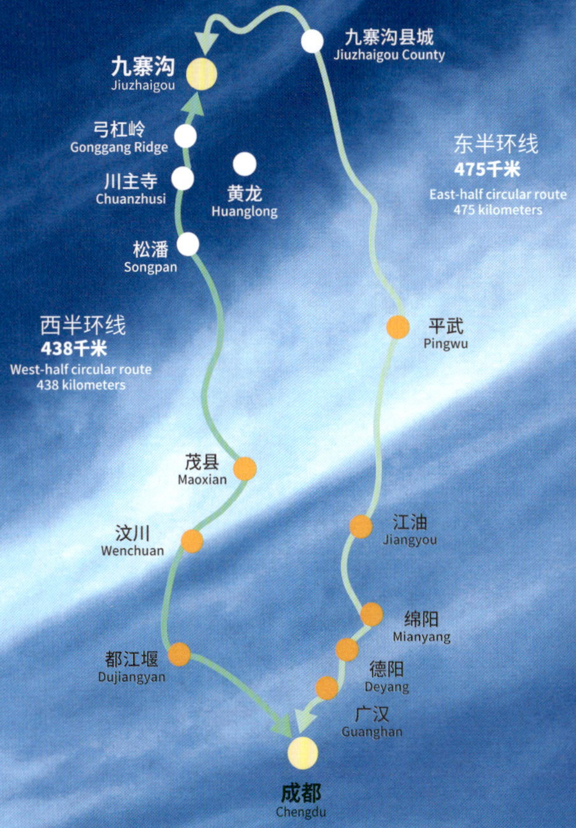

九环线示意图（2023 年，云何视觉 制图）
Diagram of the Jiuzhaigou tourist ring road (by Yunhe Vision, 2023)

九寨—黄龙机场与蓝天交相辉映（2023 年，四川九寨黄龙机场有限责任公司 供图）
Jiuzhai-Huanglong Airport under the blue sky (photo by courtesy of Sichuan Jiuzhai-Huang long Airport Co.,Ltd, 2023)

景区道路改造和修复重建

2003 年 6 月 20 日至 2004 年 4 月 20 日，九寨沟管理局先后投入 1 亿多元，按照山岭重丘二级公路一级路面标准改造完成景区公路 38140 米，路面加宽至 8.5～9 米。"8•8" 九寨沟地震后，景区部分道路出现坍塌，路基下沉、路面破损。为此，景区斥巨资实施道路及配套设施恢复重建项目。项目分 3 期进行，2021 年 8 月 30 日，三期工程（五花海至原始森林道路）实现 "初通"。

Scenic Road Improvement

From June 20, 2003 to April 20, 2004, the Jiuzhaigou Management Bureau invested over 100 million yuan in the reconstructions of the scenic roads of 38,140 meters as required of the first-class road surface of the second-class road within mountains and heavy hills, with a width of 8.5~9 meters. Part of the road (surface) collapsed and sank in the scenic area due to the "8·8" Earthquake, the restoration and reconstruction of which took huge sums of money in addition to its supporting facilities. The whole project was divided into three phases. On August 30, 2021, the third phase (from the Wuhua Lake to the Virgin Forest) got "preliminarily completed".

1 | 2
3

1 1982 年的牦牛运输队（牟航远 摄，牟薇 供图）
2 公路整治（2003 年，九寨沟管理局 供图）
3 日则公路（2011 年，周正强 摄）
1 Yak transport team in 1982 (photo by Mou Hangyuan, by courtesy of Mou Wei)
2 Road improvement (photo by courtesy of Jiuzhaigou Management Bureau, 2003)
3 Rize Highway (photo by Zhou Zhengqiang, 2011)

犀牛海栈道（2019 年，梁峰 摄）
Plank road on Rhinoceros Lake (photo by Liang Feng, 2019)

生态栈道

自 1985 年开始，九寨沟管理局先后在景区各景点修建并完善约 70 千米的生态栈道。“8・8”地震后，景区对生态栈道进行改造升级。升级后，每个景点都修建有融入现代木结构工艺和藏文化元素的休息亭和观景平台，可供游客休憩、观赏、拍摄美景。

Ecological Plank Road

Since 1985, the Jiuzhaigou Management Bureau has built and improved about 70 kilometers of ecological planks in various scenic spots. After the “8·8” Earthquake, they have been received renovation and upgrading. Each scenic spot has a rest pavilion and platforms incorporated wtih modern wooden structure techniques and Zang cultural elements. Those provide a good place to rest, to enjoy the beautiful scenery and to take photos of it.

诺日朗服务中心景区居民旅游商品售卖区（2005 年，泽仁珠 供图）
Residents tourist commodities sales area at Nuorilang Service Center (photo by courtesy of Zeren Zhu, 2015)

九寨沟诺日朗旅游服务中心

中心集旅游管理、投诉、救护、治安、消防、游客休息、购物、娱乐和餐饮于一体，占地面积 3.6 万平方米，建筑面积 12 万平方米，包括办公区、餐饮区、休息区、医务点、派出所及商品售卖区等。医务点配备医生和护士各 1 名，提供简单的吸氧、药品售卖等服务。

Jiuzhaigou Nuorilang Tourist Service Center

Integrating tourism management, complaint handling, rescue, security, fire protection, tourist rest, shopping, entertainment and catering, it covers an area of 36,000 square meters and a building area of 120,000 square meters, including office, dining, rest areas, medical services, police and commodity sales. There is a doctor and a nurse in each medical point, where simple oxygen inhalation, medicine and the like are provided.

九寨沟诺日朗旅游服务中心 (2011 年，阿冬 摄)
Nourilang Tourist Service Center of Jiuzhaigou (photo by A Dong, 2011)

1

2

1　空间信息管理子平台（2022 年，九寨沟管理局 供图）

2　智慧管理中心（2021 年，九寨沟管理局 供图）

1　Sub-platform of Spatial Information Management Platform (photo by courtesy of Jiuzhaigou Management Bureau, 2022)

2　Smart Management Center (photo by courtesy of Jiuzhaigou Management Bureau, 2022)

“数字九寨沟”体系

该体系包括基础平台层和应用系统层两个部分。基础平台层是九寨沟信息化建设基础，包括数据中心、通信系统、中心机房、电力系统；应用系统层包括办公自动化系统、门禁票务系统、网上游系统、景区 CRM、GIS 地理信息系统、多媒体展示系统、GPS 车辆调度系统、智能化监控系统、环境监测系统、规划管理系统、LED 信息发布系统、九寨沟旅游电子商务系统。

“Digital Jiuzhaigou” system

It includes two parts: basic platform and application system, the former being the foundation for its building of IT-application, including data centers, communication systems, central computer rooms and power systems. The latter includes office automation system, access control ticketing system, online travel system, scenic spot CRM, GIS geographic information system, multimedia display system, GPS vehicle dispatching system, intelligent monitoring system, environmental monitoring system, planning management system, LED information release system and Jiuzhaigou tourism e-commerce system.

文明九寨

Progressive Jiuzhaigou

在诺日朗中心站等待载客的环保观光车（2008 年，苏杰 摄）

Eco-friendly sightseeing buses waiting for passengers at Nuorilang Central Station (photo by Su Jie, 2008)

多年来，九寨沟管理局遵循“严格保护、统一管理、合理开发、永续利用”的基本原则，大力开展基础建设。

九寨沟管理局制定了一系列管理制度和详细措施，改善景区环境，规范景区内工作人员和游客活动，实现生态保护与旅游观光平衡发展。

九寨沟自然保护区设立后，当地能源结构向清洁化方向迅速发展。1998 年，九寨沟管理局投入资金 15 万元，为景区内 204 户居民安装液化石油气炉，使沟内居民生活基本实现“以气代柴”。2003 年 12 月 8 日，九寨沟景区农网全线正式带电负载试运行，沟内全面通电，居民生活全面实现“以电代柴”。

此外，九寨沟管理局还将目光投向各类新能源的开发和利用，于 2005 年开始推广可再生清洁能源的开发和利用技术。2006 年 9 月，九寨沟管理局在沟口生态广场和办公区安装太阳能、风能照明供电系统。2007 年 6 月，在箭竹海和五彩池的 2 座环保厕所安装太阳能供电系统，在环保厕所旁安装太阳能采集板，将太阳能转换成电能，标志着九寨沟在全国景区中率先在环保厕所使用绿色能源——太阳能。

九寨沟管理局采取诸多措施对传统旱厕污染物、生活污水等进行有效处理，有效控制景区内污染物排放；实施排污工程，安装排污管线，实现雨污分流；修建污水池，集中处理污水、废水；修建垃圾处理厂、中转站，实现垃圾动态清理；开展“旅游厕所革命”，实现从传统旱厕到智能环保生态厕所的转变等。

2001 年 5 月 1 日，九寨沟管理局开始实施“沟内游，沟外住”政策，整治景区内的旅游经营环境；两个月后，又率先在全国景区中实施“限量旅游”，严格控制每天进沟的人数。

《九寨沟》邮票——1998 年，中华人民共和国原邮电部发行的分别展现九寨沟“芳草海”“五花海”“树正瀑布”“诺日朗瀑布”自然景观的全套 4 枚特种邮票（薛康 供图）

Over the years, Jiuzhaigou Management Bureau has followed the basic principle of "strict protection, unified management, rational development and sustainable utilization" and vigorously carried out basic construction.

It has formulated a series of management systems and detailed measures to improve the environment of its scenic spots and to regulate the activities of staff and tourists, which has achieved a balanced development of ecological protection and tourism.

Since Jiuzhaigou Nature Reserve was established, the local energy structure has been developing rapidly towards cleanliness. In 1998, the Management Bureau spent 150,000 yuan to install liquefied petroleum gas furnaces for 204 local households, hence the basic realization of "gas in place of firewood". On December 8, 2003, all the rural power grid within the scenic area was put into trial operation with live loads and the local daily life fully realized "electricity in place of firewood".

In addition, the Management Bureau has aimed at the development and application of various new energy sources and in 2005 began to promote the development and utilization of renewable clean energy techniques. In September 2006, solar and wind energy supply systems for lightning were installed at the Entrance Ecological Square and the office area. In June 2017, solar energy power supply systems were installed in two eco-friendly toilets at the Arrow Bamboo Lake and the Wucai Pool, including some solar energy collection panels to covert solar energy to electricity. Those have made Jiuzhaigou the first across the country to use green energy in toilets in scenic spots.

It has taken many measures to effectively treat pollutants in traditional dry toilets and domestic sewage, to effectively control their discharge in the scenic area; implemented sewage projects, installed sewage pipelines and realized the diversion of rain and sewage; built sewage pools for central treatment of sewage and waste water; built garbage treatment plants and transfer stations for dynamic garbage cleaning; carried out the "Tourist Toilet Revolution" for the realization of intelligent and ecological toilets from traditional dry ones.

On May 1, 2001, it began to implement the policy of "touring in but lodging outside the valley" in the scenic area to rectify the tourism management environment in the scenic spot; two months later, it took the lead in implementing "limited tourism" required of scenic spots in China by strictly controlling the number of tourists every day.

Jiuzhaigou stamps – In 1998, the former Ministry of Posts and Telecommunications issued a set of 4 special stamps showing the natural landscape of Jiuzhaigou's "Fragrant Grass Lake", "Wuhua Lake", "Shuzheng Waterfall" and "Nuorilang Waterfall" (photo by courtesy of Xue Kang)

首批“全国低碳旅游示范区”

2012 年 9 月 16 日，全国低碳旅游发展大会暨全国低碳旅游示范区授牌仪式在北京举行，九寨沟等 19 家景区被中华环保联合会和中国旅游景区协会等单位评为首批“全国低碳旅游示范区”。

太阳能、风能照明供电系统

一种能够将光能和风能直接转换为电能，进行照明供电的系统。太阳能和风能属于可再生能源，有阳光和风就能产生电流，且使用方便安全，没有噪声和污染，九寨沟引进太阳能、风能照明供电系统，能够满足景区照明用电需求、改善景区的生态环境。

First Batch of “National Low-Carbon Tourism Demonstration Area”

On September 16, 2012, at the National Low-Carbon Tourism Development Conference and National Low-Carbon Tourism Demonstration Area Awarding Ceremony held in Beijing, Jiuzhaigou and other 19 scenic spots were rated as the first “National Low-Carbon Tourism Demonstration Area” by China Environmental Protection Federation and China Tourism Scenic Area Association.

Solar and Wind Powered Lighting System

A system that can directly convert solar and wind energy into electrical energy for lighting power supply. Solar and wind energy, renewable energy sources without noise and pollution, can generate electricity when there is sunlight and wind and is therefore convenient and safe for use. Jiuzhaigou has its supply system introduced to meet the lighting needs of scenic spots while improving the ecological environment.

1 | 2 / 3

1 2012 年 9 月 16 日，九寨沟景区被评为首批“全国低碳旅游示范区”（李淑琴 摄）

2 2018 年低碳日活动：扎如徒步环保活动（肖维阳 摄）

3 风能太阳能路灯（2011 年，九寨沟管理局 供图）

1 Jiuzhaigou Scenic Area included in the first batch of “National Low-Carbon Tourism Demonstration Area” on September 16, 2012 (photo by Li Shuqin)

2 Low-Carbon Day activity in 2018: Eco-friendly hiking at Zharu (photo by Xiao Weiyang)

3 A wind and solar powered street lamp (photo by courtesy of Jiuzhaigou Management Bureau, 2011)

新能源电动观光大巴

2021 年 11 月，九寨沟景区为实现绿色交通和生态旅游的有机融合，助推九寨沟全域绿色发展，引进 80 辆纯电动观光大巴。创造了“全国山岳型景区第一个率先规模化批量应用电动观光车”“全国第一个采取纯市场化手段购置应用纯电动观光车”两个第一。

旅游厕所革命

九寨沟管理局率先在九寨沟景区大规模引入“绿色生态旅游厕所”，并在 2001 年 10 月前拆除景区内所有的旱厕，一年内在长海、镜海等游人较密集的地方修建智能型全自动免水冲环保型生态厕所。2017 年，阿坝州在九寨沟景区召开“旅游厕所革命”现场会，推广九寨沟景区旅游厕所建设、管理、维护经验。“8・8”九寨沟地震灾后恢复重建中，九寨沟建成具有环保优先、技术领先、人性化升级、节能减排、智慧化管理 5 大亮点的 49 座真空环保智慧厕所，成为中国第一个大规模运用真空负压卫生间系统的景区。

New Energy Electric Sightseeing Bus

In November 2021, in order to realize the organic integration of green transportation and eco-tourism and promote the green development of Jiuzhaigou as a whole, the scenic area introduced 80 pure electric sightseeing buses, creating such two firsts across the country: large-scale application of electric sightseeing buses in mountain-type scenic spots and purchase and use of a pure electric sightseeing car by purely market-oriented means.

Tourist Toilet Revolution

The Management Bureau had taken the lead in introducing “green eco-tourism toilets” on a large scale in its scenic area. In place of all dry toilets before October 2001, intelligent and fully automatic toilets were built in places with dense tourists such as Long Lake and Mirror Lake within one year. In 2017, Aba Prefecture held an on-site meeting of “Tourist Toilet Revolution” in the scenic area to promote its construction, management and maintenance experience of tourist toilets. During the recovery and reconstruction upon the “8·8” Earthquake, Jiuzhaigou built 49 eco-friendly and smart vaccum toilets with 5 highlights, including the priority of environmental protection, leading technology, humanized upgrading, energy saving, emission reduction, and intelligent management. Thus it made Jiuzhaigou the first of large-scale user of vaccum tiolets.

1 | 2

1　在景区内停放整齐、统一的绿色观光车（2009 年，九寨沟管理局 供图）
2　九寨沟真空环保智慧厕所（2020 年，泽柏 摄）
1　Green sightseeing buses parked orderly and unified in the scenic area (photo by courtesy of Jiuzhaigou Management Bureau, 2009)
2　Eco-friendly and smart vaccum toilets in Jiuzhaigou (photo by Zebo, 2020)

大美九寨（2022 年，桑吉 摄）

宣传影响
Publicity and Influence

Beautiful Jiuzhaigou (photo by Sangji, 2022)

自 1984 年对外开放以来，九寨沟始终坚持以国内市场为基础，以国际市场为先导，探索并创造出九寨沟景区高质量发展典范。

九寨沟始终坚持以文塑旅、以旅彰文，持续推进文化和旅游深度融合发展。利用本地藏文化资源优势，当代文学艺术工作者创作出歌曲、舞台剧、书画、工艺美术、诗歌、散文、小说等多种以九寨沟为题材的作品，先后编著出版《九寨沟景区历史文化考察研究报告》等 10 余部民族文化书籍，拍摄《历史记忆・和谐家园》《人类的记忆・中国的世界遗产》《中国的奉献》等数十部纪录片，制作《中国・九寨沟》等 30 余册大型摄影画册，塑造“中国九寨沟国际冰瀑旅游节”节庆文化品牌，培育以容中尔甲为代表的优秀文艺人才，打造以“九寨千古情”为代表的景区品牌演出，带动地方文化产业的长足发展。

九寨沟联袂峨眉山、黄龙、都江堰、青城山等景区成立“黄金旅游走廊”联盟，不仅大大增强自身实力，还有力地带动了区域经济的快速发展，实现区域间的协同、辐射带动。

九寨沟旅游宣传从传统走向网络，再到传统宣传与网络宣传相结合，逐步提质升级。宣传的主动性、科学性、针对性、引导性和有效性明显增强，九寨沟品牌影响力持续扩大，旅客忠诚度持久延续，铸造享誉世界的旅游品牌。

Since China's opening up to the outside world in 1984, Jiuzhaigou has always adhered to the domestic market as the basis and the international one as the guide, exploring and creating a model of high-quality development of its scenic spots.

It has always insisted on shaping tourism with culture and highlighting culture with tourism and constantly promoted the in-depth integration of culture and tourism. Taking advantage of local Zang cultural resources, contemporary literary and artistic workers have created songs, stage plays, calligraphy and paintings, arts and crafts, poems, essays, novels and other literary and artistic works on the theme of Jiuzhaigou, it has edited and published over 10 national cultural books such as *A Research Report on the Historical and Cultural Investigation of Jiuzhaigou Scenic Area* and shot dozens of documentaries like *Historical Memory · Harmonious Homeland*, *Human Memory · China's World Heritage* and *China's Dedication*, produced more than 30 large-scale photo albums such as *Jiuzhaigou · China*, created the cultural brand of "China Jiuzhaigou International Icefall Tourism Festival", cultivated outstanding literary and artistic talent represented by Rongzhong Erjia and created some scenic spot brand performances represented by "Eternal Love for Jiuzhaigou", which have fueled the rapid development of the local cultural industry.

Jiuzhaigou has formed Golden Tourist Corridor Alliance with Emei Mountain, Huanglong, Dujiangyan, Qingcheng Mountain and other scenic spots, which greatly enhances its own strength and strongly promotes the rapid development of the regional economy, realizing inter-regional coordination and radiation.

Jiuzhaigou's tourism publicity has gradually upgraded its quality from traditional means to online and then to their combination. The initiative, scientificity, pertinence, guidance and effectiveness of publicity have been significantly enhanced, the influence of Jiuzhaigou brand continued to expand and the tourist loyalty continued for long, casting a world-renowned tourism brand power.

1	3
2	4
	5
	6

1　2004 年 11 月 17 日至 25 日，九寨沟管理局在泰国参加世界自然保护联盟（IUCN）第三届世界自然保护大会（九寨沟管理局 供图）

2　2011 年，九寨沟景区在韩国宣传交流（九寨沟管理局 供图）

3　2023 年 6 月，《人民日报》（海外版）报道九寨沟（九寨沟管理局 供图）

4　1985 年，《美国国家地理》报道九寨沟（张奕 供图）

5　2023 年 6 月，法国电视二台报道九寨沟（九寨沟管理局 供图）

6　“中阿之窗”脸书账号报道九寨沟（2023 年，九寨沟管理局 供图）

1　From November 17 to 25, 2004, Jiuzhaigou Management Bureau participated in the 3rd World Conservation Congress of the International Union for Conservation of Nature (IUCN) in Thailand (photo by Jiuzhaigou Management Bureau)

2　In 2011, Jiuzhaigou Scenic Area attended a promotion meeting in the Republic of Korea (photo by Jiuzhaigou Management Bureau)

3　In June 2023, *People's Daily* (Overseas Edition) reported on Jiuzhaigou (photo by Jiuzhaigou Management Bureau)

4　In 1985, *National Geographic* covered Jiuzhaigou (photo by Zhang Yi)

5　In June 2023, French TV Station 2 reported on Jiuzhaigou (photo by Jiuzhaigou Management Bureau)

6　“Window on China-Arabia” Facebook account reports on Jiuzhaigou (photo by Jiuzhaigou Management Bureau, 2023)

蜀绣《九寨风光》，178cm×101.5cm（2023 年，孟德芝 作品）
Jiuzhai Scenery, Shu embroidery, 178cm×101.5cm (by Meng Dezhi, 2023)

与九寨沟相关的文化普及作品

有关九寨沟的文化普及作品不胜枚举。早在 1983 年，电影《自古英雄出少年》就在九寨沟拍摄大量外景，使全国观众领略到九寨沟的秀丽景色。多年来，大量电影、广播、图书刊物、公益广告、纪录片等文化作品问世，如九寨沟管理局创办的《九寨沟之声》栏目、央视《祖国美・九寨沟》宣传片、2021 年上线腾讯视频・纪录片频道的《九寨沟》等。这些文化作品既是树立九寨沟形象的窗口，也是传播知识、培养人才、发展文化的重要载体。

Cultural Popularization Works Concerning Jiuzhaigou

Jiuzhaigou abounds in such works. Back to 1983, the movie of *Young Heroes* got lots of exterior scenes here, greatly impressing audiences across the country. Over the years, cultural works such as films, broadcasts, books and periodicals, public service advertisements and documentaries have been published, for example, *The Voice of Jiuzhaigou* by Jiuzhaigou Management Bureau, promotional film of *The Beautiful Motherland–Jiuzhaigou* by CCTV and *Jiuzhaigou* by Tencent Video Documentary Channel in 2021, are not only a window on the image of Jiuzhaigou, but also an important carrier for disseminating knowledge, cultivating talents and developing culture.

表 8　介绍九寨沟的书籍（部分）
Table 8 Books Introducing Jiuzhaigou (Partial)

书名 Name	作者 Author(s)	出版社 Publisher	出版时间 Year of Publication
九寨沟的神话与传说 *Myths and Legends on Jiuzhaigou*	马铁水 Ma Tieshui	四川人民出版社 Sichuan People's Publishing House	1986
九寨风景线 *Jiuzhai Scenic Line*	曾朝莹 Zeng Chaoying	中国旅游出版社 China Travel & Tourism Press	1988
九寨奇趣 *Anecdotes on Jiuzhai*	张善云 Zhang Shanyun	四川民族出版社 Sichuan Ethnic Publishing House	1988
九寨旅游指南 *Travel Guide to Jiuzhaigou*			1989
九寨沟自然交响曲 *Nature Symphony on Jiuzhaigou*	张善云、泽仁珠、章小平 Zhang Shanyun, Zeren Zhu, Zhang Xiaoping	科学普及出版社 Popular Science Press	1994
中国旅游指南九寨沟 *Chinese Tourism Guide: Jiuzhaigou*	《中国旅游指南》编委会 Editorial Board of *China TourismTravel Guide*	中华书局 Zhonghua Book Company	2000
果壳里的村寨 *Village in a Nutshell*	曾珍 Zeng Zhen	重庆出版社 Chongqing Publishing House	2006
梦幻四季九寨沟 *Dream–Like Jiuzhaigou in Four Seasons*	章小平 Zhang Xiaoping	四川民族出版社 Sichuan Ethnic Publishing House	2009
九寨沟·四川经典之旅 *Jiuzhaigou·Classic Tour in Sichuan*	墨刻编辑部 Mook Editorial Office	人民邮电出版社 Postsl & Telecom Press	2010
九寨沟的故事 *The Story of Jiuzhaigou*	邓一 Deng Yi	中国林业出版社 China Forestry Publishing House	2014
九寨沟自然保护区常见藻类图集 *Atlas of Algae in Jiuzhaigou Nature Reserve*	王全喜，邓贵平 Wang Quanxi, Deng Guiping	科学出版社 Science Press	2017
九寨沟湖泊生态环境保护与旅游可持续发展研究 *Research on Ecological Environment Protection and Tourism Sustainable Development of Lakes in Jiuzhaigou*	高丽楠 Gao Linan	四川大学出版社 Sichuan University Press	2021
九寨沟震区民族特色村寨灾后重建与常态保护的法律机制研究 *Research on the Legal Mechanism for the Post-quake Reconstruction and Normalized Protection of the Ethnic Villages in Jiuzhaigou's Quake-hit Areas*	杨鹍飞 Yang Kunfei	知识产权出版社 Intellectual Property Publishing House	2021

九寨沟相关文化作品（2022 年，云何视觉 制图）
Cultural works related to Jiuzhaigou (by Yunhe Vision, 2022)

表 9　介绍九寨沟的画册（部分）
Table 9 Albums Introducing Jiuzhaigou (Partial)

书名 Title	作者 Author/Photogragraher	出版社 Published by	出版时间 Year of Publication
神话世界九寨沟 *Jiuzhaigou–A Fairy land in China*	代安常撰文；毕凤洲等摄影 Writing/Dai Anchang; Shooting/Bi Fengzhou, etc.	四川人民出版社 Sichuan People's Publishing House	1983
九寨沟 *Jiuzhaigou*	邓一编文；谢新发等摄影 Writing/Deng Yi; Shooting/Xie Xinfa, etc	上海人民美术出版社 Shanghai People's Fine Art Publishing House	1985
中国自然保护区：九寨沟 *Jiuzhaigou–China's Nature Reserve*	林业部宣传司 Publicity Department, Ministry of Forestry	中国林业出版社 China Forestry Publishing House	1986
九寨沟 *Jiuzhaigou*	牟航远 Mou Hangyuan	四川美术出版社 Sichuan Fine Arts Publishing House	1993
中国九寨沟：世界自然遗产 *China's Jiuzhaigou: World Natural Heritage Site*	九寨沟管理局，中国旅游出版社 Jiuzhaigou Management Bureau & China Travel & Tourism Press	中国旅游出版社 China Travel & Tourism Press	1994
九寨沟·黄龙四季精粹 *Cream of Jiuzhaigou and Huanglong in Four Seasons*	于宁撰文、摄影 Writing and Shooting/Yu Ning		2002
中国神仙池：嫩恩桑措 *Nenen Sangcuo–Immortal Pond, China*	章小平主编；于宁摄影；九寨沟有限责任公司编辑 Editor-in-Chief: Zhang Xiaoping; Photo by Yu Ning; Compiled by Jiuzhaigou Co., Ltd.		2003
九寨沟·黄龙 *Jiuzhaigou–Huanglong*	王达军摄影 Photo by Wang Dajun		2007

表 10　展现九寨沟的影视作品（部分）

Table 10 Films and Televisions on Jiuzhaigou (Partial)

片名 Title	拍摄单位 Shot by	拍摄时间 Year of Shooting
风光宝石九寨沟 *Scenic Gem–Jiuzhaigou*	峨眉电影制片厂 Emei Film Studio	1982
九寨秀色 *Beautiful Jiuzhaigou*	中央电视台 CCTV	1983
九寨沟风光 *Scenic Jiuzhaigou*	峨眉电影制片厂 Emei Film Studio	1984
奇山秀水话九寨 *Unique Landscape in Jiuzhaigou*	中国科学院成都地理研究所 Chengdu Institute of Geography, Chinese Academy of Sciences	1987
九寨沟风情 *Fascinating Jiuzhaigou*	四川电视台、长龙影视联合公司 Sichuan TV & Changlong Film and Television United Company	1990
航拍中国 *Aerial Photography Over China*	中央广播电视总台央视纪录频道出品； 央视纪录国际传媒有限公司承制 Produced by CCTV Documentary Channel Undertaken by CCTV Documentary International Media Limited	2019

1 | 2

1　1999 年，由四川电视台、四川九寨沟国家级自然保护区管理处、九寨沟风景名胜管理局联合摄制的纪录片《中国的奉献：九寨沟发掘与保护史》（云何视觉 制图）

1　*China's Dedication: Exploration and Protection History of Jiuzhaigou, a documentary shot* in 1999 jointly by Sichuan TV Station, Sichuan Jiuzhaigou National-level Nature Reserve Management Office, and the Management Bureau of Jiuzhaigou Scenic and Historic Area (by Yunhe Vision, 2022)

2　蜀绣《秋韵》，60cm×60cm（2003 年，尹莉萍 作品）

2　*Autumnal Charm*, Shu embroidery, 60cm×60cm (by Yin Liping, 2003)

表 11 赞美九寨沟的歌曲（部分）
Table 11 Songs on Jiuzhaigou (Partial)

歌名 Song name	歌手 Singer	专辑 Album	发行时间 Year of Issue
神奇的九寨 *Magical Jiuzhaigou*	容中尔甲 Rongzhong Erjia	九寨沟之歌 *The Song of Jiuzhaigou*	1999
永远的九寨 *Perpetual Jiuzhaigou*			
九寨情缘 *Love in Jiuzhaigou*			
九寨沟的春天 *Spring in Jiuzhaigou*	卓依婷 Zhuoyi Ting	恭喜发财 *Wish You Prosperity*	2007
我的九寨 *My Jiuzhai*	泽尔丹 Zerdan	今生相爱·我的九寨 *Love in This Life–My Jiuzhai*	2009
九寨欢迎你 *Welcome to Jiuzhai*			
九寨姑娘 *Girls from Jiuzhai*	阿勇泽让 Ayong Zerang	不沉的红 *Unsinkable Red*	2012
九寨蓝 *Jiuzhai Blue*	格格 Gege	九寨蓝 *Jiuzhai Blue*	2019

镶嵌漆画《九寨磨坊》38cm×38cm（2014 年，司徒华 绘）

Jiuzhai Mill, mosaic lacquer painting, 90cm×90cm (photo by Situ Hua, 2014)

剪纸《九寨沟》54cm×82cm（2023 年，袁稚 作品）

Jiuzhaigou, paper-cut, 54cm×82cm (by Yuan Zhi, 2023)

1　第三届中国四川阿坝国际熊猫节（2006 年，王庆九 摄）

2　1999 年，受四川省人民政府委托，由四川省人民政府机关事务管理局负责组织制作的庆祝澳门回归四川省赠送礼品《九寨沟大熊猫图》双面绣（来源于《四川省人民政府机关事务管理局大事记（1972—2001）》）

1　The 3rd Aba International Panda Festival, Sichuan, China (photo by Wang Qingjiu, 2006)

2　Double-sided embroidery of *Giant Pandas of Jiuzhaigou*, Sichuan's gift for Macao's return to China in 1999 (from *the Memorabilia of the Sichuan Provincial People's Government Offices Administration, 1972~2001)*

中国（四川）国际熊猫节

集旅游观光、招商引资、学术研讨、艺术展示等于一体的旅游节庆活动，为期 6 天。首届活动于 2002 年 9 月 3 日在九寨沟游人中心广场开幕，至 2006 年已在九寨沟举办三届。节日期间，举办扎如沟大型开幕式、旅游摄影作品展、大熊猫生态保护专题研讨会、阿坝州国际旅游营销推介会等活动。

International Panda Festival, Sichuan, China

A 6-day tourism festival integrating tourism, investment promotion, academic seminars and art exhibitions. Its first event opened on September 3, 2002 at Jiuzhaigou Tourist Center Square. During the festival, a large-scale opening ceremony in the Zharu Gully, tourism photography exhibition, symposium on ecological protection of giant pandas and international tourism marketing promotion in Aba Prefecture were held. By 2006, the event had been held for three times in Jiuzhaigou.

中国（四川）南国冰雪节

该节由四川省人民政府主办，四川省旅游局、成都市人民政府及相关市（州）承办，是四川旅游实现跨越式发展的一个新尝试。首届活动于 2001 年 1 月 6 日在四川成都西岭雪山拉开序幕，九寨沟、峨眉山、海螺沟、龙池、卧龙大熊猫自然保护区、瓦屋山国家森林公园六地设立冰雪节分会场，九寨沟景区以“冬天里的童话——冬游九寨”为主题开展系列活动，至 2006 年已举办六届。

South China (Sichuan) Ice and Snow Festival

Sponsored by the People's Government of Sichuan Province, undertaken by Tourism Bureau of Sichuan Province, Chengdu Municipal the South China (Sichuan) Ice and Snow Festival is a new attempt to achieve leapfrog development in Sichuan tourism. The first event kicked off on January 6, 2001 in Xiling Snow Mountain, Chengdu. Six sub-venues were set up in Jiuzhaigou, Emei Mountain, Hailuo Valley, Longchi, Wolong Giant Panda Nature Reserve and Wawu Mountain National Forest Park. Jiuzhaigou Scenic Area carried out a series of activities with the theme of "Fairy Tales in Winter–Tour of Jiuzhaigou in Winter". By 2006, the event had been held for six times.

中国九寨沟国际冰瀑旅游节

2004 年 1 月 9 日，中国（四川）第四届南国冰雪节暨首届阿坝大九寨冰瀑旅游节（主会场）开幕式在九寨沟珍珠滩瀑布举办。此后改名为中国九寨沟国际冰瀑旅游节，每年举行一次，至 2023 年已举办十八届，是九寨沟冬天最盛大的节日，为平衡游客淡旺季分布起到重要作用。

China Jiuzhaigou International Icefall Tourism Festival

On January 9, 2004, the opening ceremony of the 4th Southern China Ice and Snow Festival and the 1st Aba Great Jiuzhai Icefall Tourism Festival (main venue) was held at Pearl shoal Waterfall in Jiuzhaigou. After that, it was renamed China Jiuzhaigou International Icefall Tourism Festival, the grandest winter event here, to be held on a yearly basis, playing an important role in balancing the distribution of tourists during peak and low seasons. By 2023, the event has been held for eighteen times.

九寨沟民俗风情月

2005 年 4 月 20 日至 5 月 31 日，九寨沟管理局与九寨沟县人民政府、九寨天堂联合策划举办“首届世界自然遗产九寨沟民俗风情月”活动，活动主题为“舞动炫丽民族风、体验藏羌民俗情”。此后，九寨沟每年三至四月举办为期 1 个月的民俗风情月活动，至 2014 年 3 月已举办十届。活动围绕九寨沟的美景、美食、服饰、节庆等内容展开，集中展示九寨沟区域的民族文化和宗教文化。

Jiuzhaigou Folk Customs Month

From April 20 to May 31, 2005, Jiuzhaigou Management Bureau, Jiuzhaigou Country People's Government and Jiuzhai Paradise jointly planned and held the "First World Natural Heritage Jiuzhaigou Folk Customs Month". The theme of the event was "Dancing with dazzling ethnic style and experiencing Zang and Qiang folk customs." Henceforth, this event, held from March to April every year, mainly concerning on sceneries, foods, dresses and festival customs, embodies the concentration display of ethnic and religious cultures. By March 2014, the event had been held for ten times.

中国（四川）第四届南国冰雪节首届阿坝大九寨冰瀑旅游节（2004 年，九寨沟管理局 供图）

The 4th South Country Ice and Snow Festival and the 1st Aba Greater Jiuzhai Icefall Tourism Festival, Sichuan, China (photo by courtesy of Jiuzhaigou Management Bureau, 2004)

2022 年，第十七届中国九寨沟国际冰瀑旅游节开幕式会场（九寨沟管理局 供图）

The opening ceremony of the 17th China Jiuzhaigou International Icefall Tourism Festival in 2022 (photo by courtesy of Jiuzhaigou Management Bureau)

九寨沟第八届民俗风情月民俗歌舞展现场（2012 年，胡军 摄）

Folk Song and Dance Show during the 8th Jiuzhaigou Folk Customs Month (photo by Hu Jun, 2012)

表 12　1982—2022 年九寨沟所获荣誉名录

时间	荣誉	授予单位
1982 年 11 月 8 日	第一批国家重点风景名胜区	国务院
1991 年 12 月 18 日	中国旅游胜地四十佳	国家旅游局
1992 年 12 月 14 日	世界自然遗产	联合国教科文组织
1997 年 12 月 15 日	世界生物圈保护区	联合国教科文组织
2001 年 1 月	国家 AAAA 级旅游景区标志牌	国家旅游局
2002 年 9 月	全国文明风景旅游区示范点	中央精神文明建设指导委员会办公室等
2003 年 12 月	国家重点风景名胜区综合整治先进单位	建设部
2005 年 6 月	国家“十五”科技攻关计划“城市规划、建设、管理与服务的数字化工程”项目“城市数字化示范应用工程研究”示范工程	建设部信息化工作领导小组、建设部科学技术司
2005 年 9 月	国家重点风景名胜区监管信息系统建设先进单位	建设部
2005 年 10 月	全国精神文明建设工作先进单位	中央精神文明建设指导委员会
2006 年 5 月	国家文化产业示范基地	文化部
2006 年 6 月	全国先进基层党组织	中共中央组织部
2006 年 10 月 29 日	中国最令人向往的旅游胜地	中国旅游电视协会
2006 年 11 月 22 日	九寨沟风景名胜区管理局　维护消费者权益诚信服务满意单位	中国保护消费者基金会
2006 年 11 月 22 日	九寨沟风景名胜区管理局　全国文明诚信（窗口）单位	中国保护消费者基金会
2006 年 12 月 24 日	中国最佳旅游去处	首届中国旅游品牌年会组委会
2006 年 12 月	栋梁工程扶贫助学先进单位	四川省扶贫基金会（栋梁工程）
2006 年 12 月	2006 年旅游网站中国十大优秀景区网站	中国社会科学院旅游研究中心、2006 年中国优秀旅游网站
2007 年 3 月 1 日	创建和谐旅游景区单位	四川省旅游局
2007 年 4 月 23 日	中国县域旅游品牌十强景区	品牌中国产业联盟、财经时报社、旅游杂志社等
2007 年 4 月 27 日	全国旅游系统先进集体	人事部、国家旅游局
2007 年 5 月 8 日	国家 AAAAA 级旅游景区	全国旅游景区质量等级评定委员会
2007 年 9 月 8 日	中国十佳休闲旅游风景区	联合国国际生态安全合作组织、国际休闲产业协会等
2007 年 11 月 1 日	最佳资源保护的中国十大风景名胜区	中国风景名胜区网络评选组委会、建设部风景名胜区管理办
2007 年 11 月 1 日	国家级风景名胜区综合整治优秀单位	建设部
2008 年 4 月 27 日	2008 中国旅游品牌十大景区	亚太旅游联合会、旅行杂志社、湖北新旅行杂志社等

续表 12

时间	荣誉	授予单位
2008 年 12 月	四川省风景名胜行业抗震救灾先进集体	四川省建设厅
2008 年 12 月	四川省旅游业抗震救灾先进集体	四川省旅游局
2009 年 1 月 5 日	四川九寨沟 改革 30 年——中国最佳旅游目的地	亚太地区休闲产业协会、中华民族文化促进会等
2009 年 2 月	寻找美丽的中华——西霞口·2008 中国青年喜爱的旅游目的地	中央宣传部、中央文明办、共青团中央等
2009 年 3 月 19 日	全国文明风景旅游区	中央文明办、住房和城乡建设部、国家旅游局
2010 年 12 月	全国低碳旅游实验区	中华环保联合会、中国旅游协会旅游景区分会
2011 年 12 月	全国文明单位	中央精神文明建设指导委员会
2012 年 9 月 16 日	全国低碳旅游示范区	中华环保联合会、中国旅游景区协会
2012 年 9 月 26 日	认定九寨沟生态保护国际联合研究中心为国家国际科技合作基地	科学技术部
2012 年	国家环保科普基地	环境保护部、科学技术部
2013 年 1 月 18 日	中国·九寨沟 最值得驻华大使馆向国际推荐的世界级山地生态旅游目的地	全球驻华使节文化交流合作组织
2013 年 6 月	全国中小学环境教育社会实践基地	环境保护部、教育部
2013 年 9 月	2012 年度全国旅游服务质量标杆单位	国家质检总局、国家旅游局
2013 年 10 月 22 日	民族团结进步创建示范景区	中共四川省委宣传部、中共四川省委统战部、四川省民族宗教事务委员会
2014 年 12 月	2014 年国际旅游度假目的地评选：最佳智慧旅游度假目的地九寨沟景区	人民网、国际旅游学会
2017 年 9 月 18 日	第一批“绿水青山就是金山银山”实践创新基地	环境保护部
2017 年	2013—2016 年度群众体育先进单位	国家体育总局
2019 年	国家生态环境科普基地	生态环境部、科学技术部
2020 年 12 月	《四川省志·九寨沟志》获四川省第十九次地方志优秀成果奖一等奖	四川省地方志工作办公室、四川省地方志学会
2020 年 12 月	四川省大熊猫保护突出贡献奖先进集体	四川省林业和草原局、四川省人力资源和社会保障厅
2022 年 3 月	四川省科学技术进步一等奖	四川省人民政府
2022 年 11 月	四川省“金熊猫”奖先进集体	四川省人民政府

Table 12 Honors of Jiuzhaigou from 1982 to 2022

Time	Honor	Awarded by
November 8, 1982	First Batch of National Key Scenic Spots	State Council
December 18, 1991	One of the Top 40 Tourist Attractions in China	China National Tourism Administration
December 14, 1992	World Natural Heritage	UNESCO
December 15, 1997	World Biosphere Reserve	UNESCO
January, 2001	Signboard as a National AAAA-level Tourist Area	China National Tourism Administration
September, 2002	Demonstration Site of National Civilized Tourist Scenic Area	Office of the CPC Steering Committee for Spiritual Civilization Promotion, etc.
December, 2003	Advanced Unit in Comprehensive Improvement of National Key Scenic Areas	Ministry of Construction of PRC
June, 2005	Digital Engineering of Urban Planning, Construction, Management and Service Project and Research on Urban Digital Demonstration Application Engineering: Demonstration Project under the National "10th Five-Year" Sci-Tech Research Plan	Leading Group for IT Work with Ministry of Construction and Science and Technology Department with Ministry of Construction
September, 2005	Advanced Unit in Construction of National Key Scenic Area Supervisory Information System	Ministry of Construction of PRC
October, 2005	National Advanced Unit in Promotion of Spiritual Civilization	CPC Steering Committee for Promotion of Spiritual Civilization
May, 2006	National Demonstration Base for Cultural Industry	Ministry of Culture of PRC
June, 2006	National Advanced Grassroots Party Organization	Organization Department of CPC Central Committee
October 29, 2006	China's Most Desirable Tourist Destination	China Tourism Television Association
November 22, 2006	Jiuzhaigou Scenic and Historic Area Management Bureau as a Unit of Integrity Service for Consumer Rights and Interests	China Consumer Protection Foundation
November 22, 2006	The Management Bureau of Jiuzhaigou Scenic and Historic Area as a Unit for National Civilization and Integrity (Window)	China Consumer Protection Foundation
December 24, 2006	The Best Travel Destination in China	Organizing Committee of the First Annual Conference on China Tourism Brand
November, 2006	Advanced Unit in Bridge Engineering Works for Poverty Alleviation and Education Assistance	Sichuan Poverty Alleviation Foundation (Bridge Engineering)
November, 2006	One of the Top 10 Excellent Websites of Scenic Spots in China by Tourism Website, 2006	Tourism Research Center of Chinese Academy of Social Sciences and China Excellent Tourism Website 2006
March 1, 2006	Model Unit in Creating Harmonious Tourist Attractions	Sichuan Tourism Bureau
April 23, 2007	One of the Top 10 Scenic Spots under County Tourism Brands in China	Brand China Industry Alliance, Financial Times Agency and Travel Magazine Agency
April 27, 2007	National Advanced Collective in the Tourism Sector	Ministry of Personnel, National Tourism Administration
May 8, 2007	National AAAAA-level Tourist Attraction	National Tourist Scenic Spot Quality Rating Committee
September 8, 2007	One of the Top 10 Leisure Tourism Scenic Spots in China	International Ecological Safety Collaborative Organization, International Leisure Industry Association
November 1, 2007	One of the Top 10 Scenic Spots with the Best Protection of Resources	Organizing Committee for Network Selection of Scenic Areas in China, Scenic Area Management Office of the Ministry of Construction
November 1, 2007	Excellent Unit for Comprehensive Improvement of National Scenic Spots	Ministry of Construction of PRC
April 27, 2008	One of the Top 10 Scenic Spots of China's Tourism Brands, 2008	Asia-Pacific Tourism Federation, Travel Magzine and New Travel Magazine, Hubei

Continued Table 12

Time	Honor	Awarded by
December, 2008	Advanced Collective in Earthquake Relief in the Industry of Tourist and Historic Areas of Sichuan Province	Sichuan Provincial Department of Construction
December, 2008	Advanced Collective in Earthquake Relief in the Tourism Industry of Sichuan Province	Sichuan Tourism Bureau
January 1,2009	Sichuan's Jiuzhaigou–Best Tourist Destination in China Since Its Reform Three Decades Ago	Asia-Pacific Leisure Industry Association, Chinese Culture Promotion Association
February, 2009	In Search of Beautiful China–Xixiakou–Chinese Youth Favorite Tourist Destination 2008	CPC Publicity Department, CPC Civilization Office, and Central Committee of Communist Youth League
March 19, 2009	National Civilized Scenic Tourist Area	CPC Civilization Office, Ministry of Housing and Urban-Rural Development, and China National Tourism Administration
December, 2010	National Experimental Area for Low-Carbon Tourism	All-China Environment Federation, Tourist Scenic Areas Branch of China Tourism Association
December, 2011	National Model Unit	Ministry of Science and Technology of PRC
September 16, 2012	National Low-Carbon Tourism Demonstration Area	All-China Environment Federation, China Tourist Attractions Association
September 26, 2012	International Joint Research Center for Jiuzhaigou Ecological Protection Recognized as the Country's International Sci-Tech Cooperation Base	Ministry of Science and Technology of PRC
2012	National Environmental Science Popularization Base	Ministry of Environmental Protection, Ministry of Science and Technology
January 18, 2013	Jiuzhaigou–China as a World-class Destination for Mountain Eco-tourism Most Worthy of International Recommendations by Foreign Embassies in China	Global Cultural Exchange and Cooperation Organization for Diplomatic Envoys in China
June, 2013	National Social Practice Base on Environmental Education for Primary and Secondary Schools	Ministry of Environmental Protection, Ministry of Education
September, 2013	National Benchmark Unit in Tourism Service Quality 2012	State General Administration for Quality Supervision, Inspection and Quarantine, China National Tourism Administration
October 22, 2013	Demonstration Scenic Area for Creating National Unity and Progress	The Publicity Department of CPC Sichuan Provincial Committee, the United Front Work Department of CPC Sichuan Provincial Committee, Sichuan Provincial Commission on Ethnic and Religious Affairs
December, 2014	Selection of International Tourism and Vacation Destinations 2014: Jiuzhaigou Scenic Spot, Best Destination for Smart Tourism and Vacation	People's Daily Online, International Tourism Society
September 18, 2017	First Batch of Practice and Innovation Bases for "Clear Waters and Green Mountains as Invaluable Assets"	Ministry of Environmental Protection
2017	Annual Advanced Unit in Mass Sports 2013~2016	General Administration of Sport of China
2019	National Ecological Environment Science Popularization Base	Ministry of Ecology and Environment, Ministry of Science and Technology
December, 2020	*Sichuan Local Records–Jiuzhaigou Local Records* awarded the First Prize of the 19th Excellent Achievements in Compiling Local Records of Sichuan Province	The Office of Sichuan Province Local Records, Sichuan Local Records Society
December, 2020	Advanced Collective of Sichuan for Outstanding Contributions in the Conservation of Giant Pandas	Sichuan Forestry and Grassland Bureau, Sichuan Provincial Department of Human Resources and Social Security
March, 2022	First Prize of Sichuan Science and Technology Progress Award	The People's Government of Sichuan Province
November, 2022	Advanced Collective of Sichuan "Golden Panda" Award	The People's Government of Sichuan Province

九看
Jiuzhaigou in Nine Episodes
九寨

之九

Episode Nine

涅槃重生

Nirvana and Rebirth

震后火花海（2017 年，中国科学院・水利部成都山地灾害与环境研究所 供图）

遭受重创
Heavy Sufferings

Sparkling Lake after the earthquake (photo by courtesy of Institute of Mountain Hazards and Environment, CAS, 2017)

九寨沟地处几大地质构造带接合部，西、南、北三面均有明显断裂带，构造复杂，地震活动频繁而剧烈。2017 年 8 月 8 日 21 时 19 分 46 秒，九寨沟县发生 7.0 级地震，震源深度约 20 千米，震中位于九寨沟国家级自然保护区丹祖沟北侧（北纬 33.20°，东经 103.82°），距五花海约 6 千米。

“8 • 8”九寨沟地震是目前九寨沟经历过的规模最大、震级最高、损失最严重的地震。地震造成九寨沟景区 2307 人受灾、4 人死亡；道路、电力、通信中断，公共服务用房、栈道、厕所等旅游服务设施不同程度受损；火花海溃堤，诺日朗瀑布出现裂缝……九寨沟的森林生态系统、湿地生态系统、水环境受到强烈扰动。直接损失 22.79 亿元，间接损失 183.59 亿元。

Located at the junction of several major geological structural belts, Jiuzhaigou lies in obvious fault zones on the west, south and north, where the structure is complex and seismic activities are frequent and violent. At 21:19:46 on August 8, 2017, a magnitude 7.0 earthquake occurred in Jiuzhaigou County with a focal depth of about 20 kilometers, the epicenter was located in the northern branch of the Danzu Gully in Jiuzhaigou National Nature Reserve (33.20°N, 103.82°E), about 6 kilometers off the Wuhua Lake.

In this earthquake, the largest, highest magnitude and most severe for Jiuzhaigou so far, 2,307 people were affected, 4 died. Roads, electricity and communications were interrupted, public service buildings, plank roads, toilets and other facilities were damaged to varying degrees; the Sparkling Lake dam burst, Nuorilang Waterfall cracked and forest ecosystems, wetland ecosystems and water environments of Jiuzhaigou were severely disturbed. It resulted in a direct and indirect loss of 2.279 billion and 18.359 billion yuan respectively.

被群山环绕的九寨沟树正沟（2022 年，桑吉 摄）
Shuzheng Gully in Jiuzhaigou, surrounded by mountains (photo by Sangji, 2022)

“8 • 8” 石（2017 年，肖维阳 摄）
Rock "8·8" (photo by Xiao Weiyang, 2017)

“8 · 8” 石

位于日则沟镜海上游山谷间，高 9.2 米，体积约 163 立方米，重约 522 吨，形成于 3.2 亿年前的海洋环境，因 “8 • 8” 九寨沟地震时从山体崩落而得名。这块巨石从海拔 2654 米处翻滚而下，巨大的冲击力使巨石下端深深插入谷底，所过之处植被尽毁，形成一条既宽又深的沟槽。

Rock "8·8"

Located upstream of Rize Gully's Mirror Lake, this rock is 9.2 meters high, with a volume of about 163 cubic meters and a weight of about 522 tons. Formed in a marine environment of 320 million years ago, it was thus named owing to its collapse off on August 8 when the earthquake happened. It tumbled into the bottom of the gully from an altitude of 2,654 meters with such an impact as to destroy the vegetation in its path, forming a wide and deep groove.

震中丹祖沟

丹祖沟为日则沟内左岸最大支流，“8 • 8” 九寨沟地震的震中就位于丹祖沟北侧支沟，最大烈度为 9 度。受地震活动松动破坏的影响，震中丹祖沟崩滑灾害密集发育，通行条件极差，且在余震作用下不断出现崩塌、滚石。

Epicenter Danzu Gully

Its epicenter, with a maximum intensity of 9 degrees, was located in the northern branch of the Danzu Gully, the largest tributary on the left bank of the Rize Gully. Owing to the loosening and damage of earthquake activities, landslide disasters developed intensively in the Danzu Gully, where the traffic conditions were extremely poor. And under the action of aftershocks, there were continuous collapses and rolling stones.

老虎嘴路段损毁

老虎嘴位于五花海之上，因地形险峻得名，是观赏五花海全景的最佳位置。“8・8”九寨沟地震造成景区道路损毁或掩埋 79 段。其中，箭竹海到老虎嘴路段受损最为严重，路面断裂，滑坡堆积体掩埋道路，乱石嶙峋、杂树横陈，次生灾害频发。

Tiger Mouth Section Damaged

Tiger Mouth, located over Wuhua Lake and named from its steep terrain, is the best place to enjoy the whole senery of lake. The “8·8” Earthquake damaged or buried 79 sections of road into the scenic area, of which the part from the Arrow Bamboo Lake to the Tiger Mouth was the most severely damaged, the roadway broke, landslide deposits buried the road, jagged rocks and trees lay across and secondary disasters frequently occurred.

诺日朗瀑布大裂缝

“8・8”九寨沟地震发生后，诺日朗瀑布出现一条长 16.8 米、宽 0.5 米的大裂缝。水流从裂缝中汹涌泻出，如不进行弥补，瀑布可能因余震和水流冲蚀继续坍塌，上游的诺日朗群海和镜海也会被破坏。

Great Crack in Nuorilang Waterfall

After the “8·8” Earthquake, a large crack with a length of 16.8 meters and a width of 0.5 meters appeared in the Nuorilang Waterfall, from which water flowed. If not repaired, the waterfall would continue to collapse due to aftershocks and water erosion and destroy the Nuorilang Lake Cluster and the Mirror Lake in its upper reach.

火花海决堤

火花海在“8・8”九寨沟地震中决堤，形成长 40 米、宽 12 米、深 15 米的决口，湖泊几近干涸，湖群发育裂缝 100 余条，其中 5 米及以上的有 23 条。此外，火花海上游叠瀑坝体裂缝和坍塌等次生灾害发育，湖群溃决风险增大。

Breaking of Sparkling Lake

The Sparkling Lake broke in this “8·8” Earthquake, forming a breach of 40 meters long, 12 meters wide and 15 meters deep. It went almost dry and there appeared 100-plus cracks in the lakes, 23 of which were 5 meters long and more. In addition, secondary disasters such as cracks and collapses of cascading waterfall dams on its upper reaches developed and the risk of lake break increased.

1 | 2 | 3

1 震后的老虎嘴（2018 年，桑吉 摄）
2 诺日朗瀑布大裂缝（2017 年，肖维阳 摄）
3 震后的火花海（2017 年，肖维阳 摄）

1 Post-quake Tiger Mouth (photo by Sangji, 2018)
2 Great crack in Nuorilang Waterfall (photo by Xiao Weiyang, 2017)
3 Post-quake Sparkling Lake (photo by Xiao Weiyang, 2017)

火花海修复过程——火花海溃堤坝体美化作业（2020 年，肖维阳 摄）

灾后重建
Post-quake Reconstruction

The Sparkling Lake restoration process: the beautified embankment burst of Sparkling Lake (photo by Xiao Weiyang, 2020)

“8·8”九寨沟地震发生后，中共中央领导第一时间作出重要批示，四川省委、省政府和阿坝州委、州政府主要领导带队，第一时间赶赴现场，成立“8·8”九寨沟地震抗震救灾应急指挥部，指导抗震救灾工作。九寨沟管理局工作人员迅速优先有序撤离群众，广大干部群众齐心协力、共克时艰，灾情很快得到控制，人员伤亡和财产损失等灾害损失被控制在最小范围内。

2017年11月8日，九寨沟景区灾后恢复重建全面启动。震中位于九寨沟，属国内首例、国际罕见。既要修复，又要维护遗产地突出特点及完整性不被破坏，是前所未有的世界性难题。九寨沟管理局等单位认真践行“自然修复为主、人工治理为辅，生物措施为主、工程措施为辅”要求，开展灾后恢复重建工作，为世界自然遗产地震后世界自然遗产地修复保护提供了宝贵的“九寨经验”。

核心景区之外，珍稀动物栖息地的修复工作同时展开。九寨沟管理局从“生境修复”“生境恢复”“受损山体恢复”三个方面着手，针对直接损毁和严重受损栖息地展开生态修复；针对受损山体，在不破坏山体景观美感的前提下，通过补植当地原生性和适应性树种，以及开展震后裸岩边坡苔藓人工覆绿工程进行修复。在较短时间内，将受到地震破坏的栖息地植被恢复到震前水平，同时采取良好管护措施，逐步提高栖息地质量。

Right after the “8·8” earthquake, the leaders of the CPC Central Committee immediately issued important instructions, the main leaders of the CPC Sichuan Provincial Committee, provincial government and Aba prefectural party committee and state government led the team to rush to the scene, to form the emergency headquarters for earthquake relief and the staff of the Jiuzhaigou Management Bureau quickly and orderly helped to evacuate the masses. Through the concerted efforts of cadres and the masses, the situation was quickly brought under control and the loss of casualties and property was minimized.

On November 8, 2017, the post-quake restoration and reconstruction of Jiuzhaigou Scenic Area started in full swing. The epicenter, located in the World Natural Heritage Site was the first in China and rare in the rest of the world. It was an unprecedented problem worldwide to not only restore, but also maintain its outstanding features and integrity. The Jiuzhaigou Management Bureau and other units conscientiously followed the requirements of “natural restoration first, supplemented by artificial treatment; biological measures first, supplemented by engineering measures”, carrying out the post-quake restoration and reconstruction work, which provides its valuable “Jiuzhaigou Experience” for the post-quake restoration and protection of the world natural heritage.

Outside the core scenic spots, the restoration of rare animal habitats was underway at the same time. The Jiuzhaigou Management Bureau starts from three aspects of “habitat restoration” “habitat repair” and “damaged mountain restoration” to carry out ecological restoration for directly and severely damaged habitats. As to the damaged mountains, restoration was carried out by replanting native and adaptive tree species without destroying the beauty of the mountain landscape, and by covering the bare rock slopes with artificial greening of moss after the earthquake. In a short period of time, the habitat vegetation damaged was restored to the pre-quake levels. At the same time, good management and protection measures were taken to gradually improve the quality of the habitats.

火花群海（2021 年，梁峰 摄）

Sparkling Lake Cluster (photo by Liang Feng, 2021)

熊猫海隧道内部（2022 年，易茂祥 摄）
Interior of the tunnel to Panda Lake (photo by Yi Maoxiang, 2022)

九寨沟自然保护区震后裸岩边坡苔藓覆绿（2021 年，莫进忠 供图）
Post-quake artificial greening of moss on bare rock slopes in Jiuzhaigou Nature Reserve (photo by courtesy of Mo Jinzhong, 2021)

熊猫海隧道

全长 918 米，总造价约 1.25 亿元，位于“8・8”九寨沟地震中损毁最严重的老虎嘴附近，是灾后恢复重建三期道路（五花海至原始森林段）的控制性工程。2020 年 8 月 18 日进洞开工，2021 年 8 月 11 日顺利贯通，是连接五花海至原始森林，以及打通老虎嘴瓶颈道路的关键通道，为游客提供更为安全和便捷的游览环境。

Tunnel to Panda Lake

With a total length of 918 meters at a total cost of about 125 million yuan, it is located near the Tiger Mouth, which suffered the most damage in the “8·8” Earthquake in Jiuzhaigou. As a control engineering project for the post-quake restoration and reconstruction, construction of the Phase III road from the Wuhua Lake to the Virgin Forest started on August 18, 2020 and was completed on August 11, 2021. It is a key passage connecting the Wuhua Lake to the Virgin Forest and opening up the bottleneck of the road to the Tiger Mouth, offering tourists a safer and more convenient environment for sightseeing.

裸岩边坡苔藓人工覆绿

“8・8”九寨沟地震后，九寨沟出现大面积裸岩边坡。九寨沟管理局与中国科学院成都生物研究所合作，创新利用苔藓、地衣等低等植物快速覆绿震后裸岩边坡。具体做法为：第一，成功筛选出三种适宜乡土石生藓种；第二，针对这些石生藓种研发配子体快速繁育技术；第三，攻克苔藓裸岩固着技术难关，开展野外应用试验。该项目探索了裸岩边坡生态治理新路径，对指导中国西南山区地震及地质灾害后近自然恢复具有重要的理论意义和实践价值。

Artificial Greening of Moss on Bare Rock Slopes

After the “8·8” Earthquake, a large area of exposed rock slopes appeared. The Jiuzhaigou Management Bureau, in cooperation with Chengdu Institute of Biology and Chinese Academy of Sciences, innovatively used low-level plants such as mosses and lichens to quickly cover the bare rock slopes. Its specific methods are as follows: first, successful screening of three suitable native lithophyte species; second, development of gametophyte rapid breeding techniques for these lithophyte species; and third, field testing of moss bare rock fixation despite technical difficulties. This project, as a new path for ecological management of bare rock slopes, is of theoretically great significance and practical value for guiding the near-natural restoration after an earthquake and geological disaster in the mountainous areas of Southwest China.

九寨沟大数据综合管理平台（2022 年，九寨沟管理局 供图）

Jiuzhaigou Big Data Integrated Management Platform (photo by courtesy of Jiuzhaigou Management Bureau, 2022)

智慧旅游大数据综合管理平台

九寨沟风景名胜区管理局主导的九寨沟景区灾后重建发展提升类项目之一，2018 年完成项目方案设计，2021 年底完成项目初步验收工作。是集恢复受损光缆，重建九寨沟景区旅游数据平台、智慧景区综合运营管控平台、景区监控、门禁票务等应用系统功能于一体的智慧管理中心及设施设备。

Integrated Management Platform for Intelligent Tourism Big Data

As one of the post-quake reconstruction, development and upgrading projects of Jiuzhaigou Scenic Area led by the Management Bureau of Jiuzhaigou Scenic and Historic Area, its design was completed in 2018 and preliminary acceptance by the end of 2021. It is a kind of smart management center with its facilities and equipments integrating the functions of the restoration of the damaged optical cable, the reconstruction of tourism data platform of Jiuzhaigou scenic area, the comprehensive operation management and control platform, the monitoring of scenic area, and the ticketing and access control systems.

全域发展

All-for-One Development

长海（2021 年，九寨沟管理局 供图）

Long Lake (photo by courtesy of Jiuzhaigou Management Bureau, 2021)

成为世界自然遗产地后，九寨沟每年吸引游客数百万人，创造收入数千万元，但旅游经济只能辐射影响沟口几个村寨。1998年6月19日，经国务院批准，南坪县更名为九寨沟县。文旅产业成为九寨沟县的支柱产业。

“十三五”规划以来，九寨沟县探索以“全域发展”为核心的旅游发展模式，利用发展全域旅游的资源优势，实现产业转型和精准扶贫。九寨沟景区发挥龙头带动作用，提档升级旅游链条，丰富完善旅游业态，提升旅游服务水平，牵头促成“大九寨”文旅发展联盟、中国最美黄金旅游走廊、“1+12”全域旅游布局等旅游转型升级实践落地。

九寨沟的旅游开发是川西北旅游区开发起点，也是阿坝全域旅游先行地，培育出全域共建、全域共融、全域共享的旅游生态，让单一景点游变成集生态观光、休闲康养、会议会展等功能于一体的全域综合游，坚持“旅游＋扶贫＋发展”的“大扶贫”模式。

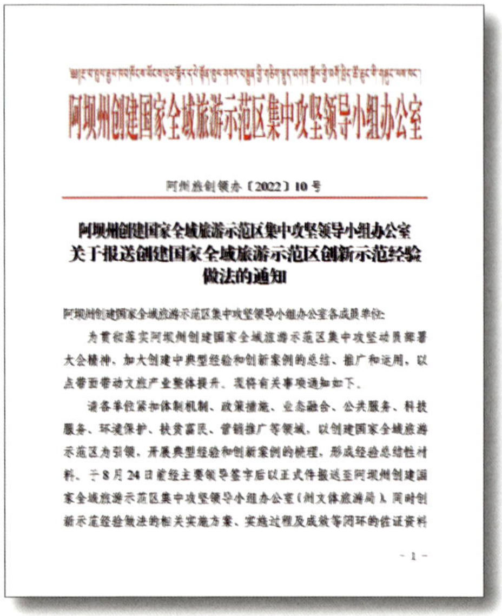

阿坝州创建国家全域旅游示范区集中攻坚领导小组办公室

阿州旅创领办〔2022〕10号

阿坝州创建国家全域旅游示范区集中攻坚领导小组办公室
关于报送创建国家全域旅游示范区创新示范经验
做法的通知

阿坝州创建国家全域旅游示范区集中攻坚领导小组办公室各成员单位：

为贯彻落实阿坝州创建国家全域旅游示范区集中攻坚动员部署大会精神，加大创建中典型经验和创新案例的总结、推广和运用，以点带面带动文旅产业整体提升，现将有关事项通知如下。

请各单位紧扣体制机制、政策措施、业态融合、公共服务、科技服务、环境保护、扶贫富民、营销推广等领域，以创建国家全域旅游示范区为引领，开展典型经验和创新案例的梳理，形成经验总结性材料，于8月24日前经主要领导签字后以正式件报送至阿坝州创建国家全域旅游示范区集中攻坚领导小组办公室（州文体旅游局），同时创新示范经验做法的相关实施方案、实施过程及成效等闭环的佐证资料

－1－

关于报送创建国家全域旅游示范区创新示范经验做法的通知（2022年，九寨沟管理局 供图）

Notice on Submitting Innovative Demonstration Experience and Practice for Creating A National All-for-One Tourism Demonstration Area (photo by courtesy of Jiuzhaigou Management Bureau, 2022)

Since it became a World Natural Heritage Site, Jiuzhaigou has brought in tens of millions of yuan in revenue owing to millions of its tourists every year. However, this tourism economy could just radiate and influence the few villages close to its entrance. On June 19, 1998, with the approval of the State Council, Nanping County was renamed Jiuzhaigou County. Since then, the tourism economy here has been developing rapidly as the county's pillar industry.

Since the "13th Five-Year Plan", this county has explored a model for tourism development centered on "all-for-one development" and utilized the resource advantages of developing all-for-one tourism to achieve industrial transformation and targeted poverty alleviation. Jiuzhaigou Scenic Area plays a leading role in upgrading its tourism chain, enriching and improving tourism models, improving tourism services and takes the lead in promoting tourism such as the "Greater Jiuzhai" Cultural Tourism Development Alliance, China's most beautiful golden tourism corridor and "1+12" all-for-one tourism layout, hence the implementation of transformation and upgrading.

Tourism development is the starting point for the development of tourism areas in Northwest Sichuan and the pioneering place for tourism in Aba as well. It has cultivated a tourism ecology of all-for-one co-construction, integration and sharing, turning a single scenic spot tour into a comprehensive one that integrates ecological sightseeing, leisure and healthcare and conferences and exhibitions, insisting the large-scale model of "tourism + poverty alleviation + development."

民族地区旅游人才培养开发示范基地办公室（2022 年，贺蜀江　摄）
Office of the Tourism Talent Training and Development Demonstration Base for Ethnic Minority Regions (photo by He Shujiang, 2022)

民族地区旅游人才培养开发示范基地

2017 年 11 月 10 日，“民族地区旅游人才培养引进五年行动暨九寨沟地震灾后恢复重建紧缺专业人才支持四大行动工作推进会”召开，九寨沟被中共四川省委组织部、四川省旅游发展委员会批准成为首批 10 个民族地区旅游人才培养开发示范基地之一。该示范基地旨在探索和推广旅游人才培养开发的经验做法，打造国内外旅游人才交流合作平台、实用人才培训基地、旅游人才会聚高地，同时为旅游扶贫、产业发展方面促成景区一体、产城融合、协同发展的红利释放效应。

Tourism Talent Training and Development Demonstration Base for Ethnic Minority Regions

On November 10, 2017, the promotion meeting on “Five-Year Action of Training and Introducing Tourism Talents in Ethnic Minority Regions and Four Major Actions to Support Post-quake Restoration and Reconstruction of Jiuzhaigou for Professionals in Shortage” was held, at which Jiuzhaigou was approved by the Organization Department of the CPC Sichuan Provincial Committee and Sichuan Tourism Development Committee as one of the 10 tourism talent training and development demonstration bases in the first batch in Sichuan Province. This base aims to explore and promote the experiences and practices in tourism talent training and development, in order to create a platform for tourism talent exchanges and cooperation at home and abroad, a practical talent training base and a highland for gathering tourism talents and, in terms of poverty alleviation through tourism and industrial development, facilitate the dividend release effect from integrations of scenic spots, interplay between the industry and cities, and coordinated development as well.

2022年3月10日，国家林草局在线组织审查《九寨沟国家级自然保护区总体规划（2022—2030）》会议现场（梁峰 摄）

On-line review of *Master Plan for Jiuzhaigou National-level Nature Reserve (2022~2030)* on March 10, 2022 by State Forestry and Grassland Administration (photo by Liang Feng)

《四川九寨沟国家级自然保护区总体规划（2019—2030）》

2018年10月30日，《四川九寨沟国家级自然保护区总体规划（2019—2030）》（以下简称《规划》）通过评审。《规划》旨在通过对生态旅游、保护管理、宣传教育、科研监测、社区共建共管等进行系统、科学规划，使九寨沟国家级自然保护区实现“建设标准化、管理信息化、经营规范化、社区先导化”，成为国家实施生态文明建设示范基地、世界一流保护区。

“大九寨”文旅发展联盟

2019年11月6日于九寨沟县成立，该联盟旨在从资源共享、品牌共创、客源共济、市场共拓、人才共育、基础共建、区域共治7个方面，加强“大九寨”品牌整体包装、策划和营销，打造环九寨国际生态文化旅游目的地品牌，协商制定联盟景区景点互惠政策和酒店餐饮等优惠政策，促进市场互相开放。

Master Plan for Sichuan Jiuzhaigou National Nature Reserve (2019~2030)

On October 30, 2018, *Master Plan for Sichuan Jiuzhaigou National Nature Reserve (2019~2030)* (*The Plan* for short) passed the assessment. *The Plan* aims to help Jiuzhaigou National Nature Reserve to realize “standardized construction, IT management, standardized operation, community as the pilot”, by means of eco-tourism, protective management, publicity and education, scientific monitoring and community co-building, so as to make Jiuzhaigou a national demonstration base for implementing ecological civilization construction and a world-class reserve.

“Greater Jiuzhai” Culture and Tourism Development Alliance

Established in Jiuzhaigou County on November 6, 2019, the alliance aims to strengthen the overall packaging, planning and marketing of the “Greater Jiuzhai” brand from seven aspects: resource sharing, brand co-creation, customer source co-help, market co-development, talent co-education, foundation co-construction and regional co-governance, create an international eco-cultural tourism destination brand around Jiuzhaigou, negotiate and formulate reciprocal policies for scenic spots in alliance and preferential policies for hotels and restaurants to promote the mutual opening of markets.

最美黄金旅游走廊

九寨沟风景名胜区、青城山—都江堰旅游景区、黄龙国家级风景名胜区三大景区将优势资源串联整合起来，形成“最美黄金旅游走廊”旅游线。这条旅游线集避暑、观光、养生等功能于一体，真正做到资源协调配合、互动分享。游客通过该黄金旅游走廊能够实现一次出行、多重体验，最大程度满足多种旅游需求。

The Most Beautiful Golden Tourism Corridor

The three major scenic areas, i.e. Jiuzhaigou Scenic and Historic Area, Qingcheng Mountain–Dujiangyan Scenic Area, and Huanglong National-level Scenic Area, integrated their superior resources that have formed a tourist route on “the most beautiful golden tourism corridor”, which plays the functions of summer escape, sightseeing and healthcare and truly achieves resource coordination, interaction and sharing. Through this corridor, tourists can get multiple experiences on one trip and satisfy their various needs to the full extent.

“1+12”全域旅游格局

“1”指享誉世界的九寨沟风景名胜区，“12”指嫩恩桑措景区、甲勿海景区、中查沟九寨·鲁能胜地旅游度假区、爱情海风景区、九寨沟熊猫研究园、柴门关景区、大录古藏寨、世外罗依度假区、白河金丝猴自然保护区、九寨云顶景区、九寨天珠景区、七里黄金小镇 12 个景点。

“1+12” Pattern of All-for-One Tourism

“1” refers to the world-renowned Jiuzhaigou Scenic and Historic Area, and “12” to 12 senic spots including Nen'en Sangcuo, Jiawu Lake, Jiuzhaigou·Luneng Resort Tourist Resort in Zhongcha Gully, Lovers Lake, Jiuzhaigou Panda Research Park, Chaimenguan, Dalu Ancient Zang Village, Shiwai Luoyi Resort, Baihe Snub-nosed Monkey Nature Reserve, Jiuzhai Yunding, Jiuzhai Tianzhu and Qili Golden Town.

1 | 2

1 2016 年 9 月 2 日，九寨沟景区参加中国最美黄金旅游走廊（北京站）宣传推介活动（刘莉 摄）

2 2021 年 9 月 28 日，第七届中国（四川）国际旅游投资大会开幕式暨九寨沟景区全域恢复开放仪式在阿坝州九寨沟县举行（九寨沟管理局 供图）

1 Jiuzhaigou Scenic Area (Beijing Station) as a participant in promoting China's most beautiful golden tourism corridor on September 2, 2016 (photo by Liu Li)

2 On September 28, 2021, the opening ceremony of the 7th China (Sichuan) International Tourism Investment Conference and the Restoration and Opening ceremony of Jiuzhaigou Scenic Area was held in Jiuzhaigou County, Aba Prefecture (photo by courtesy of Jiuzhaigou Management Bureau)

九寨沟沟口游客服务中心广场（2022 年，梁峰 摄）

震后归来
New Look After the Earthquake

Tourist Service Center Square at the entrance of Jiuzhaigou (photo by Liang Feng, 2022)

2019 年 9 月 23 日，九寨沟管理局发布《九寨沟景区关于部分区域恢复开放（试运行）的公告》，2019 年 9 月 27 日（世界旅游日）起恢复部分景观对外开放 (试运行)。开放区域为扎如沟的扎如寺、树正沟（火花海除外）、日则沟 (诺日朗至五花海段景点)、则查洼沟，并根据恢复重建情况，实行单日最大限量控制，每天最大限量为 5000 人。

2021 年 9 月 28 日，第七届中国（四川）国际旅游投资大会开幕式暨九寨沟景区全域恢复开放仪式在九寨沟沟口游客服务中心室外广场举办。至此，九寨沟景区灾后恢复重建全面完成，27 处世界自然遗产点恢复震前样貌，迎来全域开放，核定最大承载量为 4.1 万人次 / 天。

3 年多以来，九寨沟累计清理震损林地 1.67 万亩（约 1113.33 公顷），补植、补造树木 65.6 万株，点播、撒播树种、草籽 9458 千克，完成景区生境修复、恢复 5639 亩（约 375.93 公顷）；建成世界自然遗产景观与生态保护国家综合观测站，配置水质自动在线监测等系统 26 套，研发九寨沟世界自然遗产地“天—空—地”一体化监测体系，与联合国教科文组织国际自然与文化遗产空间技术中心合作建立九寨沟工作站；有效治理地质灾害隐患点 170 处，修建装板拦石墙 6480 米，拦水坝 16 座、1780 米，安装主被动网 19 万平方米，开展可视范围内绿化、美化 6.2 万平方米，安装地质灾害专业预警设备 455 套，安排监测人员 327 人次，实现景区隐患点常态化动态监测；重建道路、管网 125000 米，栈道 82000 米，重建停车场 7 个、休息亭 24 座、环保厕所 47 座、安装标识标牌 2783 个，加固维修诺日朗综合服务中心建筑面积 1.2 万平方米，重建沟口立体式游客服务设施、后勤配送中心、诺日朗换乘中心、景区沟外备用污水处理站等基础设施 35113.5 平方米。

如今的九寨沟，正在向世人展现涅槃重生的崭新面貌。这片曾在地震中“受伤”的土地，经过九寨沟人 3 年勠力同心的恢复重建，变得更加光彩夺目、美丽动人。

九寨沟景区诺日朗换乘中心（2021 年，梁峰 摄）
Jiuzhaigou scenic area Nuorilang transfer center (photo by Lang Feng, 2021)

On September 23, 2019, the Jiuzhaigou Management Bureau issued *Announcement on Restoring and Opening (Trial Operation) Part of the Scenic Area,* and some landscapes reopened to the public (trial operation) from September 27, 2019 (World Tourism Day). They were Zharu Temple in Zharu Gully, Shuzheng Gully (except Sparkling Lake), Rize Gully (scenic spot from Nuorilang to Wuhua Lake) and Zezhawa Gully. Owing to the situation of restoration and reconstruction, the largest single day limit was 5,000 tourists at most.

On September 28, 2021, the opening ceremony of the 7th China (Sichuan) International Tourism Investment Conference and the restoration and opening ceremony of the Scenic Area were held on the outdoor square of the entrance to Tourist Service Center. So far, the post-quake restoration and reconstruction of the Scenic Area had been fully completed, 27 world natural heritage spots resumed its previous appearance for full opening, namely, the approved maximum capacity of 41,000 tourists per day.

Over the past three years, Jiuzhaigou had cleared about 1,113.33 hectares of earthquake-damaged forestland, replanted 656,000 trees, sowed 9,458 kilograms of seeds for trees and grasses and completed habitat restoration and repairing of about 375.93 hectares in the Scenic Area; it had built a national comprehensive observation station for world natural heritage landscape and ecological protection, supporting 26 sets of water quality automatic online monitoring systems, “sky-air-ground” integrated monitoring system for Jiuzhaigou World Natural Heritage Site and established Jiuzhaigou Workstation in cooperation with UNESCO International Natural and Cultural Heritage Space Technology Center; effectively controlled 170 hidden danger points of geological disasters, built a slab stone wall of 6,480 meters, 16 dams of 1,780 meters, installed an active and passive net of 190,000 square meters, carried out greening and beautification within the visible range of 62,000 square meters, installed 455 sets of professional early warning equipment against geological disasters, arranged 327 person-times of monitoring personnel to realize the normal dynamic monitoring of hidden danger points in the scenic area; rebuilt 125,000 meters of roads and pipe networks, 82,000 meters of plank roads, 7 parking lots, 24 pavilions and 47 environmentally-friendly toilets, installed 2,783 identification signs, reinforced, maintained a building area of 12,000 square meters of Nuorilang comprehensive service center, reconstructed the infrastructure of 35,113.5 square meters for the tridimensional tourist service facilities at the entrance, logistics distribution center, Nuorilang transfer center, standby sewage treatment station outside the scenic area and the like.

Today’s Jiuzhaigou is showing the world a new look of nirvana and rebirth. This land that was “injured” by the earthquake has become more dazzling and beautiful through three years’ restoration and reconstruction by the people of Jiuzhaigou.

双龙海瀑布（2018 年，肖维阳 摄）
Shuanglong Lake Waterfall (photo by Xiao Weiyang, 2018)

双龙海瀑布

2018 年，高 8.4 米，长 85 米，整体呈“L”形分布。震前，双龙海瀑布隐藏在密林深处，由于规模很小，鲜为人知。震后，上游火花海决堤，湖水闯入双龙海，冲走瀑体植被，使瀑布规模扩大，形成了一处新景点。

Shuanglong Lake Waterfall

8.4 meters high and 85 meters long in 2018, it is displayed in an “L” shape as a whole. Before the earthquake, Shuanglong Lake Waterfall lay unknown due to its small scale inside the dense forest. Afterward, the upper reaches of Sparkling Lake broke and its water poured down into Shuanglong Lake, washed away its vegetations, extended the waterfall as a new scenic spot.

修复后的火花海（2020 年，肖维阳 摄）
The restored Sparkling Lake (photo by Xiao Weiyang, 2020)

火花海重生

九寨沟修复团队首次采用振冲碎石固基、糯米灰浆筑坝、竹锚加筋护坡、生态材料堵缝、本土植物绿化等措施，成功恢复火花海震前生态系统，得到联合国教科文组织、世界自然保护联盟等国际权威机构认可，并获得四川省科技进步一等奖。2020 年 8 月，九寨沟县发生百年一遇洪涝灾害，火花海修复坝体保持稳定，有效发挥减灾调控作用。

Rebirth of the Sparkling Lake

Jiuzhaigou Restoration Team adopted measures for the first time such as foundation consolidating with vibroflotation gravel, dam building with glutinous rice mortar, slope protection with bamboo anchor reinforcement, caulking with ecological materials and greening with native plant, and successfully restored the ecosystem as it had been. This was recognized by international authorities such as IUCN and UNESCO and won the first prize of Sichuan Science and Technology Progress Award. In August 2020, despite the once-in-a-century flood disaster in Jiuzhaigou County, the restored dam of the Sparkling Lake stayed stable, hence a sign of its role against disaster reduction and regulation.

九寨—松潘—成都
九寨售票處

立体式游客服务设施

位于九寨沟沟口，西至荷叶宾馆，东至四号桥，南至贵宾楼饭店，西北侧临国道544线，为2021年9月建成的全新游客服务设施，包含游客服务中心、展示中心、国际学术交流中心、智慧管理中心、人防应急避难场所、世界自然遗产景观及生态保护国家级综合观测站等。九寨沟管理局率先采用立体式交通、曲线建筑造型、钢结构装配等施工工艺，将沟口立体式游客服务中心打造成绿色环保、人文相融、功能齐全、设备先进、进出快速的标志性建筑和门户，极大提高了服务水平、效率和游客进出通行分流的舒适度与满意度。

Tridimensional Tourist Service Facility

Located at the at the entrance to Jiuzhaigou, it abuts on Heye Hotel in the west, No. 4 Bridge in the east, Guest House Hotel in the south and National Highway 544 in the northwest. As a new tourist service facility completed in September 2021, it includes a tourist service center, an exhibition center, an international academic exchange center, a smart management center, a civil air defense emergency refuge, world nature heritage landscapes and a national comprehensive observation station for ecological protection. The Jiuzhaigou Management Bureau took the lead in adopting tridimensional traffic, curved architectural shapes, steel structure assembly and other construction techniques for the building of this tourist service center into a landmark with green environmental protection, humanistic integration, complete functions, advanced equipment and fast access. Its portal has greatly improved the service level, efficiency and comfort and satisfaction of tourists.

1	2	3
	4	

1 1982年的九寨沟沟口（来源于《四川省志·九寨沟志》）
2 1985年的九寨沟沟口（来源于《四川省志·九寨沟志》）
3 2013年的九寨沟沟口游人广场（建措 摄）
4 立体式游客中心（2021年，梁峰 摄）

1 Entrance to Jiuzhaigou in 1982 (photo from *Sichuan Provincial Records–Jiuzhaigou Records*)
2 Entrance to Jiuzhaigou in 1985 (photo from *Sichuan Provincial Records–Jiuzhaigou Records*)
3 Tourists' Square at the entrance to Jiuzhaigou in 2013 (photo by Jiancuo)
4 Tridimensional Tourists' Center (photo by Liang Feng, 2021)

水墨画《九寨胜景图》（节选 / 全图），2570cm×48cm（2004 年，童昌信 作品）

Scenery of Jiuzhaigou (sectional/full image), ink painting, 2,570cm×48cm (by Tong Changxin, 2004)

诺日朗瀑布（2023 年，梁峰 摄）
Nuorilang Waterfall (photo by Liang Feng, 2023)

附录：重要文件

附表 1

时间	单位	文件名
1978 年 8 月	中国科学院成都生物研究所	《关于建议在四川建立几个自然保护区的报告》
1978 年 10 月	中国科学院	《转送我院成都生物研究所关于建设在四川建立几个自然保护区的报告》
1978 年 12 月	国务院批转国家林业总局	《关于加强大熊猫保护、驯养工作的报告》
1979 年 3 月	四川省革命委员会	《关于加强自然保护区建设的通知》
1979 年 7 月	四川省林业局	《关于请求解决自然保护区管理机构及人员编制的报告》
1979 年 9 月	四川省革命委员会办公厅	《关于解决自然保护区管理机构及人员编制问题的批复》
1982 年 10 月	四川省林业厅	《关于在年底前将 124、126 林场撤出九寨沟保护区的函》
1982 年 11 月	国务院批转城乡建设环境保护部等部门	《关于审定第一批国家重点风景名胜区的请示的通知》
1983 年 9 月	四川省人民政府	《关于加强南坪九寨沟自然保护和风景名胜区管理工作的决定》
1987 年 1 月	中华人民共和国城乡建设环境保护部	《关于九寨沟风景名胜区规划的批复》
1993 年 1 月	中国联合国教科文组织全国委员会秘书处	《关于我遗产项目列入〈世界遗产名录〉的通知》
1994 年 7 月	中华人民共和国林业部	《关于确认九寨沟等四个自然保护区为国家级自然保护区的函》
1997 年 11 月	中国人与生物圈国家委员会	《关于丰林、九寨沟自然保护区被批准纳入联合国教科文组织世界生物圈保护网络的函》
2000 年 3 月	国家林业局	《关于进一步加强自然保护区管理工作的通知》
2004 年 1 月	国土资源部	《关于批准河南王屋山等 41 处国家地质公园的通知》
2007 年 5 月	国家旅游局	《关于批准发布北京市故宫博物院等 66 家景区为国家 AAAAA 级旅游景区公告的决定》

Appendices: Key Documents

Attached Table 1

Time	Unit	Document Name
August, 1978	Chengdu Institute of Biology, Chinese Academy of Sciences	*Report on Suggesting the Establishment of Several Nature Reserves in Sichuan*
October, 1978	Chinese Academy of Sciences	*Report on the Establishment of Several Nature Reserves in Sichuan Submitted to Chengdu Institute of Biology*
December, 1978	Approved by State Council and transferred to State Forestry Administration	*Report on Strengthening the Protection and Domestication of Giant Panda*
March, 1979	Sichuan Revolutionary Committee	*Announcement on Strengthening Construction of Nature Reserves*
July, 1979	Sichuan Provincial Forestry Bureau	*Request Report on Addressing Nature Reserve Management Agencies and Staffing*
September, 1979	General Office of Sichuan Revolutionary Committee	*Reply to Addressing Nature Reserve Management Agencies and Staffing*
October, 1982	Sichuan Povincial Department of Forestry	*Official Letter on* No. *124 and 126 Forest Farms' Withdrawal from Jiuzhaigou Nature Reserve*
November, 1982	Approved by State Council and transferred to Ministry of Urban and Rural Construction and Environmental Protection	*Announcement on the Request for Rating First Batch of National Key Scenic Spots*
September, 1983	The People's Government of Sichuan Province	*Decision on Strengthening Management of Jiuzhaigou Nature Conservation and Scenic Area in Nanping County*
January, 1987	Ministry of Urban and Rural Construction and Environmental Protection of PRC	*Reply to Planning of Jiuzhaigou Scenic Area*
January, 1993	Secretariat of Chinese National Commission for UNESCO	*Announcement of Jiuzhaigou Scenic Area on the World Heritage List*
July, 1994	Ministry of Forestry of PRC	*Official Letter on Confirming Four Nature Reserves Including Jiuzhaigou as National Ones*
November, 1997	Chinese National Committee for Man and the Biosphere Programme	*Official Letter to Inclusion of Fenglin and Jiuzhaigou Nature Reserves into UNESCO World Biosphere Reserve Network*
March, 2000	National Forestry Administration	*Announcement on Further Strengthening the Management of Nature Reserves*
January, 2004	Ministry of Land and Resources	*Announcement on Approving 41 National Geoparks Including Wangwu Mountain in Henan Province*
May, 2007	National Tourism Administration	*Decision on Approving the Release of 66 Scenic Spots Including the Palace Museum of Beijing as National AAAAA-level Tourist Attractions*

附录：主要参考文献

[1] 四川省地方志编纂委员会 . 四川省志 • 九寨沟志 [M]. 北京：方志出版社，2019.

[2] 四川省阿坝藏族羌族自治州南坪县地方志编纂委员会 . 南坪县志 [M]. 北京：民族出版社，1994.

[3] 九寨沟县地方志编纂委员会 . 九寨沟县志（1986—2005）[M]. 北京：方志出版社，2011.

[4] 四川省地方志编纂委员会 . 四川省志 • 气象志（1986—2005）[M]. 北京：方志出版社，2013.

[5] 四川省地方志编纂委员会 . 四川省志 • 旅游志（1840—1985）[M]. 成都：四川人民出版社，1996.

[6] 四川省地方志编纂委员会 . 四川省志 • 旅游志（1986—2005）[M]. 北京：方志出版社，2014.

[7] 四川省地方志编纂委员会 . 四川省志 • 林业志（1986—2005）[M]. 北京：方志出版社，2014.

[8] 四川省地方志编纂委员会 . 四川省志 • 黄龙志 [M]. 北京：方志出版社，2017.

[9] 四川省地方志编纂委员会 . 四川省志 • 大熊猫志 [M]. 北京：方志出版社，2018.

[10] 四川省地方志编纂委员会 . 四川省志 • 环境保护志（1986—2005）[M]. 北京：方志出版社，2018.

[11] 四川省地方志编纂委员会 . 四川省志 • 地震志（1840—1985）[M]. 成都：四川人民出版社，1998.

[12] 四川省地方志编纂委员会 . 四川省志 • 地震志（1986—2005）[M]. 北京：方志出版社，2018.

[13] 四川省地方志编纂委员会 . 四川省志 • 地理志（上下册）（1840—1985）[M]. 成都：成都地图出版社，1996.

[14] 四川省地方志编纂委员会 . 四川省志 • 林业志（1840—1985）[M]. 成都：四川科学技术出版社，1999.

[15] 四川省地方志编纂委员会 . 四川省志 • 国土资源志（1986—2005）[M]. 北京：方志出版社，2017.

[16] 四川省地方志工作办公室 . 四川年鉴（2018）[M]. 成都：四川年鉴社，2018.

[17] 四川省地方志工作办公室 . 四川年鉴（2019）[M]. 成都：四川年鉴社，2019.

[18] 四川省地方志工作办公室 . 四川年鉴（2020）[M]. 成都：四川年鉴社，2020.

[19] 四川省地方志工作办公室 . 四川年鉴（2021）[M]. 成都：四川年鉴社，2021.

[20] 四川文化和旅游年鉴编辑委员会 . 四川文化和旅游年鉴 2021[M]. 成都：四川科学技术出版社，2022.

[21] 阿坝州地方志办公室 . 阿坝州年鉴（2018）[M]. 成都：四川科学技术出版社，2018.

[22] 阿坝州地方志办公室 . 阿坝州年鉴（2019）[M]. 北京：开明出版社，2019.

[23] 阿坝州地方志办公室 . 阿坝州年鉴（2020）[M]. 北京：新华出版社，2020.

[24] 阿坝州地方志办公室 . 阿坝州年鉴（2021）[M]. 北京：方志出版社，2021.

[25] 九寨沟县史志办公室 . 九寨沟县年鉴（2018）[M]. 北京：中国市场出版社，2019.

[26] 九寨沟县史志办公室 . 九寨沟县年鉴（2019）[M]. 北京：开明出版社，2019.

[27] 九寨沟县党史研究和地方志编纂中心 . 九寨沟县年鉴（2020）[M]. 北京：开明出版社，2020.

[28] 九寨沟县党史研究和地方志编纂中心 . 九寨沟县年鉴（2021）[M]. 北京：中华工商联合出版社，2021.

[29] 本书课题组 . 九寨—黄龙核心景区景观水系统及生态地质环境可持续发展综合应用研究 [M]. 成都：电子科技大学出版社，2009.

[30] 刘少英，章小平，曾宗永 . 九寨沟自然保护区的生物多样性 [M]. 成都：四川科学技术出版社，2007.

[31] 四川大学考古系，九寨沟风景名胜区管理局，等 . 九寨沟景区历史文化考察研究报告 [M]. 成都：巴蜀书社，2016.

[32] 张善云 . 九寨沟存照 [M]. 北京：团结出版社，2018.

[33] 王庆九 . 九寨凝眸 [M]. 成都：四川民族出版社，2021.

[34] 邓一 . 永远的九寨沟：第一任局长亲述 [M]. 北京：中国林业出版社，2009.

[35] 赵德猛，徐荣林，向宝云 . 归来：九寨沟恢复重建实录 [M]. 成都：天地出版社，2021.

[36] 向宝云，李怡 . 造化：九寨沟的神奇与美丽 [M]. 成都：天地出版社，2021.

[37] 向宝云，徐荣林 . 探秘：九寨沟的生物与文化 [M]. 成都：天地出版社，2021.

[38] 孙庚，类延宝，陈珂，等 . 九寨沟国家级自然保护区苔藓植物图鉴 [M]. 成都：四川科学技术出版社，2021.

[39] 叶欣梁，温家洪，孙瑞红 . 旅游地自然灾害风险评价研究——以九寨沟为例 [M]. 北京：清华大学出版社，2014.

[40] 星球研究所，中国青藏高原研究会 . 这里是中国 [M]. 北京：中信出版社，2019.

[41] 唐思远 . 九寨沟生态导览手册 [M]. 北京：清华大学出版社，2016.

[42] 四川省林业和草原局 . 自然之赐：发现四川本来的样子 [M]. 北京：中国林业出版社，2020.

[43] 曹亚楠 . 绝色四川 [M]. 成都：四川人民出版社，2017.

[44] 马夫、陈慧 . 美不胜收：九寨沟 [M]. 长春：吉林出版集团有限责任公司，2011.

Appendices: Bibliography

[1] Sichuan Provincial Local Records Compilation Committee. *Sichuan Provincial Records–Jiuzhaigou Records* [M]. Beijing: Publishing House of Local Records, 2019.

[2] Nanping County Local Records Compilation Committee, Aba Zang and Qiang Autonomous Prefecture, Sichuan Province. *Nanping County Records* [M]. Beijing: The Ethnic Publishing House, 1994.

[3] Jiuzhaigou County Local Records Compilation Committee. *Jiuzhaigou County Records (1986~2005)* [M]. Beijing: Publishing House of Local Records, 2011.

[4] Sichuan Provincial Local Records Compilation Committee. *Sichuan Provincial Records–Meteorological Records* (1986~2005) [M]. Beijing: Publishing House of Local Records, 2013.

[5] Sichuan Provincial Local Records Compilation Committee. *Sichuan Provincial Records–Travel Records (1840~1985)* [M]. Chengdu: Sichuan People's Publishing House, 1996.

[6] Sichuan Provincial Local Records Compilation Committee. *Sichuan Provincial Records–Travel Records (1986~2005)* [M]. Beijing: Publishing House of Local Records, 2014.

[7] Sichuan Provincial Local Records Compilation Committee. *Sichuan Provincial Records–Forestry Records (1986~2005)* [M]. Beijing: Publishing House of Local Records, 2014.

[8] Sichuan Provincial Local Records Compilation Committee. *Sichuan Provincial Records–Huanglong Records* [M]. Beijing: Publishing House of Local Records, 2017.

[9] Sichuan Provincial Local Records Compilation Committee. *Sichuan Provincial Records–Ailuropoda melanoleuca Records* [M]. Beijing: Publishing House of Local Records, 2018.

[10] Sichuan Provincial Local Records Compilation Committee. *Sichuan Provincial Records–Environmental Protection Records* (1986~2005) [M]. Beijing: Publishing House of Local Records, 2018.

[11] Sichuan Provincial Local Records Compilation Committee. *Sichuan Provincial Records–Earthquake Records (1840~1985)* [M]. Chengdu: Sichuan People's Publishing House, 1998.

[12] Sichuan Provincial Local Records Compilation Committee. *Sichuan Provincial Records–Earthquake Records (1986~2005)* [M]. Beijing: Publishing House of Local Records, 2018.

[13] Sichuan Provincial Local Records Compilation Committee. *Sichuan Provincial Records–Geographical Records (Volumes 1 and 2) (1840~1985)* [M]. Chengdu: Chengdu Cartographic Publishing House, 1996.

[14] Sichuan Provincial Local Records Compilation Committee. *Sichuan Provincial Records–Forestry Records (1840~1985)* [M]. Chengdu: Sichuan Publishing House of Science & Technology, 1999.

[15] Sichuan Provincial Local Records Compilation Committee. *Sichuan Provincial Records–Land Resources Records (1986~2005)* [M]. Beijing: Publishing House of Local Records, 2017.

[16] Sichuan Provincial Local Chronicle Work Office. *Sichuan Yearbook (2018)* [M]. Chengdu: Sichuan Yearbook Society, 2018.

[17] Sichuan Provincial Local Records Work Office. *Sichuan Yearbook (2019)* [M]. Chengdu: Sichuan Yearbook Society, 2019.

[18] Sichuan Provincial Local Records Work Office. *Sichuan Yearbook (2020)* [M]. Chengdu: Sichuan Yearbook Society, 2020.

[19] Sichuan Provincial Local Records Work Office. *Sichuan Yearbook (2021)* [M]. Chengdu: Sichuan Yearbook Society, 2021.

[20] Sichuan Culture and Tourism Yearbook Editorial Committee. *Sichuan Culture and Tourism Yearbook (2021)* [M]. Chengdu: Sichuan Publishing House of Science & Technology, 2022.

[21] The Office of Aba Prefecture Local Records. *Aba Prefecture Yearbook (2018)* [M]. Chengdu: Sichuan Publishing House of Science & Technology, 2018.

[22] The Office of Aba Prefecture Local Records. *Aba Prefecture Yearbook (2019)* [M]. Beijing: Kaiming Press, 2019.

[23] The Office of Aba Prefecture Local Records. *Aba Prefecture Yearbook (2020)* [M]. Beijing: Xinhua Publishing House, 2020.

[24] The Office of Aba Prefecture Local Records. *Aba Prefecture Yearbook (2021)* [M]. Beijing: Publishing House of Local Records, 2021.

[25] Jiuzhaigou County History Office. *Jiuzhaigou County Yearbook (2018)* [M]. Beijing: China Market Press, 2019.

[26] Jiuzhaigou County History Office. *Jiuzhaigou County Yearbook (2019)* [M]. Beijing: Kaiming Press, 2019.

[27] Jiuzhaigou County Party History Research and Local Records Compilation Center. *Jiuzhaigou County Yearbook 2020* [M]. Beijing: Kaiming Press, 2020.

[28] Jiuzhaigou County Party History Research and Local Records Compilation Center. *Jiuzhaigou County Yearbook 2021* [M]. Beijing: China Industry & Commerce Associated Press, 2021.

[29] Research Group of This Book. *Comprehensive Application Research on Waterscape System and Sustainable Development of Ecological Geological Environment in Jiuzhai-Huanglong Core Scenic Area* [M]. Chengdu: University of Electronic Science and Technology of China Press, 2009.

[30] Liu Shaoying, Zhang Xiaoping, Zeng Zongyong. *Biodiversity of the Jiuzhaigou National Nature Reserve* [M]. Chengdu: Sichuan Publishing House of Science and Technology, 2007

[31] Department of Archeology, Sichuan University, et al. *Research Report on Historical and Cultural Investigation of Jiuzhaigou Scenic Area* [M]. Chengdu: Bashu Publishing House, 2016.

[32] Zhang Shanyun. *The Literature on Jiuzhaigou Preservation* [M]. Beijing: Unity Press, 2018.

[33] Wang Qingjiu. *A Look at Jiuzhaigou* [M]. Chengdu: Sichuan Ethnic Publishing House, 2021.

[34] Deng Yi. Eternal Jiuzhaigou: *Personal Account by the First Director* [M]. Beijing: China Forestry Publishing House, 2009.

[35] Zhao Demeng, Xu Ronglin, Xiang Baoyun. *Return: Record of Jiuzhaigou Restoration and Reconstruction* [M]. Chengdu: TianDi Press, 2021.

[36] Xiang Baoyun, Li Yi. *Good Fortune: Magic and Beauty of Jiuzhaigou* [M]. Chengdu: TianDi Press, 2021.

[37] Xiang Baoyun, Xu Ronglin. Quest: Biology and Culture of Jiuzhaigou [M]. Chengdu: TianDi Press, 2021.

[38] Sun Geng, Lei Yanbao, Chen Ke, et al. Illustrated Book of Mosses in Jiuzhaigou National Nature Reserve [M]. Chengdu: Sichuan Publishing House of Science and Technology, 2021.

[39] Ye Xinliang, Wen Jiahong, Sun Ruihong. *Research on Risk Assessment of Natural Disasters in Tourist Destinations–Taking Jiuzhaigou as an Example* [M]. Beijing: Tsinghua University Press, 2014.

[40] Planetary Research Institute, China Qinghai-Xizang Plateau Research Association. *Hi I'm China* [M]. Beijing: CITIC Publishing House, 2019.

[41] Tang Siyuan. *A Field Guide to Nature and Culture of Jiuzaigou* [M]. Beijing: Tsinghua University Press, 2016.

[42] Forestry and Grassland Bureau of Sichuan Province. *The Gift of Nature: Discover Original Sichuan* [M]. Beijing: China Forestry Publishing House, 2020.

[43] Cao Yanan. *Stunning Sichuan* [M]. Chengdu: Sichuan People's Publishing House, 2017.

[44] Ma Fu, Chen Hui. *So Beautiful: Jiuzhaigou* [M]. Changchun: Jilin Publishing Group Co., Ltd., 2011.

后记　志载九寨

志书是中国独特的记载地方自然、地理、历史、人文的传统著述，图志则是当代对传统志书形式的创新。2022 年 5 月，四川省地方志工作办公室、阿坝州地方志办公室和九寨沟风景名胜区管理局三方协同，并引入专业编纂服务机构，以图文并茂、以图为主的形式，编纂出版全球首部全方位展现九寨沟独特性的图志——《九寨沟图志》。

《九寨沟图志》力图充分展现九寨沟的生态保护、科学研究和旅游美学，向广大读者传递九寨沟的文化深度和视觉美感。我们期望通过本书的编纂出版，既为四川方志事业再添创新成果，又为巴蜀文旅全球推广和四川全域对外开放提供助力，更有利于世界进一步认识九寨沟，认识四川，认识中国。

《九寨沟图志》的编纂出版，有助于为四川其他风景区旅游资源的开发、利用和保护工作提供借鉴；有助于提升九寨沟的品牌影响力，为推动“熊猫家园 • 净土阿坝”全域旅游提档升级贡献方志力量；有助于释放四川魅力、打响四川文旅品牌，服务巴蜀文旅全球推广计划。

在一年多的图志编纂过程中，我们有序统筹组织、多方征集资料、精心编纂文稿、高度重视审改，最终如期完成了编纂任务。为给读者带来良好的阅读体验，我们力求在史志性与大众化之间掌握平衡，确保图志语言既专业科学，又通俗易懂。图志中收录的每一幅图照，都是我们在成千上万幅图照中反复精选才最终确定的，兼具知识性与艺术性，目的是为读者带来一场视觉盛宴。

《九寨沟图志》的付梓，离不开多方力量的全力支持。在此，我们向参与图志编纂工作的个人和单位致以最真挚的谢意。

首先，感谢各位专家学者，感谢他们不辞辛劳，多次严谨、细致地审核图志内容，为图志编纂提供专业指导并严格把关。其次，要感谢各位摄影家，感谢他们心怀对九寨沟的热爱，用镜头发现并记录九寨沟的旧貌新颜，为图志贡献了大量珍贵、精美的照片。再次，感谢提供资料的单位与个人，感谢他们高度重视、通力配合，为图志编纂搜集、整理了大量的一手资料和图片，并提出宝贵的修改意见。特别感谢章玉钧先生为本书作序，特别感谢四川省民族宗教事务委员会和阿坝州民族宗教事务委员会给予项目资金支持，感谢天下志鉴公司团队为本书编纂付出的心血汗水。感谢所有为保护九寨沟作出贡献的人士，正因为他们的远见卓识与不懈努力，才使宛如仙境的九寨沟走出高山深谷，走至人前，走向世界。

四川省地方志工作办公室
阿坝州地方志办公室
九寨沟风景名胜区管理局
2023 年 8 月 31 日

Epilogue: A Record of Jiuzhaigou

The local record, a unique traditional Chinese work that records local nature, geography, history and humanities and the integration of pictures in it is a contemporary innovation. In May 2022, Sichuan Province Local Records Office, Aba Prefecture Local Records Office and the Management Bureau of Jiuzhaigou Scenic and Historic Area, in cooperation with one another, invited service agencies for professional compiling, editing such a tome, in hopes of presenting the uniqueness of Jiuzhaigou–the world's first of such annals in the form of essays mainly accompanied with pictures–in an omnibearing way, so *Jiuzhaigou Pictorial Annals* have come into being.

Striving to fully demonstrate the ecological protection, scientific research and aesthetic tourism of Jiuzhaigou, realize the role and value of senior management and historical preservation and convey its cultural depth and visual beauty to readers, we hope, through the compilation and publication of the annals, to add not only more innovations to Sichuan's local records, but also assist global promotion of cultural tourism and help the world better understand Jiuzhaigou, Sichuan and China.

The compilation and publication of *Jiuzhaigou Pictorial Annals* will be of great help to the development, utilization and protection of tourism resources in other scenic spots in Sichuan, to the improvement of Jiuzhaigou's brand influence and to the promotion of local records in upgrading the all-for-one tourism of "Home to Panda–Pure Land Aba", to the endeavor to further unleash Jiuzhaigou's charm, to the elevation of the brand of Sichuan's cultural tourism, and eventually to the ambitious plan for the global promotion of Ba-Shu cultural tourism.

For more than a year, we have orderly coordinated organizations concerned, collected materials from various sources, carefully dealt with manuscripts, attached great importance to its review and revision. Finally, the compilation task was completed as scheduled. In order to fill readers with a good reading experience, we have been striving for its historical and popular balance and ensuring that its language is both professional and easy to understand. Each of its picture, finalized upon repeated selection, from thousands of pictures, can be both knowledgeable and artistic, hence a visual feast to whoever reads this book.

The publication of *Jiuzhaigou Pictorial Annals* cannot be separated from the full support of various forces. Here, we would like to express our most sincere thanks to all individuals and organizations that have ever participated in the endeavor of compiling this book.

First of all, our thanks go to all the experts and scholars for their tireless efforts to review the contents of the pictorial annals for many times as well as their professional guidance and strict check and review. Secondly, we would like to thank all photographers for their love of Jiuzhaigou, for the discovery and recording of its past and present appearance with their lenses and for offering this book so many precious and exquisite photos. Thirdly, we are indebted to all organizations and individuals that provided the information for their great attention and cooperation, for collecting and sorting out plenty of first-hand materials and photos for the annals and for putting forward valuable suggestions to its revision. Besides our special thanks to Mr. Zhang Yujun for his preface to this book, we would also like to thank Sichuan Ethnic and Religious Affairs Commission and Aba Prefecture Ethnic and Religious Affairs Commission for their financial support on the project and the team of Tianxia Zhijian Company for their hard work in compiling this book. We would like to give our hearty thanks to all those who have contributed to the conservation and protection of Jiuzhaigou. It is because of their foresight and unremitting efforts that this earthly fairyland has come face to face to the world from behind the high mountain and deep valley.

The Office of Sichuan Province Local Records
The Office of Aba Prefecture Local Records
The Management Bureau of Jiuzhaigou Scenic and Historic Area
August 31, 2023

四川省地方志工作办公室
阿坝州地方志办公室 编著
九寨沟风景名胜区管理局

Compiled by The Office of Sichuan Province Local Records
The Office of Aba Prefecture Local Records
The Management Bureau of Jiuzhaigou Scenic and Historic Area

九寨沟是大自然以鬼斧神工之力精心雕琢而成的杰出作品，被誉为“童话世界”“人间仙境”，在四川省旅游发展中居于核心地位。2023 年，四川省地方志工作办公室、阿坝州地方志办公室、九寨沟风景名胜区管理局三家单位联合编写全球首部《九寨沟图志》，旨在以通俗简洁的语言、数百幅精美图照，全方位展示九寨沟的水、山、植物、动物、民俗文化、科研、保护、旅游、灾后重建的情况。

翻开此书，我们不仅能欣赏到九寨沟的奇绝景观生态，感受人类对九寨沟的开发与管理，更能领略政府与民间等各方保护力量对九寨沟这一人间瑰宝的珍视与呵护。

Jiuzhaigou, an outstanding work carved by nature with uncanny craftsmanship and reputed as a Fairytale World and Fairyland on Earth, occupies a core position in Sichuan's tourism development. In 2023, the Office of Sichuan Province Local Records, the Office of Aba Prefecture Local Records and the Management Bureau of Jiuzhaigou Scenic and Historic Area jointly compiled the world's first *Jiuzhaigou Pictorial Annals*, meant for a full display of the valley's waters, mountains, flora and fauna, folk custom, scientific research, protection, tourism, post-quake reconstruction.

On opening this book, one can not only appreciate its unique landscape and ecology and feel its human development and management, but also better understand its cherishment and care as a global treasure.

读者服务
Reader Service
4000213677 （028）87575393

编纂机构

四川省地方志工作办公室

四川省地方志工作办公室是四川省人民政府直属参照公务员法管理的正厅级事业单位，主要负责本行政区域内地方志工作的组织、管理、指导和督促检查。

The Office of Sichuan Province Local Records

An organization that is a department-level public institution directly under the People's Government of Sichuan Province with reference to the civil service law, committed to the compilation, management and use of its local records and yearbooks.

阿坝州地方志办公室

阿坝州地方志办公室是阿坝州政府直属参照公务员法管理的正县级事业单位，主要负责本行政区域内地方志书、地方综合年鉴的组织编纂、管理、开发利用工作。

The Office of Aba Prefecture Local Records

Is a county-level institution directly under Aba Prefectural Government in accordance with the civil service law, which mainly organizes, compiles, manages, develops and uses the local records and yearbooks within its administrative area.

九寨沟风景名胜区管理局

九寨沟风景名胜区管理局（九寨沟国家级自然保护区管理局、九寨沟世界遗产管理局、九寨沟国家地质公园管理局、九寨沟国家 AAAAA 级旅游景区管理局）是阿坝州人民政府直属正县级事业单位，现实行“五块牌子、一套班子”的管理体制。主要负责九寨沟自然保护区、风景名胜区、世界遗产、地质公园、国家 AAAAA 级旅游景区的保护、利用和管理等工作。

The Management Bureau of Jiuzhaigou Scenic and Historic Area

The Management Bureau of Jiuzhaigou Scenic and Historic Area, which consists of Jiuzhaigou National-level Nature Reserve Management Bureau, World Heritage Management Bureau, Jiuzhaigou National-level Geological Park Management Bureau, and National AAAAA-level Tourist Scenic Area Management Bureau, is a county-level institution under the administration of Aba Prefectural People's Government. They function under five names but on one team of personnel, who are responsible for the conservation, protection, utilization and management of Jiuzhaigou Nature Reserve, scenic areas and places of historic interest, world heritage sites, geological parks, and National AAAAA-level tourist attractions.

联合编纂机构

九寨沟县党史研究和地方志编纂中心

九寨沟县党史研究和地方志编纂中心为县委直属参照公务员法管理的正科级事业单位，主要工作任务是在县委、县政府的领导下，统一组织、指导负责本行政区域内党史、县志和各部门志的组织编纂，管理和开发利用工作。

Party History Research and Local Records Compilation Center of Jiuzhaigou County

This center, directly under the CPC Jiuzhaigou County Committee, is a department-level public institution managing as per the civil service law. It performs its duty under the leadership of the CPC County Committee and the County Government in arranging and guiding the compilation, management, development and utilization of the Party history and local records of the county and its departments within the administrative region.

协作团队

天下志鉴
Tianxia Zhijian

四川天下志鉴文化传播有限公司是一家专业从事志书年鉴修编的机构，主要为政府机构和企事业单位提供编纂出版志书和年鉴的全流程服务。

Sichuan Tianxia Zhijian Cultural Communication Co., Ltd provides professional whole process service of editing and publishing annals for government, enterprises and public institutions.

书服家
Forbooks

书服家是一个专业的内容出版团队，致力于优质内容的发现和高品质出版，并通过多种出版形式，向更多人分享值得出版和分享的知识，以书和内容为媒介，帮助更多的人和机构发生联系。

A professional content publishing team committed to the discovery and publication of high-quality contents, sharing worthwhile ideas with people through multiple forms of publication, and thus acting as a bridge between people and institutions.

特邀编创：天下志鉴　书服家
装帧设计：云何视觉（汪智昊　漆孟涛）　华著设计

Specially-invited creator: Tianxia Zhijian, For Books
Binding designers: Yunhe Vision (Wang Zhihao, Qi Mengtao), Huazhu Design

图书在版编目（CIP）数据

九寨沟图志 / 四川省地方志工作办公室，阿坝州地方志办公室，九寨沟风景名胜区管理局编著 . — 北京 : 方志出版社，2023.8

ISBN 978-7-5144-5769-8

Ⅰ . ①九… Ⅱ . ①四… ②阿… ③九… Ⅲ . ①九寨沟县—地方志—图集 Ⅳ . ① K297.14-64

中国国家版本馆 CIP 数据核字 (2023) 第 140106 号

责任编辑：陈菁
责任校对：刘玉霞
责任印制：梅中英
出 版 者：方志出版社
地　　址：北京市朝阳区潘家园东里 9 号（国家方志馆 4 层）
邮　　编：100021
网　　址：http://www.zgfzcb.cn
发　　行：方志出版社图书营销中心（010-67110500）
设计制作：四川天下志鉴文化传播有限公司　重庆云庄文化传播有限公司（书服家）
印　　刷：成都市金雅迪彩色印刷有限公司
开　　本：889 毫米 ×1194 毫米 1/16
印　　张：22.75　插页：4
字　　数：247 千字
版　　次：2023 年 8 月第 1 版
印　　次：2023 年 8 月第 1 次印刷
定　　价：520.00 元